Meaningful Work and Workplace Democracy

Meaningful Work and Workplace Democracy

A Philosophy of Work and a Politics of Meaningfulness

Ruth Yeoman
Research Fellow, Saïd Business School, University of Oxford, UK

First published 2014 by
PALGRAVE MACMILLAN

Palgrave Macmillan in the UK is an imprint of Macmillan Publishers Limited, registered in England, company number 785998, of Houndmills, Basingstoke, Hampshire RG21 6XS.

Palgrave Macmillan in the US is a division of St Martin's Press LLC, 175 Fifth Avenue, New York, NY 10010.

Palgrave Macmillan is the global academic imprint of the above companies and has companies and representatives throughout the world.

Palgrave® and Macmillan® are registered trademarks in the United States, the United Kingdom, Europe and other countries

ISBN: 978-1-137-37057-0 hardback

This book is printed on paper suitable for recycling and made from fully managed and sustained forest sources. Logging, pulping and manufacturing processes are expected to conform to the environmental regulations of the country of origin.

A catalogue record for this book is available from the British Library.
Library of Congress Cataloging-in-Publication Data

Yeoman, Ruth, 1964–
    Meaningful work and workplace democracy : a philosophy of work and a politics of meaningfulness / Ruth Yeoman.
        pages cm
    Summary: "Meaningful Work and Workplace Democracy is a timely revival of the social and political importance of meaningful work. Drawing upon moral philosophy, political theory and sociology of work, this book creates a philosophy of work based upon the value of meaningfulness, and addresses contemporary concerns that work has become irretrievably degraded by evaluating how this understanding of meaningfulness remedies alienation, domination and distorted social recognition. In order to retrieve the emancipatory potential of all kind of work, this book argues for the institution of a new politics of meaningfulness through a system of workplace democracy which combines democratic authority with participatory practices, concluding that making work meaningful is both the legitimate and achievable object of political and social action" – Provided by publisher.

ISBN 978-1-137-37057-0 (hardback)

1. Work environment—Philosophy. I. Title.
HD7261.Y46 2014
658.3'8—dc23

                                            2014021116

This book is dedicated to the memory of Jonathan Chenoweth

Contents

Acknowledgements

To embark upon doctoral research as a mature student presents particular challenges. Somehow, in the midst of raising children, caring for friends and family, shouldering teaching duties and coping with the unexpected, the work has to get done. I was extremely fortunate in my intellectual mentors who encouraged me to take up the task in the first place, and then steered me towards what seemed, at many times, an unattainable goal. I would like to thank all my colleagues and fellow students at the Department of Politics and International Relations at Royal Holloway, the University of London who provided sustaining personal and academic support. Through his teaching on Rawls and Nozick, Emeritus Professor John Edwards introduced me to the addictive challenges of political theory, and set my direction for advanced study. My supervisor, Dr Jonathan Seglow, provided clarity of thought and insight, gentle but precise guidance, and vital injections of resolve at times when I thought I would be overwhelmed by the scholarly and personal effort needed to continue. With my friend and fellow student, Dr Michelle Springfield, I shared the joys and trials of being a mature PhD researcher. I am grateful to those I met during the University of Manchester Political Theory Workshops who provided intellectual provocation and a sense of community. My thanks to Dr Keith Breen of Queen's University, Belfast, Professor Nicholas Smith, Macquarie University, Australia, and especially to Russell Keat, Emeritus Professor of Political Theory at the University of Edinburgh. Professor Keat examined my thesis together with Professor Laura Spence of the School of Management, Royal Holloway, and they encouraged me to seek publication. I am delighted with new colleagues at the University of Oxford who are interested in the value and character of work, particularly Professor Duncan Gallie and Dr Marc Thompson, and at the University of Sussex, Professor Katie Truss and Dr Adrian Madden. I look forward to a long and fruitful association.

Aside from this indispensable intellectual nourishment, I would never have completed this book without the support of my family. During some very difficult times, my parents, Marie and David Yeoman, devoted themselves to caring for myself and my daughters. My sister, Kay and my brother-in-law, JC, together with my nephews, Alex and Georgie, loved and encouraged us. My daughters, Hannah and Abigail Chenoweth, saw the start of this work when they were children. They are now young women, with working and family lives of their own just around the corner. You have my love and admiration. Finally, I would like to express my deep gratitude to my partner, Roger Harrison, who would not allow me to give up.

Introduction

In advanced industrialised societies, work occupies a peculiarly ambivalent position – simultaneously valued for providing the means for self-realisation and disvalued for being burdensome and compulsory. Shershow (2005) describes work as consisting of a 'double necessity', whereby 'we see ourselves both as *working to* live and as *living to work*' (ibid: 13, original emphasis). On the one hand, work is a source of expressive human action, one of 'the hopes of civilisation' (Morris, 1993 [1890]), fulfilled in a correctly ordered society which enables all persons to do decent, humane and dignified work. On the other hand, work is an experience of oppressive degradation, which must be minimised, if not eliminated, since the worker deprived of worthwhile activities 'generally becomes as stupid and ignorant as it is possible for a human creature to become' (Smith, 1999 [1776]), resulting in him or her becoming 'a crippled monstrosity' (Marx, 1978 [1867]). We can be in no doubt that our survival and our ability to flourish depend upon our being able to work together to produce the material and social goods which satisfy individual and collective human needs. But acknowledging that work is unavoidable for most people leaves us with limited resources for investigating whether work is simply what is necessary to sustain life, or whether it can add to the experience of a full and meaningful human existence. However, even though the meaning of work as compulsion has left little space for the meaning of work as free, expressive, and creative action (Spencer, 2009a), we have not entirely lost hope in work which is fruitful for human emancipation. Despite the many ways in which our daily experience of work falls short of meaningfulness, the ideal of meaningful work retains a strong hold upon our imagination, motivating us to seek work which adds to the personal meaning of our lives, and even to aspire to a society

1

transformed by each person being able to do the work which he or she finds worth doing. Moreover, engaging in the hunt for meaning in work sharpens critical attentiveness to how the contemporary organisation of work, rather than being a natural inevitability, is a consequence of socio-historical contingencies which still contain remnant potentialities for a more humanised experience of work. For example, Ciulla (2000) provides the following description of meaningful work which indicates how the content of work and the social organisation of work operate together to promote or impair our sense of work being meaningful.

> Meaningful work, like a meaningful life, is morally worthy work undertaken in a morally worthy organization. Work has meaning because there is some good in it. The most meaningful jobs are those in which people directly help others or create products which make life better for people. Work makes life better if it helps others; alleviates suffering; eliminates difficult, dangerous, or tedious toil; makes someone healthier or happier; or aesthetically or intellectually enriches people and improves the environment in which we live. All work that is worthy does at least some of these things in some small or large way. Still, not all people will find worthy work personally meaningful to them (Ciulla, 2000: 226).

In the spirit of critical attentiveness to emancipatory possibilities, I aim to show that the conceptual evaluation of meaningful work is not simply an exercise in remote abstraction, but directs us toward a pragmatic political programme for ensuring that all work possesses the structure for meaningfulness. Furthermore, not only can the value of meaningfulness in the concept of meaningful work be described, but social institutions can be arranged according to normative principles conducive to enabling all persons to attribute meaning content to their lives because of the work they do. To this end, I take work, following Kovacs (1986), to be 'a basic mode of being in the world', where 'to work means to humanise the world and to produce something' (ibid: 198). In this sense, work functions to create and to sustain values and meanings beyond the realm of its economic productivity: work is a mode of being in the world which transcends the employment relation to include all the activities which contribute to producing and reproducing a complex system of social cooperation. But if work is to humanise the world, it must at the same time humanise the one through whom the work takes place. In Morris's terms: 'Nothing should be made by man's labour which is not worth doing; or which must be made by labour degrading to the makers' (Morris, 1884). Work cannot be meaningful if it requires the enslavement of the worker, the deformation of her human capabilities, or the misrecognition of her vital commitments. This means that some work is morally desirable and some work is not, requiring that the improvement of individuals and of society depends upon work having a certain interior content, which I argue is given by the value of meaningfulness. Furthermore, to aim at the meaningfulness of individual lives because of the work people do is a proper moral and political project – and a necessary element in addressing the many challenges of our times, including how increasingly unequal societies unevenly distribute the benefits and burdens of the work of social cooperation.

I ground my reasons for making meaningful work for all a political project in a normative argument that being able to experience one's life as meaningful is a fundamental human need, which, under present economic arrangements, is extremely difficult for most people to satisfy if their work lacks the structure for meaningfulness. In justifying meaningful work as an object of political action, I start by making the strong claim that, because being able to experience work with the relevant structure is of such importance for living a fully human life, then it is a fundamental human need, requiring the organisation of society to eliminate non-meaningful work from the work of social cooperation. I go on to argue that proliferating meaningful work requires two capabilities for objective valuing and affective attachment, supported by our status as co-authorities in the realm of value. These capabilities and status enable us to join with others in the social construction of an enriched stock of positive meanings of work, which we draw upon in order to create stable practical self-identities. I show that the objective content of meaningful work is constituted by three core values of autonomy as non-alienation, freedom as non-domination, and social recognition as dignified work. These values already operate to a lesser or greater degree in most forms of work, producing pre-political interpretive differences in meanings and values which can be mobilised to enhance the meaningfulness potential of work within a system of workplace democracy. I specify two dimensions to this system: democratic authority at the level of the organisation and democratic practices with agonistic characteristics at the level of the task, and I argue that such a system can be realised in a programme of political action through an entitlement to the Capability for Voice.

Meaningful work has always been available to the few who occupy social roles allowing them to exercise socially valuable capabilities in contexts of personal autonomy which aim at a worthwhile purpose. But a just social order will be concerned that meaningfulness in work is so unevenly distributed, and will seek to ensure, not only that there is equal opportunity in the competition for the most desirable roles, but that all work provides for the development and exercise of complex capabilities (cf. Gomberg, 2007). However, I shall not be proposing that society is organised to ensure that each person is able to access an elite ideal of exceptional meaning, but instead that everyday human action is structured to ensure that work provides the context for creating objects which are worth pursuing, and for developing human capacities for intersubjective meaning-making. Hence, I pursue an egalitarian conception of ordinary meaning which is already at hand in much of the work we do together, provided that we make certain adjustments to our institutional arrangements and the organisation of work in the basic structure of society.

Attending to work

I engage with moral philosophers, critical social theorists, and liberal political theorists for whom the concept of meaningful work, and its implications for public policy, has been of marginal interest. I also draw upon the empirical literature from psychology, employee engagement, and organisational studies more broadly. However, the empirical research on meaningful work remains limited. This book therefore concentrates upon a theoretical engagement with the concept of meaningful work in the anticipation that this will aid the operationalisation of the experience and practice of meaningfulness.

In moral philosophy, the normative content of work is rarely the object of analytical consideration, because work is dismissed as a norm-free zone of human activity governed by technical rationality. In critical social theory, the interior content of work is seen as having been degraded to such a degree that it no longer supports the worthy objects necessary for us to find our lives to be meaningful. In liberal political theory, meaningful work is treated as a preference in the market, because the irredeemably subjective content of meaningfulness threatens the maintenance of neutrality between different conceptions of living. Yet, the centrality of work in modern societies makes construing meaningful work as a preference, dismissing it as irretrievably degraded, or treating it as a realm from which ethical considerations of value and worth are absent, normatively unsatisfactory.

Despite this, I acknowledge concerns that liberal neutralists may have with the way in which I make meaningfulness dependent upon taking part in democratic deliberation, since not everyone has the taste for democratic participation – some people may be reluctant co-operators. Others may have constrained opportunities for participation in publicly recognised practices because their activities are undertaken in obscurity or the domestic realm, such as the artist who remains unrecognised in her lifetime or the full-time, unpaid carer. If meaningfulness is realised only when individuals engage in activities which are valued through public deliberation, then this would limit the opportunities for the unknown artist to receive validation of her work as meaningful or for the carer to gain the self-confidence to speak publicly about her labour. In the case of the reluctant co-operator, much contemporary work is now organised along participatory lines, making participation an ordinary necessity for getting the work done. Although much of this participation may be of the pseudo-participatory variety (Pateman, 1970), such practices nonetheless sketch a line in the sand for 'bleak houses' organised through command and control (Brogger, 2010). In order to provide for the reluctant co-operator, I propose that participatory practices which are constitutive of the meaning content of work must be plural, including both direct/individual and indirect/representative forms of participation (cf. Pyman et al, 2006). This provides multiple channels for people to choose the form of their participation, perhaps delegating participation to their representatives, if they have no taste for direct involvement. In the case of the unknown artist and the unpaid carer, I argue that we must define work more broadly than paid work, so as to include an individual's own identification of what counts as work. Since the unknown artist is part of an honourable tradition of the unrecognised innovator in all fields of human endeavour, this allows her to claim that her identification of her activity as work places her within an established public practice. Finally, the unpaid carer has often developed her confidence and capabilities through public service and civic engagement.

Democracy at work

I argue that work is more likely to enable people to experience the bipartite value of meaningfulness (BVM) when it is organised democratically in social practices containing subjectively attractive worthy objects, where agonistic democratic practices at the level of the task are combined with democratic authority at the level of the organisation. Agonism realises the emancipatory potential of the interior content of work by bringing into public deliberation interpretive differences which arise out of acts of work, but which are more likely to remain as pre-political potentials in hierarchically organised enterprises. Such practices are able to bring into public view the irreducible autonomy of workers by: firstly, enabling deliberation over acts of meaning-making which overcome technical reason by extending knowledge, developing skill, and re-uniting ends and means to complete necessary tasks, and secondly, enabling deliberation over the diversification and individual-isation of the subjective formations which underpin positive self-relations. By bringing invisibilised interpretive differences which arise from meaning-making into conscious collective deliberation, we can make available to all enriched sources of positive values which can be incorporated into a person's identity. Hence I argue that realising the value of meaningfulness in work for all requires a system of workplace democracy at the level of the task and at the level of the organisation. At the level of the task, a political mode of being structured by agonis-tic democratic practices has the potential to foster a form of workplace democracy which reveals the necessary autonomy in every act of work. At the level of the organisation, democratic authority contests the pre-sumption of hierarchical authority. As a consequence, the individual worker is re-presented as an irreplaceable contributor imbued with expressive political agency, and situated in cooperative relations with others.

The Capability for Voice

I shall argue that bringing the value of meaningfulness though demo-cratic participation into the practicalities of everyday working lives requires an opportunity structure for the Capability for Voice which combines collective institutional and regulatory arrangements with personal resources, abilities, and sense of confidence. The political object is not to guarantee that every person's life will be actually mean-ingful, but that the organisation of work will secure for each person the Capability for Voice in the work they do with others, thus ensuring that the individual will not find her search for meaning unfairly hin-dered by social structures which benefit only a few. This means that realising meaningful work for all is not an unachievable ideal provided that the interior content of work is organised to allow people to express the political mode of being through participation in democratic practices. Hence, I make democratic practices in the work we do together constitutive of the meaning content of work, arguing that they become the object of justice when we seek to institute the value of meaningfulness in the basic structure of society. It is not fair that some people are able to accrue meaning content to their lives because of the work they do, whereas others must endure a lifetime of meaningless activity because society has limited the available supply of the most attractive work. It is therefore a matter of justice that all work be structured by the value of meaningfulness, and that everyone be equipped with the capabilities for experiencing the value of meaningfulness in the work they do with others.

I begin by arguing that meaningful work is a fundamental human need and describing the content of meaningful work using Susan Wolf's (2010) distinct bipartite value of meaningfulness which unites objective and subjective dimensions of valuing. I use this analysis to specify a positive critical conception of work which will allow us to distinguish between desirable and undesirable forms of work, and to identify the latent emancipatory potentials in all kinds of work. In order to judge between the worthiness of different kinds of activities, I propose that we use an ethic of care as a standpoint for assessment. I go on to describe the core values of meaningful work which are autonomy as non-alienation, freedom as non-domination, and social recognition as dignified work. From this discussion, I show how interpretive differences in meaning-making arising from within the experience of working can be drawn upon, through democratic authorisation and participation more broadly, to multiply the range of positive values we can use to create practical identities giving us a sense of dignity. I fill out the direct participatory practices needed for inclusion and plurality using agonistic democratic theory. Finally, I outline the institutional features needed to establish an opportunity structure for the Capability for Voice, concluding that this provides the basis for a compelling programme of political action.

1

Conceptualising Meaningful Work as a Fundamental Human Need*

I begin by claiming that the widespread institution of meaningful work is a proper moral and political project, which is attentive to contemporary concerns for the nature and organisation of work.[1] My reasons for making meaningful work for all a political project is grounded in a normative argument that being able to experience one's life as meaningful is a fundamental human need, which, under present economic arrangements, is extremely difficult for most people to satisfy if their work lacks the structure for meaningfulness. I shall argue that meaningful work is a fundamental human need because it satisfies our inescapable interests in being able to experience the constitutive values of autonomy, freedom, and dignity. By requiring social organisation to ensure that all work is structured for meaningfulness, I distinguish my approach from liberal political theorists, for whom meaningful work, whilst an important ideal, is an individual preference which may or may not be expressed in any particular conception of the good life, and thus cannot be the legitimate target of state intervention without coming into conflict with the principle of liberal neutrality. Instead, I propose that meaningful work is a fundamental human need within a liberal perfectionist framework (cf. Roessler, 2012). I go on to evaluate the conceptual content of meaningfulness using Wolf's (2010) concept of a bipartite value of meaningfulness, arguing that, in order to experience our lives as meaningful, we require certain capabilities for objective valuing and affective attachment, supported by the recognition of our equal status as co-authorities in the realm of value. This makes the possibility of experiencing meaningfulness in work dependent upon our becoming valuers, situated in social structures allowing us to develop the relevant capabilities (Sen, 1999a) and enabling us to join with others in interpretive sense-making (see for example

8

Wrzesniewski & Dutton, 2001; Wrzesniewski et al, 2003; Bechky, 2003; Weick, 1995).[2]

Meaningfulness in work: Preference or need?

I claim that meaningfulness is a fundamental human need which liberal political theorists have subordinated to their commitment to the principle of liberal neutrality. As a result, our need for work which is free, autonomous, and dignified has been relegated to the status of an individual taste or preference, which is no business of the state's to promote. But this settlement is normatively inadequate as the centrality of work in modern societies makes it increasingly difficult for individuals to remedy non-meaningful work in other action contexts.

The argument for meaningful work as a preference

Meaningful work, liberal political theorists complain, is an immodest ideal, because, by making work central to the possibility of a meaningful life, individual preferences for meaning in other action contexts, such as the family, community, or political life, are crowded out (Arneson, 1987). Moreover, since meaningful work is constituted by substantive normative commitments to what it is to live a good life, variously including values such as autonomy (Schwartz, 1982), expressive freedom and self-realisation (Marx, 1978[1844]; see also Gewirth, 1988), complex activities (Rawls, 1999[1971]; Elster, 1986a; see also Walsh, 1994), or self-respect (Honneth, 1995b), then it arbitrarily specifies the content of the good life for all (see also Michaelson et al, 2013; Rosso et al, 2010; Steger & Dik, 2010). As a result, the substantive normative content of meaningful work violates the liberal principle of neutrality, which maintains that a liberal democratic state must remain neutral between different conceptions of living. Since people possess a diversity of subjective preferences for the kind of work they wish to undertake, then the state has no legitimate role in specifying whether or not that work should be meaningful.

The liberal neutralist is concerned that to legislate for the character of work means that one kind of good will be prioritised over other equally valuable goods. If the state were to privilege meaningful work, then the range of values which people might incorporate into their conception of living would be narrowed. So, even though we can acknowledge the importance of meaningful work for living a good life, meaningful work must be restricted to the status of an individual preference (Kymlicka, 2002; Miller, 1999; Christman, 2002). To do otherwise is to support state sponsored perfectionism which promotes one conception of living, constraining options for finding meaning in other activities. In arguing against both a strong and a weak right to meaningful work, Arneson (1987) says: 'implementing a right to meaningful work elevates one particular category of good, intrinsic job satisfaction, and arbitrarily privileges that good and those people who favour it over other equally desirable goods and equally wise fans of those other goods' (ibid: 524–5). For Arneson, meaningful work is a perfectionist ideal which 'assumes objective knowledge of the good life for human beings, the activities that constitute human flourishing' (ibid: 520).

As a consequence of similar anxieties, Rawls (1999[1971]) acknowledges the value of meaningful work (ibid: 463–4) from the point of view of human flourishing and autonomy (it is one of the human goods), but does not make meaningful work a primary good because to do so would result in the good of meaningful work being prioritised over equally valuable human goods. For Rawls, meaningful work is crucial to justice as fairness, because work with the requisite structure supports the self-respect of citizens, but it need not be part of the good for everyone – and to make it so is to advocate perfectionism which breaches the priority of liberty. Since to legislate for the interior content of work would require interference in the available range of values which society allows to be constitutive of the good life, a liberal democratic state ought to have no interest in the normative content of work, except to ensure that work meets basic humane standards, such as health and safety, employment rights, or welfare support for the unlucky, and that society is organised to secure justice in the equality of opportunity for the available supply of meaningful work. Where equality of opportunity pertains, we do not require guarantees for the interior content of work because the market will sort out individual preferences for meaningful or non-meaningful work (cf. Nozick, 1974). Thus, provided individuals are able to satisfy their preferences for meaning in other spheres of living, we need have no further concerns for the normative content of the work they choose to do.

The compensation argument

But constructing meaningful work as an individual preference which can be satisfied in the market does not entirely eliminate the intuition that liberal political theory should have something more to say about the interior content of work. We are uncomfortable concurring with Henry Ford's conclusion that 'to some types of mind [...] the ideal job is one where the creative instinct need not be expressed' (Breen, 2011: 9).[3] Surely preferences for some kinds of work over others do not extend to the desire to do work where no expressive human faculty need be exercised? Instead, I argue that it is incumbent upon a liberal democratic state to take seriously the moral concern that the interior content of much contemporary work stunts the human flourishing of workers by failing to meet their fundamental human interests in autonomy, freedom, and social recognition. This is because non-meaningful work visits extensive harms upon those who have to do it, which for most people cannot be offset by compensations in other spheres of action.

If people are harmed by having to do non-meaningful work, then liberal complacency with respect to the availability and distribution of meaningful work becomes difficult to maintain. After all, despite the remarkable growth in varieties of work, as well as persisting expectations that work should be attractive or meaningful, work often fails to provide even a basic standard of living, let alone meets minimal standards for a humane and dignified experience of working. A common response to these concerns is some variant of the Compensation Argument: that work does not have to be meaningful, provided we can find our lives as a whole to be meaningful because of our activities in other spheres of living, such as our status in a community of interest (see Gomberg, 2007). Whilst I admit this to be a possibility, I argue that, in contemporary societies, such a strategy is extremely difficult for most individuals to pursue, because of the ways in which the burdens and benefits of the work we do shape our lives as a whole. Work provides access to the roles, practices, and social institutions of society which allocate resources for the development of the capabilities necessary to secure our social position and economic participation over the life course. Furthermore, such social structures embody the values we can potentially incorporate into our practical identities, grounding the sense that our lives have meaning (Roessler, 2012; cf. Korsegaard, 2009). This means that, in no small way, the work we do determines 'the distribution of lives' (Walzer, 1994). Indeed, to such an extent that, when our work lacks the requisite content in a system which restricts the supply of meaningful work, then we suffer from constrained opportunities to develop the human capabilities necessary for equal participation over the life course, with the result that our lives as a whole are less likely to be structured for meaningfulness.

I argue that the Compensation Argument fails to address three kinds of concerns arising from a social organisation of work which generates a scarcity of meaningful work: firstly, the injustice of an unfair distribution of the most attractive work; secondly, harms to the capability formation necessary for equal participation in making one's contribution; and thirdly, the diminishing of human well-being.

Firstly, the injustice of an unfair distribution of the most attractive work – all societies provide forms of meaningful work, but it has been meaningful work for the few and not for the many: Lane (1991) comments that it is the 'privileged class' for whom work offers 'self-direction, substantive complexity and challenge, variety, little supervision, and intrinsic satisfaction of excellence or self-determination' (ibid: 302). But liberal political theory has had little to say on the subject of elite expropriation of the most 'attractive work' (Fourier, 1983), nor has remedying the harms of non-meaningful work been central to theories of liberal egalitarian justice – and particularly of how social structures operate to shape an individual's search for meaning by enabling or disabling his capabilities for experiencing meaningfulness. Schooler (2007) theorises that one way in which social structure directly affects psychological functioning is through occupational conditions, where she defines social structure as 'the patterned interrelationships upon a set of individual and organisational statuses, as defined by the nature of their interacting roles' (ibid: 371). Schooler concludes that being able to undertake complex work, that is, work requiring self-direction, thought, and judgement, depends upon where the job is located in the social structure of society (ibid: 375). The unequal distribution of good quality work results in uneven health and well-being outcomes. In her review of health inequalities, Bambra (2011) shows that 'work and the socio-economic polarities it creates play a fundamental role in creating inequalities in the distribution of morbidity and mortality' (ibid: 187). She finds that the damage of harmful psychosocial work environments can be mitigated by doing work which allows for control over tasks, in organisations which consult workers over changes and underpinned by social welfare systems which support an individual's capacity to cope with stress and reversal. Taken together, such research provides a strong basis for concluding that the way society arranges the work of social cooperation is unjust, because it unfairly allocates and unnecessarily constrains the kind of work which is most likely to enable individuals to satisfy their fundamental human interests in exercising thought and judgement.[4] Given the importance of the nature of work for the development of human capabilities, justice requires that all work be organised to allow each person to experience the beings and doings which foster vital human capacities for thinking and feeling (cf. Sen, 2009).

Secondly, the harms of non-meaningful work to the capability formation necessary to secure equal participation over the life course – such harms are not mere inconveniences to be remedied elsewhere, because, from poorly developed human capabilities to physical, mental, and psychological deterioration, they affect the flourishing of an individual in every dimension of her life (Kohn & Schooler, 1983). Drawing upon Kohn and Schooler, Schwartz (1982) argues that the prevailing structure of work is degrading because it fails to provide for the exercise of autonomy which is vital to moral personhood (Schwartz, 1982: 636). Lack of autonomy whilst at work affects a person's ability to lead an autonomous life as a whole, because diminished autonomy at work cannot be made up for by full autonomy elsewhere: 'When persons work for considerable lengths of time at jobs that involve mainly mechanical activity, they tend to be made less capable of and less interested in rationally framing, pursuing and adjusting their own plans during the rest of their time' (Schwartz, 1982: 637). Autonomy is not simply having the capability to form one's own plans and purposes – it is also being able to exercise those capacities throughout all aspects of one's life. Schwartz (ibid) argues that action contexts cannot be artificially separated, and we cannot assume that if a person is able to practice autonomy in one sphere, then it does not matter if a person is deprived of autonomy in another. Kohn and Schooler (1983) find that the structure of work affects the development of abilities to sustain thought and exercise judgement, and that the loss of these abilities carries over into the rest of the person's life so that those who undertake challenging and creative market work also demonstrate a preference for leisure work with similar characteristics. Kornhauser (1965) in his study of factory workers in Detroit found that: 'factory employment, especially in routine production tasks, does give evidence of extinguishing workers' ambition, initiative, and purposeful direction toward life goals' (ibid: 252).

Specifically, the harms of non-meaningful work undermine an individual's ability to participate in the work of social cooperation over a lifetime by: stunting the development of her capabilities for free and autonomous action; undermining her sense of self-esteem and self-worth, of her standing relative to others; and thwarting her sense of efficacy, of being able to act with others upon the world. Together, these harms to capabilities, status, and efficacy reduce a person's ability to build the practical identity necessary to securing a sense that her life has meaning (cf. Korsegaard, 2009). Thus work with the right content for avoiding such harms is an essential experience for those living in contemporary societies who have an interest in the development of their human capabilities, the securing of their social status, and their sense of being able to act with others – which is all people.

Thirdly, the diminishing of human well-being – the psychology of work and organisational studies literatures provides compelling empirical evidence that being involved in 'satisfying work' is fundamental for psychological well-being 'across various domains of human functioning' (Blustein, 2008). Being able to experience meaningful work is linked to greater reported levels of well-being (Arnold et al, 2007) and to higher levels of job satisfaction (Sparks & Schenk, 2001). Kohn and Schooler (1983), in their studies of how occupational conditions affect cognitive and psychological functioning in a 1970s longitudinal research of male workers in the US, present evidence for the pervasive impact of the interior content of work upon an individual's sense of competence and self-respect: 'Hence, doing substantially complex work tends to increase one's respect for one's own capacities, one's valuation of self-direction, one's intellectuality (even in leisure-time pursuits), and one's sense that the problems one encounters are manageable' (ibid: 304). Kohn and Schooler (1983) looked at occupational self-direction in terms of substantial complexity, closeness of supervision, and routinisation, of which substantive complexity was the core concept. They define substantively complex work as 'work that, in its very substance, requires thought and independent judgement' (ibid: 106), and identify a positive link between the substantive complexity of work and intellectual flexibility. They observed that job conditions shape personality (ibid: 47): jobs differing in complexity and self-direction were occupied by people with differing levels of cognitive functioning, but over time the nature of the job led to changes in the intellectual flexibility of job holders. Kohn and Schooler (1983) conclude: 'The structural imperatives of the job – particularly those conditions that facilitate or restrict the exercise of self-direction in work – affect workers' values, orientations to the self and society, and cognitive functioning primarily through a direct process of learning from the job and generalising what has been learned to other realms of life' (ibid: 62–6, 126; see also Kornhauser, 1965).

The Kohn-Shooler hypothesis receives strong confirmation from a 1978 study of Polish workers (Kohn & Slomczynski, 1990), and a Japanese study of employed males (Naoi & Schooler, 1985). More recently, Hauser and Roan's (2007) evaluation of the Wisconsin Longitudinal Study shows there are moderate, but significant, effects of work complexity upon abstract reasoning abilities in mid-life. Additionally, Kornhauser (1965) identifies how the mental health of workers deteriorated 'as we move from skilled, responsible, varied types of work to jobs lower in those respects' (ibid: 75–6). Physical as well as mental health is affected by the interior content of work: for example, the Whitehall I and II studies showed that lack of control in the work environment, indicated by low job status, was associated with an increase in heart disease amongst government office workers (Bosma et al, 1997). Importantly, Bosma et al find that the objective state of low job control, independent of subjective reporting of the experience of low job control, has a deleterious impact upon health. They conclude that the harmful effects of disease can be ameliorated by increasing task variety and providing enriched opportunities for having a voice in decision-making.[5]

Such studies are highly suggestive of the way work affects the shape of a life, making the harms experienced at work difficult to remedy elsewhere. Taken together, evidence for the harms of non-meaningful work compels us to re-consider the claims of liberal theory – that the promotion of meaningful work is not state business because it violates liberal neutrality. Of course, such research does not allow us to claim that a particularly forthright, reflective, and capable individual doing non-meaningful work cannot find their lives to be meaningful because of their activities in other action contexts. But if the present organisation of work unjustly distributes, and constrains the supply of, meaningful work, resulting in distorted capabilities and diminished well-being, then having to do non-meaningful work does present formidable barriers to most people being able to do so.

In sum, the Compensation Argument fails because, firstly, our experiences in work shapes the capabilities, status, and identities which structure our lives as a whole and, secondly, the course of our life is influenced by the associations we belong to, and the social and economic positions we occupy (Young, 1990). But even though being able to do work with the requisite content structures an individual's life as whole, the supply of meaningful work is restricted. This means that a just society should seek to make available to everyone work which secures the opportunity to develop important human capabilities through being able to do something worthwhile in mutually respectful relations with others.

The need for meaningfulness argument

The harmfulness of non-meaningful work is derived from its inability to satisfy inescapable human interests in experiencing freedom, autonomy and dignity. Given the centrality of work in modern societies, the fundamental human need for meaning implied by such interests justifies institutional guarantees for meaningful work. Indeed, Terkel (1975) identifies the important relationship between meaningfulness and the everyday experience of working when he says 'Working is about the search for daily meaning as well as daily bread, for recognition as well as cash, for astonishment rather than torpor; in short, for a sort of life rather than a Monday through Friday sort of dying' (ibid: 1). Frankl (1978, 1988) claims that the search for meaning, or the 'will to meaning', is a universal human motivation which addresses a fundamental need for a sense that one's life is worth living (see also Maddi, 1970). In similar vein to Terkel, he says that the need for meaning is satisfied by active engagement with ordinary human living: 'Life ultimately means taking the responsibility to find the right answer to its problems and to fulfil the tasks which it constantly sets for each individual' (Frankl, 1984: 98). In a similar vein: meaning is 'the ontological significance of life; making sense of life situations, deriving purpose in existence' (Martsolf & Mickley, 1998: 294). Frankl acknowledges that although there is a givenness to everyday problems which appears to undermine our personal autonomy, this does not mean that we are not choosers. Instead, it is incumbent upon us to take responsibility for resolving the struggles of everyday living, demanding that we make reflective judgements when choosing the modes of acting and being appropriate to the situations in which we find ourselves. However, the necessity for an individual to choose how she responds to everyday situations does not imply that she bears all the responsibility for finding her life to be meaningful, since the Kohn-Schooler research shows us how social structures can enable or disable capabilities, status and efficacy, thereby determining the resources which society makes available to any particular individual in her search for meaning.

Our need for meaning is confirmed by a number of different sources. From *psychology*, Baumeister (1991) identifies four needs for meaning: a sense of purpose; a sense of efficacy; being able to view oneself as having positive value or being morally justified; and a sense of positive self-worth. Blustein (2006) identifies three fundamental needs for survival, self-determination, and relatedness, consistent with the harms of non-meaningful work already discussed: stunted capabilities, damaged self-worth, and an inhibited sense of efficacy in acting with others upon the world and in forming a practical identity. From *moral philosophy*, Wolf (2010) suggests that meaningfulness may be *'felt* to answer to a certain kind of human need' (Wolf, 2010: 26), one where we experience the need for meaningfulness as urgent and inescapable, because it addresses vital human interests which are necessary for human flourishing:

> Our interest in being able to see our lives as worthwhile from some point of view external to ourselves, and our interest in being able to see ourselves as part of an at least notional community that can understand us and that to some degree shares our point of view, then, seems to me to be pervasive if not universal. By engaging in projects of independent value, by protecting, preserving, creating, and realizing value the source of which lies outside of ourselves, we can satisfy these interests. *Indeed, it is hard to see how we could satisfy them in any other way* (ibid: 31, emphasis added).

From *political theory*, Holbrook (1977) describes the need for meaning as a 'primary human need' which he claims has been insufficiently recognised in political deliberation. According to Holbrook, reductionist philosophies have recast men and women into the roles of social functionaries in which our human worth has degraded into the value our roles and status positions have within the formal economy. Holbrook suggests that the frustrated will to meaning manifests itself in dysfunctions such as compulsive consumerism: 'If we reduce men to their functions, both in their life and the predominant philosophy of their existence, they are doomed [...] For man reduced to functional man, there is no possibility of finding any meaning in his life' (ibid: 183).

From *organisation and labour studies*, workers are not motivated purely by external goods – they act also out of a fundamental need for living a human kind of life, which goes beyond their need for survival. In the absence of a functioning politics of meaningfulness, workers will seek some outlet for their frustrated will to meaning. For example, denied the experience of autonomy, workers will invent simulations of autonomy in the form of games, or even make deliberate mistakes, which Burawoy (1979) describes as the art of 'making out'. Amongst numerous testimonies to such practices, is that of the worker who said: 'Yes, I want my signature on 'em too. Sometimes, out of pure meanness, when I make something, I put a little dent in it. I like to do something to make it really unique. Hit it with a hammer. I deliberately fuck it up to see if it'll get by, just so I can say I did it' (Mike Levevre, Steelworker, in Terkel, 1975: 22).

Organisation studies which have explored what meaning work has for people and what values are experienced as meaningful theorise how sources of meaning are multiple, and issue in a diversity of positive and negative values. For example, Rosso et al (2010) identify four sources of meaning in work: the self, others, the work context and spiritual life, and seven categories through which people experience their work as meaningful: authenticity, self-efficacy, self-esteem, purpose, belongingness, transcendence, and cultural and interpersonal sense-making. Michaelson et al (2013) argue for interdisciplinary research in meaningful work which combines organisational studies research on good outcomes from meaningful work for employees (job satisfaction, engagement, well-being) and for organisations (increased job performance, organisational citizenship, organisational commitment and identification, occupational identification, and customer satisfaction) with business ethics approaches which argue that meaningful work is of moral concern.

Employee engagement

In organisation studies, concern for meaningful work is, mainly, prompted by the desire of organisations to create schemes of work which will elevate employee engagement for improved organisational performance. In other words, management concern for meaningful work is instrumentally attentive to organisational needs – and to the needs of employees only so far as their satisfaction promotes financial outcomes. This is manifested in practitioner anxiety that the empirical evidence shows low and declining levels of employee engagement with possible impact upon business performance (Chalofsky, 2010; Gebauer & Loman, 2008).[6] Alfes et al (2010) report that 'the two most important drivers of [employee] engagement are meaningfulness of work and employee voice' (ibid: 36). Theoretically, they derive the link between meaningful work and employee engagement from Kahn's (1990) original paper which defines personal engagement as 'the harnessing of the organization members' selves to their work roles; in engagement people employ and express themselves physically, cognitively and emotionally during role performances' and personal disengagement as 'the uncoupling of selves from work roles; in disengagement, people withdraw and defend themselves physically, cognitively, or emotionally during role performances' (ibid: 694). Drawing on Goffman (1959), Kahn finds from his ethnographical studies of American holiday camps and an architecture firm that people have preferred selves that they bring to or withdraw from performance in their work roles. Thus, 'people who are personally engaged keep their selves within a role, without sacrificing one for the other' (ibid: 700), resulting in them becoming:

> [...] physically involved in tasks, whether alone or with others, cognitively vigilant, and empathetically connected to others in the service of the work they are doing in ways that display what they think and feel, their creativity, their beliefs and values, and their personal connections to others (ibid: 700).

This positive state of affairs is mediated by contexts which foster three psychological conditions: meaningfulness, safety, and availability (ibid: 703), where the sense of meaningfulness is

> a feeling that one is receiving a return on investments of one's self in the currency of physical, cognitive, or emotional energy. People experienced such meaningfulness when they felt worthwhile, useful, and valuable – as though they made a difference and were not taken for granted. They felt able to give to others and to the work itself in their roles and also able to receive (ibid: 704).

Employees are drawn to experiences which provide them with a sense of meaning (Shuck et al, 2011: 441; cf. Brown & Leigh, 1996; May et al, 2004), and those who perceive their work to be meaningful demonstrate higher levels of engagement (Harter et al, 2002; Fredrickson, 1998). In an empirical study of the psychological conditions of meaningfulness, May et al (2004) show that meaningfulness fully mediates the relationship between job enrichment and engagement, and also between role fit and engagement. Such studies are motivated by a desire to understand how to harness 'the human spirit at work' (ibid: 19). But the project of achieving elevated economic performance by means of social and organisational technologies to harvest the human soul seems a dubious, if not illegitimate, use of power. Purcell (2012) asks us to consider how employees benefit from having to conform to the normalising model of the engaged employee:

> In engagement, organisation members harness their full selves in active, complete work role performances by driving personal energy into physical, cognitive and emotional labours. Engaged individuals

are described as being psychologically present, fully *there,* attentive, feeling, connected, integrated, and focussed in their role performances. They are open to themselves and others, connected to work, and focussed in their role performance (Rich et al, 2010: 619 original emphasis).

The effort to maintain the appearance of high levels of engagement is not only inconsistent with Kahn's theory that engagement results from the unity of the individual's preferred self with their public role, but potentially issues in harms such as burnout and health problems (Welbourne, 2011).

Welbourne (2011) proposes that employee engagement, and therefore by implication meaningful work, is helpful to a company 'only if it leads to behaviours that the organization needs in order to execute its strategy and to be successful' (ibid: 89). Companies then can choose to ignore their employees' fundamental need for meaningful work, if they can gain their objectives by other means. Shuck and Wollard (2010) define employee engagement as 'an employee's cognitive, emotional and behavioural state directed towards desired organisational outcomes' (ibid: 15). However, the desired organisational outcomes are usually selected and promulgated by a managerial elite. Yet, the demand for 'above and beyond behaviours' can only be legitimated by establishing goals which are worthy of a person's engagement, and endorsed by that person as worthy of their effort. May et al (2004) suggest that the experience of meaningfulness is linked to judgements people make as to 'how valuable a work goal is in relation to an individual's own ideals or standards' (ibid: 19). Goals should earn our attention. Moreover, to be consistent with the intrinsic value of meaningfulness, they should be democratically authorised. Even in the absence of authorisation, goals, and purposes are never taken up automatically, but are instead subject to interpretation, contestation, resistance, and revision, giving rise to pre-political differences which can either be silenced (Milliken et al, 2003) or made productive for a common cause.

My claim is that individuals who undertake non-meaningful work are less likely to be able to satisfy their need for meaning, and are thereby made unacceptably vulnerable to the harms of non-meaningful work. Remedying such harms demands a politics of meaningfulness, enabled by collective deliberation over the ways in which the interior content of work can be structured to alleviate unfreedom, heteronomy, and misrecognition. Holbrook proposes that the fundamental question for politics is: 'what opportunities do societies provide for the satisfaction of the human need for meaning, and how should societies be organised in order to provide those opportunities?' (ibid). Hence, in a liberal democratic society, the expressive need for meaning is mobilised through a politics of meaningfulness, which seeks to ensure that people are not prevented from experiencing their lives as meaningful because of the work they do. I ground this mobilisation in the experience of work itself by making democratic practices constitutive of meaningfulness. I propose that the starting point for such a politics of meaningfulness is to understand meaningful work, not as a preference in the market, but as a fundamental human need.

Meaningfulness is a fundamental human need

My claim is that meaningfulness is a fundamental human need because it identifies and satisfies what is of profound importance for living a human kind of life: 'human needs are the things that must be if human life is to be' (Reader, 2005: 135). Thomson defines a fundamental need as:

> a non-derivative [...] inescapable necessary condition in order for the person A not to undergo serious harm (2005: 175).

A fundamental need directs us to what constitutes the normative outlines of a person's life: 'A person's needs have a bearing on how he ought to live, but drives have no such relevance' (Thomson, 1987: 14). A person is harmed when their fundamental needs remain unmet because, in such circumstances, they are 'deprived of activities and experiences that answer such interests' (Thomson, 2005: 177). Thomson (1987) argues that a fundamental need addresses vital interests that are characteristic of a person's essential nature. Vital interests are reasons which lie behind our 'non-instrumental desires' (ibid: 64), where an interest 'defines the range and type of activities and experiences that partly constitute a meaningful, worthwhile life, and it defines the nature of their worth' (ibid: 76). This means that harm is not to be understood simply in terms of thwarted desire satisfaction. Instead, harm arises when the unavoidable interests a person has in her life being a certain way are ignored or misrecognised, independent of whether or not her desires have been met. Interests may be unfulfilled even when desires are satisfied, because people adapt their expectations to the constraints of their circumstances (Elster, 1983): 'the poor who have never had money are deprived and harmed, even though their standard of living has never actually fallen' (Thomson, 1987: 26). This is because a continually unchanging, low quality of living, whilst it may keep life going, damages a person's potential to lead a life of human flourishing. Wolf (2010) suggests that the value of meaningfulness addresses several important human interests: an aspiration to objectivity or being connected to something larger than ourselves; a need for self-esteem or being able to judge ourselves and our projects as worthwhile; a sense of belonging or a wish not to be alone; and existential security (ibid: 28). Our self-esteem depends upon being able to assess ourselves and our situation from an external point of view, and then being able to judge our lives as 'good and valuable' against the standards generated by that exterior standpoint (ibid) which then becomes a 'rightful source of pride' (ibid). Meaningful work is a fundamental human need in this sense because it addresses our inescapable interest in living a life of human quality. And in modern societies, such inescapable interests are satisfied or thwarted in the work we do together in a system of social cooperation.

So, fundamental human needs are not simply what are required (negatively) if harm is to be avoided, but are necessities (positively) for a flourishing life. Furthermore, the fundamental needs which we attribute to a person depend on what we understand to be their value as human beings. Reader (2005) defines entrenched needs as needs which are determined by relatively unchangeable facts of nature, facts which generate a need for work of a certain kind. She argues that what we understand by need is grounded in what we understand the human being to be: for example, in the same way that food is not simply what sustains the human body, work is not simply what provides necessities for continuing to exist. If the human being is merely biological then work can be provided in any way which simply sustains life, it will not matter if the work is of poor quality. However, if the human being is essentially free, rational, and social, then this generates a demand that he is treated with respect in relation to work, which, given the kind of creature he is, requires that the work he does possesses the requisite interior content (see also Camus, 1955). Thus, providing a person with any kind of work which sustains human existence is not sufficient for satisfying the need for meaningful work, since a person who has become inured to non-meaningful work will still have inescapable interests in the goods of freedom, autonomy, and dignity. A useful illustration is a study of mid-life Australians which indicates that poor quality work involving job strain and insecurity may be as bad for health outcomes as unemployment (Broom et al, 2006).

I conclude that meaningful work is an 'inescapably valuable' (Thomson, 2005: 84) fundamental human need, because it answers our unavoidable interests in work being structured by freedom, autonomy, and dignity.[7] Therefore, to argue for the political importance of meaningful work is to make the claim that each individual ought to be treated as a certain kind of being, one possessing dignity and worth. Hence, in contemporary societies, the centrality of work for securing a life of human flourishing makes evaluating how work inhibits the development of capabilities, status, and efficacy a political priority. If we accept this claim, then meaningful work is not a mere preference in the market, but is a regulatory ideal requiring societies to pay attention to how work meets the fundamental human needs of its members by ensuring that the interior content of work has the requisite structure for meaningfulness.

Liberal perfectionism and a politics of meaningfulness

Adopting institutional guarantees for the content of work breaks with liberal neutrality, but this does not entail that the state is entitled to impose a perfectionist notion of work upon its members. Rather, several writers have identified that it is possible for a meaningful work ideal to operate within a framework of liberal perfectionism (Roessler, 2012; Keat, 2006, 2009b; Hsieh, 2008; Muirhead, 2004),[8] which Dzur (1998) describes as 'an effort to escape the shortcomings of the predominant liberal conception of the state as neutral in matters of life-choices without falling into the overreaching perfectionism of neoconservative writings' (ibid: 668; cf. Raz, 1986; cf. Sher, 1997). In a liberal perfectionist framework, meaningful work is an open-ended ideal containing an extensive range of values, allowing for the development of a diversity of capability formations and practical identities. So, although a liberal perfectionist framework for meaningful work will 'reject the role of state agents in channelling a person into a particular life' it will allow 'the "mild illiberality" of preventing the degradation or truncation of capabilities' (Dzur, 1998: 678). However, the protection of capabilities does not prevent there being a very wide range of activities, embodying a plurality of values – although excluding those which are likely to result in capability deformation of self or others. Consequently, institutional guarantees for meaningful work will permit many worthwhile activities containing a plurality of attractive values, thereby making available a wide diversity of individual interpretations of meaningfulness.[9]

Since people can continue to pursue a broad range of options for living, with the added security of capability protection, then liberal concerns that institutional guarantees for meaningful work will limit those options are overstated. Instead, setting meaningful work within a liberal perfectionist framework ensures that no person's efforts will be rendered futile by finding themselves in work which is structured by heteronomy, unfreedom, and misrecognition. However, the concerns of liberal neutralists may not be so easy to set aside, because any kind of perfectionism runs the risk of compromising our autonomy. Dzur (1998) addresses these anxieties by making the legitimacy of a liberal perfectionist framework dependent upon a general capability for collective self-determination in forming the values embodied within the framework of acting and being. By allowing for deliberative engagement in the interpretation of what values add to the meaningfulness of an individual life, the form that meaningful work might take for any individual remains available for amendment, ensuring that individuals are not coerced into taking work which is subjectively unappealing or objectively valueless. Furthermore, deliberation provides, not only for the interpretation and multiplication of values, but also for engagement with others over which of these values add to the meaning content of a life, disagreeing with them, being challenged, and challenging in return. Through deliberative engagement over values, people develop and exercise the political mode of being, opening up possibilities for personal and social change, in the process finding that being able to express the political mode of being can add, in itself, to the meaning content of a life.

Of course, simply securing institutional guarantees for the availability of meaningful work for all does not ensure that all individuals will experience their work as meaningful: 'no one can make a success of another person's life' (Raz, 1996: 8). Hurka (1993) calls this the problem of asymmetry where 'governments can provide necessary but not sufficient conditions for the realization of good lives' (Dzur, 1998: 677). In defending perfectionism, Hurka (1993) says that seeking the fulfilment of one's human potential requires the deliberate engagement of one's own self in projects and persons: it 'involves doing things, forming goals and realizing them in the world. And each person's doing must be largely her own, reflecting her energy and commitment' (ibid: 64). But even though the individual herself must engage actively with meaning possibilities, governments can ensure that social structures do not inhibit the individual's search for meaning by encouraging a diversity of organisational forms, such as mutuals, social enterprises, charities, and trade unions, which express a wide range of positive values conducive to meaning attribution. In sum, liberal perfectionism legitimated by a deliberative framework requires: firstly, an active orientation of the self towards the values embodied in substantive ideals, ensuring that values are not simply received, but interpreted, made, accepted or rejected; supported by, secondly, state action to ensure that social structures enable people to develop the capabilities and acquire the status for becoming co-authorities in the creation and maintenance of positive values. Finally, this implies a reordering of economic life to ensure widespread access to democratic participation at work.

The value of meaningfulness

We might argue that, in the absence of God, or some transcendental standpoint, the individual search for meaning in life is nonsensical (Nagel, 1971; Hare, 1972), and our lingering need for meaning simply 'a kind of hangover produced by overindulgence in the potent brew of metaphysics' (Kekes, 1986: 79). Whilst acknowledging that we can no longer rely upon a transcendental standpoint to satisfy our need for meaning, I argue, with Frankl (2004), Kekes (1986), and Wolf (2007), that this does not entail having to dispense with all possibility of being able to attribute meaning to our lives. Wolf (2007) says that 'an appropriate response to our status as specks in a vast universe is a concern and aspiration to have one's life wrapped up with projects of positive value' (ibid: 19–20; see also Metz, 2001a; Wong, 2008). Frankl (2004) says that the search for meaning is satisfied by the ordinary, everyday experiences towards which we adopt positive and active orientations: 'The perception of meaning boils down to becoming aware of a possibility against the background of reality, or, more simply, becoming aware of what can be done about a given situation' (ibid: 84). This indicates that meaningfulness, if such exists or can be created, must be sought in the mundane realities of our human lives, in our acting and being together in the messy everyday of human experience: 'Our lives have such meaning as we give to them. Meaning is made, not received or found; it is a human contribution to the world' (Kekes, 1986: 75). Even though meaningfulness is not given, but must, instead, be patched together from our experiences of living together, this does not force us to conclude that the value of meaningfulness is either illusory or cannot be described. Nor is the search for meaningfulness a purely personal affair for which we have no collective responsibility because we have already seen how social structures can inhibit or support meaning-making capabilities, rendering us more or less vulnerable to the harms of non-meaningful work, and unfairly distributing the available range of positive values. When interpretive differences become subject to public evaluation and judgement through a system of workplace democracy in which workers have the status to be co-authorities in the creation and interpretation of meaning, then such differences become a public resource of positive values, from which we can all draw to create meaningful self-identities. Thus, despite the loss of a transcendental standpoint, the search for meaningfulness remains a legitimate personal and social objective, where a politics of meaningfulness acts to ensure that all work has the requisite structure for meaningfulness (Levy, 2005).

Structuring the value of meaningfulness

Because work with the structure for meaningfulness shapes our lives as a whole, an individual seeking to find her life meaningful will be concerned to ensure that work contributes to 'the meaningfulness of her life, in virtue of the way it furthers her life story', rather than simply 'the sum total of good things in life' (Kauppinen, 2008: 2). I show that activities with the structure for meaningfulness combine objective valuing with subjective attachment in actions which promote what is good for the objects of our actions, whether a person, an animal, an institution, or a practice. In Wolf's work on the value of meaningfulness, meaningfulness has an overarching structure, given by what has independent value beyond its value to the individual (Wolf, 2010; see also Wolf, 1982, 1997a, 1997b, 2002, 2007). Wolf (2010) says:

> Our interest in living a meaningful life is not an interest in a life *feeling* a certain way, but rather an interest that it *be* a certain way, specifically, that it be one that can be appropriately appreciated, admired, or valued by others; that it be a life that contributes to or realizes or connects in some positive way with independent value (Wolf, 2010: 32).

Wolf describes a bipartite value of meaningfulness which unites objective valuation with subjective satisfaction: 'meaning arises when subjective attraction meets objective attractiveness' (ibid: 9), where the experience of meaningfulness is more likely to occur when a person becomes actively connected to a worthy object, or something or someone of value, such that they are 'gripped, excited, involved by it'

(Wolf, 1997a: 208; see also Starkey, 2006). She distinguishes the bipartite value of meaningfulness from morality (duty) or happiness (feelings of goodness), where meaningfulness is 'a category of value that is not reducible to happiness or morality, and that is realized by loving objects worthy of love and engaging with them in a positive way' (Wolf, 2010: 13). Wolf argues that a bipartite value for meaningfulness is necessary because the morality/self-interest distinction fails to describe all that is normatively significant about our actions and our relations. In particular, the morality/self-interest distinction is unable to account for the special ties we feel towards our 'ground projects' – projects which help us to answer the question 'what reasons do we have for living?' (Wolf, 2010: 56). Williams (1981) refers to ground projects as 'closely related to [one's] existence and [...] to a significant degree give meaning to [one's] life' (ibid: 12; see also Smart & Williams, 1983). The special significance for meaningfulness of ground projects comes from how they organise our values and frame our practical identities. Having ground projects provides us with the material for the narrative formation of our lives, directing us to the responsibilities we have to act appropriately towards the objects for the sake of which such projects exist. Thus, meaningfulness does not come from the aggregation of individual goods, but from long-lasting, *appropriate orientations* towards particular objects, such as persons, animals, or activities, where orientations are appropriate when they point us towards the responsibilities we have to further the good for those objects.

Wolf's bipartite value of meaningfulness integrates the objective and subjective dimensions when affective feelings of attachment, satisfaction, or fulfilment are united to an assessment of the worthiness of the object at which the feelings aim. This implies that in order for our ground projects to be meaningful, then what we subjectively feel to be meaningful must be joined to considerations of what is of independent value: 'A meaningful life is a life that a) the subject finds fulfilling, and b) contributes to or connects positively with something the value of which has its source outside the subject' (ibid: 20). Wolf argues that a purely subjective view of meaningfulness as the pursuit of feelings of fulfilment fails to address our intuitions concerning the meaningfulness of objects and activities. She illustrates her argument with Taylor's (1970) adaptation of the figure of Sisyphus, condemned to stone rolling, but who is given a drug to change him into someone who enjoys the activity of stone rolling (Wolf, 2010: 17). The reason Wolf gives for the continued meaninglessness of Sisyphus' life is that his efforts are objectively futile and their futility cannot be redeemed simply because they have become subjectively satisfying (see also Joske, 1974). In Wolf's bipartite view, the life of 'Sisyphus Fulfilled' cannot be meaningful without the objective dimension of being involved in activities which have independent value in a 'source *outside of* oneself' (Wolf, 2010: 19).[10]

This implies that how ground projects add to the meaning content of a life is not given automatically by the objective values they represent. Although a project may be acknowledged by all, including the one whose life is structured by the project, as valuable, this does not mean that the individual doing the project will have an affective sense of that project being meaningful. Objectively, there are 'many different kinds of lives that are good, many different activities and relationships that are valuable and can contribute to a life that is worth living' (Keat, 2009a: 360), but, subjectively, there is 'variability with respect to what is good for the different subjects' (ibid). Consequently, finding meaning in ground projects requires the exercise of 'subjective judgement' (Hicks & King, 2009: 643), involving 'a confirmatory search for information suggesting that one's life is meaningful' (ibid: 644). The search for information is the search for validation, for affirmation of one's judgements, out of which we construct the objective value of our doings and beings.

Subjective satisfactions contribute to a life of meaning when they arise from engagements with worthy objects: 'what is valuable is that in one's life we actively (and lovingly) engage in projects that give rise to this feeling, when the projects in question can be seen to have a certain kind of objective value' (ibid: 27). This includes what is appropriate for the particular kinds of creatures we are. 'Sisyphus Fulfilled' fails to meet the objective condition of the value of meaningfulness, but the full explanation for the continued meaninglessness of Sisyphus's activities lies, not just in the structure of the action, but in the failure to be attentive to the kind of creature Sisyphus is. Even though Sisyphus is now subjectively satisfied, the pointlessness of the task makes it unworthy of a creature who is capable of more complex and meaningful feats, and to whom violence had to be done in order to make him into the kind of creature who would experience such work as fulfilling. It is disrespectful of our status as human beings if the meaning of our valued activities or ground projects is reduced to manipulated feelings of satisfaction. This suggests that fulfilment which is worth experiencing must contain 'a cognitive component that requires seeing the source or object of fulfilment as being, in some independent way, good or worthwhile' (Wolf, 2010: 24). Some actions are inappropriate for a creature whose fundamental needs are not to be met in any way whatsoever, but in a manner consistent with the kind of creature he is – that is, one who has a fundamental human need to express free, autonomous acts directed towards worthy objects in respectful association with others.[11]

The capability for objective valuing: Worthy objects in the objective dimension

Whilst the bipartite value of meaningfulness provides us with the means to identify which activities have the structure for meaningfulness, it does not tell us how these activities translate into the actual experience of meaningfulness for any particular individual. I propose that to experience meaningfulness, we need to become valuers, able to recognise what has objective worth, and to affectively appropriate positive values to our lives. When we become valuers, we provide ourselves with the opportunity to become 'appropriately related to what has worth' (Wolf, 2010: 179) by developing the capabilities for objective valuation and subjective attachment, through which we learn to appreciate what objects have value, and to generate the *relevant orientations* towards those objects. I argue that the relevant orientations are those which motivate the right actions consistent with the nature of the object: for example, unconditional love when parenting a child or respectful care when looking after an aged relative. In addition, becoming a valuer must be incorporated into our practical identities, where we see ourselves as having the status as co-authorities entitled both to make judgements upon the worthiness of objects and to decide upon how to act towards those objects appropriately. However, developing the capabilities and practical identity necessary for becoming a valuer depends upon our being able to engage in activities which connect us to things that matter: 'connecting with something of worth in a way that enables the direct appreciation of the value of one's activity' (ibid: 189). This is because, by investing their objects with meaning and positive values, and educating our capacities for judging and feeling, these connections are intrinsically valuable: 'we flourish through (meritorious) activity such as parenting and music making, because these activities involve an appreciation of things that matter, things with worth' (ibid: 179). Although purposes derive from the needs and characteristics of worthy objects, they are not just read off from worthy objects, but are shaped and created by processes of interpretation, disagreement, and consensus. In turn, objects themselves are socially constructed: for example, in contrast to earlier historical periods, the object of modern parenting is the child who is entitled to an extended period of care, education, and development, exempting them from hard labour, early marriage, or adult responsibilities.

The purpose of work

The purposes we create to attend to worthy objects are shaped, in part, by what we understand to be the final ends of work. If work is just to ensure survival or to provide a surplus for leisure, then work is simply a means to an end, and activities can be structured in any way which achieves the relevant ends, including by 'unpleasant toil' (Sayers, 2005: 608). Drawing upon Marx's concept of alienated work, in which we 'relate to our own product or activity as if it is something independent or hostile' (ibid: 609), Sayers opposes this instrumental view of work to work as an end-in-itself, that is 'productive, creative activity' which should be 'an expression and confirmation of our creative powers' (ibid: 610; see Marx 1978 [1867]). Thus, in work as an end-in-itself, the purpose of work is to achieve self-realisation by becoming productive and creative beings. However, an important feature of non-alienated work is that it is not arrived at through individual effort alone, but through inter-dependency and cooperation, specifically through the reconciliation and repair (Spelman, 2003) of our relations to self, others, our products, and the world. In alienated work, the worker is divorced from his skills and capabilities when the content of work inhibits his sense of autonomy over his actions. He is separated from his own self when the relations and circumstances of work fail to support his sense of identity as an efficacious, distinct person; and he is divided from others, such that he values the other person only for her position in the division of labour, making the mutual needs, which should be a source of solidarity, 'a source of tactical advantage' (Miller, 2003). In work as an end-in-itself, the purpose of work is to restore our alienated relations by making of the world a home, where 'our coming to be at home in our world is not our natural and initial condition; rather it is an achievement, a result of human activity and work, both individual and social' (Sayers, 2005: 613). Meaningful work is therefore work which has both the object and the activity in mind. By developing the capability for objective valuing, we become participants in constructing purposes consistent with the interests of worthy objects, through activities which are characterised by autonomy, freedom, and dignity. And by attending to both the object and the activity, we create and repair the human world, making it a habitation suitable for human flourishing.

Creating purposes

A life of meaning is a life with a *purpose*: 'A life has point when it is oriented toward goals which transcend the limits of the individual, goals which are more valuable than the subjective concerns of any one person' (Levy, 2005: 178). But the life of a person does not reduce to her goals or purposes: 'It is degrading for a man to be regarded as merely serving a purpose' (Baier, 2000 [1957]: 120). Besides, not all purposes are equally worthwhile – some goals are trivial, reprehensible, or even wicked. Furthermore, a life defined by its goals is vulnerable to devaluation, as a consequence either of failure, or of over-achievement. For example, Wiggins's (1998) farmer, trapped in a cycle of endless achievement in which the farmer buys land to grow corn to feed pigs, illustrates the pointlessness of the repetitive recreation of the same goal without resolution, unconnected to a wider structure of value. Even though 'lives do not acquire meaning just in case they achieve goals' (Levy, 2005: 178), goals can add to the meaning content of a life. This is so, even where the activities concerned lack intrinsic merit, as is the case with many kinds of hard work (Walzer, 1983), since those engaged in dirty, hard, or menial work are not unjustified in claiming meaning for those activities when their ends benefit society; for example, cleaning sewers is vital for public health. In case study research of several workplaces from banks to retail, Doherty (2009) found that work interpreted from 'the outside' as unskilled, poor quality work, was often seen by workers themselves as invested in complex social interactions and meaning: 'The job I'm doing now (customer service) is mostly pluses because I like dealing with people and I like arguing! I love the job I'm doing now (Deirdre)' (ibid: 92). Thus, when sufficient political space is given to interpretive sense-making, then even purposes judged as less worthwhile by society can acquire valuable meaning for those doing them – and when these judgements are brought into public deliberation through democratic practices, they have the potential to reframe society's valuation of the worthiness of activities.

Democratic deliberation

Democratic deliberation provides a way to construct the objective basis for independent value, allowing individuals to deploy meaning-making capabilities in interpreting, shaping, and ordering purposes. Lawrence (1977) suggests that people in the same organisation will pursue different types of primary purposes. They will pursue the *normative* primary task, or the official version of the task; the *existential* primary task or the one they believe they are doing; or the *phenomenal* primary task or the task which can be deduced from their behaviour. The distances between formal description of the purpose, beliefs about the purpose, and actual behaviours open out the deliberative space for contestation and interpretive differences over purposes. This directs us to the potential of democratic practices at the level of the task to bring into public view interpretive differences over values, meanings, and purposes. We should be careful, however, not to conclude that, just by filtering the meaning of poor quality work through deliberative public evaluation, we have satisfied all normative concerns with respect to the content of work, since 'boring work is boring work' (Carter, 2003: 179). If the work fails to provide sufficient meaning in an objective sense, then it must be reorganised to ensure that it contains a sufficient range of worthy objects embodying attractive values, where activities, to be consistent with the ends of work as self-realisation and reconciliation, are structured by autonomy, freedom, and dignity. Moreover, to be susceptible to meaning appropriation, purposes need to be contained within wider structures of value, such as the roles, practices, and institutions which make up the fabric of a system of social cooperation, where to be a practice participant or institutional member is also to be afforded a vantage point for deliberation with others over the value of those objects through accessing information about the worthiness of objects, and assessing whether our actions and orientations are appropriate for the objects in question (cf. MacIntyre, 1981).

In sum, the purposes of work are concerned both with the object and the activity. The object is constructed through interpretive sense-making, and the activity is both a mediator for self-realisation and a means to attend to the needs of worthy objects. The capability for objective valuing is formed and exercised through institutional structures of value which enable us to engage with others in determining the purposes and ends of work. Through the practice of objective valuing, we join with others in creating and maintaining positive values, which in turn generates both objects and activities consistent with the value of meaningfulness, thereby affirming and validating our appropriation of worthy objects to the meaning content of our lives.

The capability for subjective attachment: Affective appropriation in the subjective dimension

Recognition of the value of worthy objects, and even active involvement with those worthy objects through public practices, does not guarantee that a person will find those objects and activities to be personally meaningful – what is also needed is their affective incorporation into the meaning content of that person's life. Practices and projects are sources of worthy objects and sites for the development of the relevant capabilities for meaningfulness, but to secure the value of meaningfulness to their lives, a person must also experience those worthy objects as subjectively attractive. Realising subjective attractiveness requires that a person be able to incorporate worthy objects into her life, such that her life is shaped by the orientations and actions promoting the good for the worthy objects in question. But there may be occasions when, although we may recognise the objective value of things, we may be unable to experience them as valuable for our own lives. Raz (2001) says that the attempt to revive the mood of a depressed person by pointing out to them the beauties and treasures of the world is unlikely to be successful: 'Their problem is not the absence of value in the world but the absence of meaning in their lives' (ibid: 19). In short, without affective attachment, worthy objects cannot, on their own, add to the meaning content of a life: 'Concrete attachments are good for those whose attachments they are; their value is within the sphere of personal meaning. The uniqueness of an object or pursuit established by an attachment is uniqueness to one person, not uniqueness impersonally judged' (Raz, 2001: 39). This means that, for worthwhile activities to add to the meaning content of our lives, we need to experience them as subjectively attractive: 'A housewife and mother, a doctor, or a bus driver may be competently doing a socially valuable job, but because she is not engaged by her work ... she has no categorical desires that give her a reason to live' (Wolf, 1997a: 211). And this implies limits to public practices as a source of meaningfulness because, although public acknowledgement of value or worthiness reinforces our affective engagement with values, public acknowledgement will not compensate for a person finding an activity insufficiently attractive. An achievement can be objectively and publically valued as a genuine contribution, but still be subjectively disvalued by the individual whose achievement it is. Arneson (2000) claims that the slave's achievements are not diminished by his state of slavery

– they can still add to the perfection of his life, although he qualifies this by adding 'no doubt achievement does more to enhance an agent's life, other things being equal, when the agent wholeheartedly endorses the doing and properly rates its value' (ibid: 57). Arneson does not find that the absence of subjective endorsement prevents an exceptional achievement from counting towards the *perfection* of a person's life, but, in my application of the bipartite value of meaningfulness to work, it would constitute a formidable barrier to the *meaningfulness* of that person's life.

Appropriation and affective attachment

I argue that for persons, objects, and activities of value to be constitutive of the meaning content of our lives, we must make them our own through a process of affective appropriation. Affective appropriation in the bipartite value of meaningfulness implies legitimate emotional engagement with worthy objects where legitimacy is given by how our emotions direct us toward what is good for worthy objects. As a consequence of affective appropriation, we acknowledge them as ours because of the particular place they have within our lives, giving us reasons to regard our life as worth living. But we also acknowledge them as ours because their objective value confirms that we are right to give them such prominence in our lives:

> The personal meaning of objects, causes and pursuits depends upon their impersonal value, and is conditional upon it. But things of value have to be appropriated by us to endow our lives with meaning, meaning which is a precondition for life being either a success or a failure (Raz, 2001: 20).

Drawing on Raz's identification of the need for appropriation of 'things of value', I understand appropriation not in the pejorative sense of exploitation, but as an active orientation of one's self to the particular value of worthy objects, requiring a form of emotional engagement which does not seek to secure in ourselves a satisfying state of mind, but seeks instead what is good for worthy objects. Consequently, not just any kind of emotional state will do for meaning appropriation – some emotions directed at worthy objects are not legitimate if they lead to abuse, or simply misrecognition, of what constitutes the good for the object. This suggests that we need an account of emotional engagement which describes the kind of affective appropriation of worthy objects capable of fostering the correct orientations towards the objects in question. Nussbaum (2001) characterises emotions as 'forms of judgement' (ibid: 22) which, in their intensity and particularity, are 'acknowledgements of neediness and lack of self-sufficiency' (ibid). Because they are directed at objects (goals, projects, persons) constituting our vital interests in our conception of the good life, such emotions indicate where we are vulnerable to reversion, loss, or harm: 'The emotional importance of the projects that one values is revealed in the whole complex array of feelings to which one becomes vulnerable by virtue of one's engagement with them' (Scheffler, 2006: 254; see also Reader, 2007). Our sense of meaning, our place in the world, is dependent upon the flourishing of the worthy objects we have appropriated to the meaning content of our lives, where the type and intensity of our emotions indicate the relative importance of various objects, and how they structure our lives as a whole. Nussbaum specifies the normative dimensions of the relevant emotions in relation to their objects which explains also the nature of our vulnerability: firstly, our emotions have an object (and in the value of meaningfulness, it is a worthy object); secondly, the kind of emotion which it is appropriate for us to experience is 'internal' to the object (Nussbaum, 2001: 27), in other words, it is not only the place the object occupies in our lives, but also the nature of the object itself which specifies the correct emotional orientation; thirdly, our beliefs about the object generate types of emotions, for example, the anger we experience if a loved one is threatened (ibid: 29); and fourthly, the kind and intensity of our emotions signals the value of the object, they are 'concerned with value, they see their object as invested with value or importance' (ibid: 30). Hence our emotions alert us to what is important in our lives: in their intensity and persistence they indicate the shape of our lives, and direct us to how the judgements we make are legitimate when they are structured by what is good for the worthy objects to which we are affectively engaged.

But our emotions do not simply happen to us, rendering us out of control and unable to exercise freedom of choice (cf. Wallace, 1993). Instead, emotions are susceptible to change in the light of new evaluations and judgements, potentially leading to reassessments of the worthiness of objects: 'Transformation in feeling for oneself is a transformation in judgements about the self' (Gilligan, 1982). Developed emotions are person-specific, as well as object-appropriate; that is, they are constituted by the place the object has in the life of the person whose emotions they are, as well as by the nature of the object: 'they insist on the real importance of their object, but they also embody the person's own commitment to the object as a part of her scheme of ends' (Nussbaum, 2001: 33). They are eudaimonistic (ibid: 31) because they are concerned with both the person's, and the object's, flourishing, and they specify the appropriate actions we should take towards worthy objects, such as deciding, making, preserving, caring, and restoring (cf. Spelman, 2003). This means that emotions which enable legitimate affective appropriation of worthy objects are 'merited emotions' (Kauppinen, 2008), that is, they are emotions which are structured by the recognition that the objective worthiness of the object *merits* our emotional engagement with the object (Kauppinen, 2008). In addition, they are merited because they reflect legitimate attachments; for example, unmerited emotions include feelings of attachment which keep us in destructive personal relationships, or foster misplaced loyalty to dysfunctional practices or institutions. 'Merited emotions' help us to forgo personal welfare maximisation: they support our recognition that our vulnerability to loss or harm of worthy objects is alleviated if we act to fulfil our responsibilities towards these objects, even if such actions are not maximally beneficial to ourselves. In sum, emotional engagement enables legitimate affective appropriation of worthy objects in two ways: firstly, when the objects are worthy of our emotional engagement, and secondly, when our emotions direct our attention and actions towards what is good for worthy objects.

Equal co-authorities in the realm of value

In my account of the bipartite value of meaningfulness, I show that being able to experience meaningfulness depends not only upon our becoming valuers, able to exercise the capabilities for objective valuing and affective attachment, but also upon our equal status as co-authorities in the realm of value. This is because to be involved in the co-creation of meaning, we need to experience ourselves as worthy of the entitlement to speak and be heard, where participating in meaning-making is necessary for experiencing our lives as worthwhile: 'human beings denied the opportunity to exercise their world-building capacities live an impoverished life, a life that is somehow less human, a life without freedom, without happiness' (Honig, 1993: 112). Christiano (2005) proposes that the fundamentally relevant feature of the person which grounds the principle of egalitarian justice is 'their authority in the realm of value' (ibid: 49) and it is in virtue of each person's status as authorities that we give each person their due (ibid). Potentially, all persons possess the capabilities for objective valuing and subjective attachment, including being able to appreciate, engage with, and produce values. This means that being a valuer applies to all persons with no distinctions which are relevant to a theory of justice.

But although developing one's human potential contributes to an activity being meaningful, simply realising one's capacities is not the same as having a sense of one's life being worth living, since 'a slave might be forced to do theoretical physics and to do it surprisingly well' (Arneson, 2000: 44). For meaningfulness, we must also find the project to be subjectively attractive, as well as judged objectively worthwhile against the values we have incorporated into our practical identities – and we maintain a sense of meaning by continuing to care about what we are doing in relation to worthy objects. Indeed, it is in the interlocking of the objective and subjective dimensions of the bipartite value of meaningfulness that we ensure a meaningful activity is not only recognised as objectively valuable and subjectively engaging, but is experienced as such by the individual whose activity it is: 'meaning consists of engagement in an activity that is not only subjectively engaging, but that is also subjectively experienced as being meaningful' (Kekes, 1986: 97). This requires a 'fittingness between certain kinds of activities and the potential for fulfilment' which Wolf calls Fitting Fulfilment (Wolf, 1997a: 216–17; see also Muirhead, 2004). Fitting Fulfilment arises when there is a match between activities with the requisite structure for capability formation and the individual's own valuations of which activities and capability formations are worth pursuing. I argue that Fitting Fulfilment is more likely to be realised when we become valuers: that is, when we develop the capabilities relevant to realising the bipartite value of meaningfulness, given by the capabilities for objective valuing and subjective attachment, and where we possess a sense of our worthiness to be valuers.

In sum, we need both the capabilities for meaningfulness and a sense of our status as co-authorities to give us confidence that we are entitled to engage with others in the co-creation of values; this means that we must be situated in social contexts which affirm our equal status as co-authorities, and support our development of the 'human capacity for building, preserving, and caring for a world that can survive us and remain a place fit to live in for those who come after us' (Arendt, 1977 [1954]: 95). Thus, the two capabilities united to status specify the manner in which the objective and subjective dimensions of the bipartite value of meaningfulness can be integrated in actual human lives.

In Chapter 2, interpretive meaning-making, using the capabilities and status of being a valuer, is an aspect of the critical evaluation of the content and organisation of work. In order to help us distinguish between desirable and undesirable work, I specify a positive critical conception of meaningful work using an ethic of care as the standpoint from which to judge between different kinds of activities.

2
Proliferating Meaningful Work: Meaning-Making and an Ethic of Care

Serious political attention to the organisation and content of work is lacking. To remedy this neglect, my objective is to outline the normative content of a political and social agenda which aims at proliferating the experience of meaningfulness in all kinds of work, where meaningfulness is structured by the bipartite value of meaningfulness. To that end, I identify the importance of each person being able to engage in the creation and maintenance of a repertoire of positive meanings, from which they draw to create the practical identities giving them a sense that their lives are worth living. Widespread participation in positive value generation requires an opportunity structure which fosters the relevant capability formation and status equality through institutional arrangements for democratic participation. Furthermore, positive value generation depends upon our being able to distinguish between more or less meaningful work, for which we require a critical conception of meaningful work constituted by a standpoint from where we can reflect and make judgements between different kinds of meanings and values. In order to provide the tools for evaluative meaning-making in the content of work, I draw upon critical social theory to specify a positive critical conception of meaningful work which distinguishes between meaningful and non-meaningful work from the standpoint of an ethic of care.

The meaning potential of all work

Engaging with positive meaning by creating, nurturing, and promoting the values embodied in worthy objects such as persons, animals, material things or institutions is something we all do – indeed, we *must* do, if we are to be human. All work, even the most unpromising, contains

39

positive meanings and values. These meanings, however, are not given automatically: instead, they arise out of inter-relations between self, others, and the material world (Dejours, 2006). As we interact with people and things in order to get the work done, then we find ourselves struggling with resistances and differences – struggles which give rise to new understandings of the work we do, and of the people we do it with and for. For example, a study of hospital cleaners found that, despite the low social valuation of their work, some cleaners sought to positively re-value their work as skilled and worthwhile by actively engaging in tasks which supported patient recovery, including interacting with patients, visitors, and nurses (Wrzesniewski & Dutton, 2001). But in power-laden hierarchies, where the organisation of work – and indeed, interpretive meaning-making more broadly – is assumed to be a management prerogative, such differing interpretations of meaning and value often remain as pre-political potentials, unless they are brought into public evaluation through democratic deliberation. When interpretive differences become subject to public evaluation and judgement through a system of workplace democracy in which workers are co-decision-makers, then they have the potential to generate a public resource of positive values, from which we can each draw to create meaningful self-identities. Hence, the organisation of work is an important political project because, not only do we make work, but to the extent we diminish or enhance work as a source of positive values, then work makes us, giving narrative shape to our lives by grounding our identities and forming our capabilities. The creation and promotion of meanings in work, however, is riven by the uses and abuses of power. In other words, work is replete with politics and difficult choices, demanding that we *work out* what justice demands with respect to what kind of work is made available to whom, how it is to be organised, and how we are to determine what it means to us. Therefore, making interpretive difference productive of positive meaning requires a politics of meaningfulness, instituted by a system of workplace democracy, where economic citizenship is rooted not only in paid employment, but in all the work – paid and unpaid – we contribute to the maintenance of a complex system of social cooperation.

Positive and negative meanings of work

Raz says: 'meaning comes through a common history and through work' (Raz, 2001: 20). Part of our common history is our meanings of work repertoire – the reserve of meanings and values, both positive and negative, which is in continuous interpretive movement, but which provides a vital resource for collective and personal identity formation. However, this resource of meanings is frequently exploited by political ideologies or managerial discourse to achieve conceptual closure for the purpose of maintaining the existing hierarchy of valuations. Hence we find, in contemporary ideological formations of work, meanings being co-opted to distinguish between different kinds of activities so that some work is rendered invisible, demoted to mere leisure, or simply designated non-work, obscuring the fact that work encompasses an enormous diversity of activities necessary to the reproduction of society, many of which evade fixed categorisation, and over which there is no final agreement. Moreover, positive and negative meanings of work inform the value we give to work as a human activity. So, the negative meaning of work as a curse informs both the economic conception of work as a disutility and the various 'end of work' theses (cf. Granter, 2009), whereas the positive meaning of work as expressive, creative self-realisation informs concepts of work based upon the craft ideal (Sennett, 2008). In turn, the craft ideal is criticised for excluding some groups, such as women, from desirable, higher paid occupations, and prospects for the 'end of work' can be viewed positively as opening up new dimensions of human activity, such as serious leisure.

How we use our meanings of work repertoire reflects our underlying normative assumptions: work can be presented as morally neutral when it is theorised as part of an instrumentalised system of economic exchange (Smith, 2009: 48), or as morally negative when it is conceived as degrading and unfit for human beings (Spencer, 2009b). Normatively negative meanings of work allow work to be presented as irretrievably compromised as a source of moral action, competing with more meaningful forms of human activity, such as political action. Negative conceptions of work prompt propositions that work must be contained because it has colonised too much of human life, or eliminated because it has failed to fulfil its promise as a site of human expressiveness. Conversely, positive conceptions of work promote strategies to broaden work to undervalued human activities, or to advance work as the pre-eminent site for the formation of a virtuous citizenry (Spencer, 2009a). I make use of an ethic of care within a positive critical conception of meaningful work to provide normative resources for distinguishing between values which are more or less promoting of the experience of meaningfulness.

Creating meanings through dissent, difference, and deliberation

By treating meaningful work as a regulative ideal we are able to retrieve a positive critical conception of work which can be distinguished from other conceptions of work, such as decent work or work as an economic activity. But although a positive critical conception of meaningful work supports an enriched plurality of positive values in a liberal perfectionist framework, being able to experience work as actually meaningful depends also upon our individual meaning-making capabilities, combined with the opportunity structure made available to us by society. A crucial dimension of the meaning-making opportunity structure is the deliberative democratic practices which promote disagreement and struggle over the meanings of work. Moreover, the process of deliberative engagement with others is productive of our sense of self, forming our subjective attachments (or de-attachments) to the work we do together, constituting a vital dimension of our practical identities, and making democratic participation itself one of the worthy objects. Therefore, to participate in creating differences in meaning we must become, and identify ourselves as being, valuers, able to exercise the two capabilities for objective valuing and subjective attachment, in addition to having confidence in our equal status as co-authorities.

Meanings are made through joint working. For example, Wrzesniewski et al (2003) describe how the engaged intersubjective sense-making activities of workers shape their understanding not only of *what* they do, but also the *significance* of what they do: 'Employees actively notice, interpret and seek out cues in the course of daily interaction that convey evaluation and worth [...] the creation, alteration and destruction of meaning at work occur in concert with others on a daily basis' (ibid: 126–7). Rather than a rational separation between the worker and the work, 'worker and work form one entity through the lived experience of work. Competence is thus seen as constituted by the meaning of the work takes on for the worker in his or her experience of it' (Sandberg, 2000: 11). Making intersubjective encounters central to the meaningfulness of work is essential to recognising how dimensions of shared agency and cooperation contribute to the objective valuing and subjective attractiveness of meaningful work. Deliberating over meanings and values is a joint undertaking with others, requiring status and capability equality. To deliberate under conditions of equality with others, we must be situated in social structures, such as practices, roles, and institutions, conducive to supporting intersubjective relations with the relevant normative characteristics for supporting our status as co-authorities in meaning-making and for developing our meaning-making capabilities. When structured by democratic practices – and because it involves so many of us, whether paid or unpaid – work provides a particularly rich value-generative environment. As a consequence of moments of deliberative meaning-making through joint working, democratically organised work settings foster positive intersubjective relations which are not merely functional or incidental, but are in themselves constitutive of the possibility of work being able to contribute to the meaning content of a life (see Stacey, 2005). However, contemporary work, whether formally in the market or informally defined by the market, is vulnerable to an impoverishment of positive meanings.

Impoverishing work as a source of meaningfulness

The standard economic conception of work

The standard economic conception of work is one of consumption rather than production, where work is 'the sacrifice that makes the purchase of commodities possible' (Lane, 1992: 48). In standard economics, work is understood positively as the maximum level of wages which a worker can exchange for their labour, and negatively as a disutility which workers will prefer to trade for leisure. But such assumptions shackle us to a narrow understanding of work as paid employment – as market work which is carried out in the formal economy. Work in the production paradigm (Gurtler, 2005: 124) takes workers to be rationally self-interested individuals, and assumes that the social product issues from measurable economic activity. Consequently, human development is valued when it produces economic outputs, but is disvalued when it takes place in other action contexts, such as the family and civic society (Meda, 1996: 639). In turn, work as a vital source of positive meanings is diminished and marginalised as a means to positive identity formation.

Neglecting the interior content of work

In the standard economic concept of work, once we have satisfied the requirements of justice for equality of participation in the open competition for paid employment and desirable work, what goes on *inside* the experience of work is of little philosophical interest. Hence, Nozick (1974) reduces the philosophy of work to the economic argument that market efficiency mediates the supply of meaningful work which is created by employers when they divide work into more satisfying segments, create work teams, and employ task rotation (ibid: 248). Meaningful work will then become more or less available according to whether the organisation of work used to generate meaningful work promotes productive efficiency. If productivity rises, then owners will reorganise to make work meaningful, but if productivity stays the same, then worker preferences for meaningful work will generate competition for labour, thereby forcing owners to reorganise work. There are no normative considerations in these two cases because market efficiency will determine sufficient availability of meaningful work to satisfy expressed preferences. The only situation where normative considerations arise is when reorganising work for meaningfulness results in reduced efficiency, giving owners no incentive to create meaningful work. In circumstances where the market fails to satisfy workers' preferences for meaningful work, then normative considerations may direct us to compensatory mechanisms, such as: workers being able to trade off pay for more meaningful work; customers being prepared to bear the extra costs; or state prohibition of non-meaningful work (Nozick, 1974: 247–9). In the end, since the market will sort out preferences for meaningful work, supported by some compensatory mechanisms in cases of market failure, political theorists need have no further concerns for the interior content of work (Schwartz, 1982: 635).[1]

Conceptual closure in liberal political theory

Liberal political theorists have, with notable exceptions, neglected the conceptual evaluation of the interior content of work. Where meaningful work has been the subject of theoretical research, the result has generally been to constrain the variety of positive values by which we conceptualise meaningful work, in order to strengthen arguments that the concept of meaningful work is irredeemably substantive, and therefore inconsistent with the liberal commitment to neutrality.

One consequence of liberal political theory's narrow determination of the conceptual content of meaningful work has been to marginalise, and even eliminate, the value of intersubjectivity from the meaning content of work. For example, Elster (1986a) says that it is the element of 'mental challenge' (ibid: 113)[2] which distinguishes work conducive to self-realisation from work which is not. Such work is best promoted under conditions given by: the possibility of engaging 'in full-time concentration on one complex task' (ibid: 113) rather than rotating amongst a number of simple tasks; matching workers to jobs (ibid:

114) in a social order where 'for each individual there is some ability he can develop that will meet an effective demand' (ibid: 115); and where work is freely chosen, autonomously carried out, and enables social recognition (ibid: 115). Elster discounts 'spontaneous inter-personal relations' on the basis that they 'can be deeply satisfying but have no purpose beyond themselves' (ibid: 100). But his argument that inter-relations cannot support self-realisation because they are not intrinsic to the purposes of work is not supported by the empirical evidence, which reveals how intersubjective relations are essential if workers are to get their work done.[3] Complex socio-technical settings, such as operating theatres, air traffic controllers, factory work teams, R&D labs, are characterised by collaborative working where 'one encounters flows of choreographed attending, prescient anticipation, mutual adjustment, and entwined action, out of which routinely emerge without remark a stream of decisions that often have life or death implications' (Barley & Kunda, 2001: 89). By removing intersubjective relations from the meaning content of work, Elster describes a conception of meaningful work which constrains unnecessarily the range of positive values available for appropriation to the meaning content of a life. Consequently, not only does this reduce the plurality of values which might be made available for meaning appropriation, but it fails also to provide us with the theoretical resources to describe how intersubjective relations are inherent to the ability of workers to get their work done through the joint creation of meanings. Moreover, Elster's move cannot account for how economic and social arrange-ments render unjust the applications of power which lend meaning-making authority to a management elite.

In a sophisticated account of meaningful work which provides support to his theory of justice, Rawls (1999) makes meaningful work a human good because of its importance for generating self-respect in the political conception of the person – although, to avoid violating the principle of liberal neutrality, he does not make meaningful work one of the social goods. However, Rawls's concept of meaningful work ends up limiting the potential range of positive values because he ties the importance of meaningful work to the Aristotelian Principle (AP) – a psychological fact about human nature which explains how our desire for the primary goods motivates us to come together to form and sustain a just system of social cooperation. Rawls defines the AP as:

> The Aristotelian Principle states that, other things equal, human beings enjoy the exercise of their realised capacities (their innate or

trained abilities), and this enjoyment increases the more the capacity is realised or the greater its complexity (Rawls, 1999: 374).

But by constraining the conceptual core of meaningful work to complex activities, Rawls is in danger of violating his own commitment to neutrality, opening him up to the charge that he has introduced into the AP itself perfectionism by the backdoor. Proudfoot (1978) suggests that: 'the determination of simplicity and complexity, or of richness and poverty among human activities, may well depend upon prior conceptions of the good' (ibid: 265). Judgements about what activities are simple or complex are socially determined and subject to valuations based upon factors such as the social status of the kinds of people who normally undertake those activities in particular societies (ibid: 266). If the AP cannot be taken to be an incontestable natural fact about persons, then, at most, it becomes a kind of capability which we may or may not include in a worthwhile plan of living, since it may not be the only meaningful way to lead one's life. In the end, the determination of what is complex or simple, and how it contributes to a life which is worth living, is a critical judgement, the determination of which requires the capabilities for objective valuing and subjective attachment in the bipartite value of meaningfulness.

Constraining meaningful work to variety as opposed to specialisation

In an instructive example of conceptual closure, Arneson (1987) identifies meaningful work with variety, which he opposes to specialisation, in order to argue that meaningful work contains substantive normative commitments, making it a perfectionist ideal. Arneson (1987) argues against a right to meaningful work, as proposed by Schwartz (1982) and Doppelt (1984), on the grounds that this would require the state to promote a perfectionist ideal of what constitutes a good life. Under a regime of market socialism,[4] a right to meaningful work is objectionably paternalistic because people will form differing conceptions of living which may or may not include meaningful work. Some people may prefer non-meaningful work because the conceptions of living they have chosen include attributing meaning to their lives through activities other than work. Given the diversity of ways in which work can play a part in individual conceptions of living, it is illegitimate for the state to promote only those plans which contain meaningful work.[5] In any case, state perfectionism is redundant because market socialism is a system that is able to compensate those who must undertake unavoidable, boring, or dangerous work: 'in a well-regulated market economy that fairly distributes the benefits and burdens of economic cooperation, there is no ground for assigning individuals a further right to meaningful work beyond whatever array of meaningful work options the market happens to generate' (ibid: 536). This does not mean, however, that Arneson rejects the ideal of meaningful work. He suggests rather that meaningful work be 'considered as a regulative ideal that a socialist society – or any decent political economy – should regard as part of its mission gradually to fulfil' (ibid: 537).

In his conceptual understanding of meaningful work as interesting work, Arneson employs what he characterises as a 'narrow' definition of meaningful work, where the use of the descriptor 'interesting' is understood to be dependent upon individual tastes and preferences:

> What I am calling 'meaningful' is work that is interesting, that calls for intelligence and initiative, and that is attached to a job that gives the worker considerable freedom to decide how the work is to be done and a democratic say over the character of the work process and the policies pursued by the employing enterprise. The term 'meaningful work' might rather be thought to suggest work that serves a good cause as contrasted with work that serves trivial or pernicious aims (making and marketing hula hoops or mustard gas). No doubt it is better that people's work should objectively serve good causes and on the subjective side no doubt it is desirable that people should experience their work as making a contribution to the goals they support (ibid: 522–3).

Describing the concept of meaningful work in terms of 'interesting' work, allows Arneson to identify the perfectionist ideal of meaningful work with the positive values of variety and the freedom to choose one's occupation.[6] Arneson reads the ideal of 'meaningful work as variety' from Marx's critique of the division of labour: for Marx, the division of labour is harmful because it reduces our freedom to decide how to lead our life and frustrates our natural human preference for variety and challenge in work: 'Owing to the extensive use of machinery and to division of labour, the work of the proletarian has lost all individual character, and consequently, all charm for the workman' (Marx, 1948 [1848]). But by agreeing with Marx that the division of labour is harmful, we assume we can know what it is to experience the good life, where the good life consists in variety rather than specialisation: 'Narrow specialization is bad whether or not people want it'

(Arneson, 1987: 520). Arneson claims, plausibly, that if we then try to maximise meaningful work as variety, we end up by reducing the scope to satisfy human desire for other forms of living which may include specialisation – and, for Arneson, this kind of perfectionism is harmful, independent of the harms engendered by the technical division of labour.

From this position, Arneson critiques Schwartz (1982) for implying that we should have a 'state-mandated meaningfulness standard for all jobs' (Arneson, 1987: 523), which is mediated by meaningfulness as democratic participation: 'we are therefore committed to demanding that this hierarchical division be replaced by a meaningful or democratic, division of labour that will ensure that no one is employed mainly at routine operations' (Schwartz, 1982: 644). Arneson characterises Schwartz's proposal as unacceptable perfectionism which marginalises other kinds of goods people may wish to acquire from their work, such as those related to productive values where 'a worker might derive satisfaction from being a contributing member of an enterprise that efficiently serves vital human needs' (Arneson, 1987: 525).[7] A worker adhering to such values may find demands to participate in management decision-making in the democratic division of labour proposed by Schwartz a frustrating limitation upon achieving their preferences in work. Therefore, the value of meaningfulness, understood as the 'satisfactions intrinsic to the laboring process' (ibid: 525), competes with and, when embodied in a right to meaningful work, crowds out alternative values. But, in many contemporary work environments, participation is not a bolt-on, optional extra, but inherent to the joint action necessary for getting the work done. Achieving the goals of service, care, and effectiveness depends upon the intrinsic content of work being shaped by participatory practices and solidaristic relations between persons (Smith & Laitenen, 2009).

In sum, there is not the competition between the value of meaningfulness and other values which Arneson presumes, because part of what makes work meaningful is expressed through those other values of service, production, or contribution. Moreover, in a liberal perfectionist framework, the value of meaningfulness is not narrowly described by variety, but is rightly expansive, allowing for a diversity of values, including many of the goods listed by Arneson, such as solidarity, interpersonal relationships and responsible, skilful work. As a result, by attempting to avoid the perceived harms of state perfectionism, Arneson has failed to describe an adequate account of meaningful work, and diminished meaningful work as a rich source of the values we might wish to appropriate to our lives. Rather than preserving the widest field for freedom of interpretation in our subjective preferences for work which we can claim to be meaningful, Arneson has reduced our scope to make such claims to one-dimensional 'variety', with the consequence that our freedom to appropriate meanings has been circumscribed. This can be remedied by adopting a positive critical conception of work which pluralises the range of positive values, increasing our freedom to appropriate meanings of work to the meaning content of our lives, whether based on variety, specialisation, complex activities or some other value, such as caring.

Enriching work as a source of positive values

In order to identify strategies able to resist conceptual closure, I turn to feminist theory which has engaged in the difficult task of attempting to re-imagine how work might transcend a hierarchy of valuation circumscribed by the standard economic conception of work. Feminist theorists have drawn upon a more capacious understanding of the variety of activities constituting the work we do together in a system of social cooperation, including family and community work. Consequently, feminism has alerted us to the plurality of values and meanings already present in work, which are potentially available to enrich the possibility of work being meaningful within a liberal perfectionist framework. For instance, Cameron and Gibson-Graham (2003) argue that feminist strategies for reordering work take one of three directions: firstly, the separate spheres of economic activity are retained, but the sphere of reproduction is added in, leading to calls for women's unpaid work to be given a monetary value; secondly, the range of activities which count as work are expanded, but with the consequence that women's work, although now publicly recognised, occupies a subordinate status in the formal division of labour; and thirdly, economics itself is redefined, so that the economic landscape is conceived as diverse, made up of a variety of capitalist and non-capitalist enterprises, in which 'multiple and unfixed economic identities can be conceived' (Cameron & Gibson-Graham, 2003: 151). By reconceiving the work of social cooperation in this manner, we can start to perceive and to explore the values-resource of invisibilised work, making such values available for meaning appropriation through public deliberation which aims at proliferating positive meanings within a liberal perfectionist framework.

A productive concept for reordering our understanding of the work people do, as well as challenging conventional economic notions of work, is 'provisioning'. Provisioning consists of the everyday activities required to provide the necessities and goods that sustain families and individuals (Neysmith & Reitsma-Street, 2005; see also Power, 2004; Glucksmann, 1995), which, by being attentive to the variety of activities women undertake in their daily lives, 'breaks down distinctions between market, familial and social activities' (ibid: 381). It is complex and time consuming, requiring the provisioner to form networks and relationships which secure, not only the material survival of provisioners and their dependents, but also a sense of identity and belonging. Moreover, provisioning questions the way in which conventional economics treats citizens as undifferentiated labour participants and job holders, thereby casting those who are without paid employment into the category of welfare dependents, or rendering their work invisible as a form of social contribution. This makes the concept of provisioning useful for illuminating how people negotiate time/space boundaries in order to fulfil the requirements of their multiple social roles.

To theorise such work in the service of pluralising values in a concept of meaningful work, we need to come to a new understanding of time/space boundaries and our assumptions with respect to private/public distinctions.[8] Gal (2002) theorises the public/private binary using a process of 'fractal distinction' (ibid: 81), where the same space, through continuous recalibration signalled by different physical behaviours or linguistic symbols, is recast as private or public. Cal proposes that we imagine public/private distinctions recurring repeatedly inside the same space, and, rather than visualising them as boundaries carving up a territory, we should think of them as subdivisions nested inside one another according to the relations between persons and their social, economic, and political context. Increasingly, people must manage fluid spaces and unstable boundaries (where the very concept of boundaries is in doubt) as they move in and out of roles, or simultaneously occupy different roles – and such active management is a form of discursive and symbolic *work*. For example, a conversation in the playground may be about arranging a play date for children, the agenda for a meeting to campaign against a school/hospital closure, or the exchange of business ideas. Such discursive work, undertaken in rich intersubjective encounter, is generative of positive and negative values, making them available for incorporation into the meanings, and meaningfulness, of work (see also Halford & Leonard, 2006; Landes, 1995).

As the terms of reference between persons shift, the playground might be constituted in one moment as a public space, and in the next moment as a private space (see Coole, 2000). Ettlinger (2003) takes a relational and microspace approach to 'the spaces of interaction among people and nodes (workplaces) in networks of social interaction' (ibid: 146) which enables analyses across spheres of life. By so doing, she reveals the multiplicity of work timespaces, where 'workplaces can be situated in a firm, in a state-supported or governed office, in one's home, or some 'place' in the informal economy' (ibid: 150; see also Halford & Leonard, 2006). Leach (1998) documents how meanings of work are 'constructed and manipulated in the context of industrial homework' (ibid: 99) where 'the separation of home and work is largely a fiction' (ibid: 107). Homeworking blurs conventional space/time boundaries, leading to long working hours for women who have domestic responsibilities during the day, and homeworkers being treated as flexible labour because all their work – paid and unpaid – is symbolically domestic labour (ibid: 114). Thus, what work means to people cannot be captured by taking the formal workplace to be the only context in which work happens (see England & Lawson, 2005). Instead, what work is and what it means to us is socially constructed and intersubjectively negotiated, shaped by the context in which the work takes place and the purpose for which it is performed.

A value-generative conception of work: Timespaces, interwoven spheres, and materiality

In order to identify resources for a value-generative conception of meaningful work, I investigate and challenge treatments of work in the critical social theory tradition, specifically Hannah Arendt, Jurgen Habermas, and Axel Honneth. I use critical social theory to identify three strategies for re-imagining work: first, that work takes place in multiple timespaces; second, that work involves the exercise of different modes of being (and particularly, the political mode of being); and third, that work is constituted by intersubjective relations in joint action, including relations to materiality. Together, these themes help us to overcome the narrowed conceptual understandings of meaningful work offered by liberal political theorists for the sake of liberal neutrality. Rather, timespaces, modes of being, and intersubjectivity expand the range of positive values in work by allowing us to consider: *what* activities are to be counted as work, *when/where* work takes place, and *who* does what work. These are ethico-political questions which do not submit to final resolution, but remain contestable and therefore susceptible to collective deliberation over differences in meaning interpretation. They produce answers which do not reduce work to the employment relation, but instead enfold a wide range of productive and reproductive activities necessary to the work of social cooperation. Within a positive critical conception of meaningful work, they help us to understand how work can be made generative of positive values which are then made available for practical identity formation.

Multiple timespaces

Work cannot be confined to a simple understanding of bounded space, circumscribed by an employment contract. Instead the activities and roles of work traverse timespace boundaries in complex, sometimes paradoxical ways. A timespace boundary can be thought of as a 'container of meaning' (Thompson & Bunderson, 2001: 18), framing how we 'address the nature of the activities that occupy our time, including the significance that they assume' (ibid). Thinking about work as being enacted in timespaces allows us to conceive of workers as active agents, who incorporate diverse values of work into practical identities, becoming re-interpreters of the temporarily settled meanings which lend significance to the activities they do. Even so, how timespace dimensions influence perceptions of meaningfulness remains poorly understood. From an examination of two occupations (street sweepers and cathedral stonemasons), Truss & Madden (2013) find that the experience of meaningfulness depends upon temporal perceptions of forward looking and backward looking as workers seek to make sense of the meaning of their work. The internal experience of meaningfulness is constructed by workers in the midst of their activities, and whilst immersed in social structures and materiality which can act to foster or inhibit this psychological processing of meaningfulness.

Arendt (1958) identifies three existential categories and three conditions describing what it means to be in association with other human beings. These are: labour and life, work and worldliness, action and plurality.[9] Taking labour and work: labour produces things for consumption and work produces things for use, but labour and work do not consist merely in the kinds of objects produced. More fundamentally each enables different modes of being human, in the form of *animal laborans* and *homo faber*. The realm of *animal laborans* is where the biological processes of the human body – of birth, decay, and death – are managed. Labour and life replicate the processes of nature and is characterised by repetitive, ceaseless activity which produces consumable objects – it is the realm of the perishable, the ephemeral, and the impermanent. Labour is marked out by leaving 'nothing behind, that the result of its effort is almost as quickly consumed as the effort is spent' (Arendt, 1958: 87). It is necessary because it reproduces life and creates a private realm for renewal of mind and body, but to live one's whole life within it is to experience a darkened, instinctual existence. By contrast, the realm of *homo faber* is structured by activities which make the material things that differentiate the human world from the natural world. Objects are produced through repetitive processes of fabrication which have a definite beginning and end, but unlike the end results of labour these objects are durable and permanent, to be used or enjoyed rather than consumed. By breaking out of the biological processes of nature, they have an existence beyond their makers, establishing a stable world for humans to be at home. Despite this positive necessity, the usefulness and enjoyment of things encourages objectification and instrumentalism, leading to 'a growing meaninglessness where every end is transformed into a means' (Arendt, 1958: 157).[10] Consequently, the realm of *homo faber*, instead of being the site of emancipation and a fully human experience, has become colonised by the realm of *animal laborans* through the processes of automatism: 'the automatism of labor and the instrumentalism of work – conspire in the modern world to obliterate the human capacity for action' (Dietz, 2002: 131).

For Arendt, action is the sphere in which it is possible to be fully human and fully free – only in the realm of action can we experience the mode of being expressive of our distinctiveness and diversity. But although the realm of action reveals human beings in their plurality, Arendt characterises this sphere as lacking the means to institute politics with a practical purposefulness.[11] All practical activity is subsumed under *animal laborans* and *homo faber*, which leaves Arendt without the resources for identifying where the programmes for emancipatory change in the political arena are going to come from, or how they are going to be implemented. This presents us with a conundrum. We depend upon the realm of action to experience our full humanity. In turn, the realm of action depends upon our being able to satisfy the demands of life as *animal laborans* and establish a stable world as *homo faber*. But despite being indispensable, both labour and work pose a threat to the possibility of becoming fully human, either by absorbing us into biological processes leading to an eclipse of the mind, or by instrumentalisation, leading to objectification and 'world alienation'. Yet, for most people, it seems unlikely that the experience of being fully human in the realm of action can compensate for the experience of diminished humanity in the realms of work and labour. Moreover, acting which is stripped of working risks becoming reduced to a mere spectacle, a space of performance in which nothing actually gets done.

In order to overcome the dichotomy between necessary working and humanising acting, Dietz (2002) retrieves a 'making in politics' based upon the collective wisdom of citizens in identifying problems and consideration of methods (ibid: 178), and a 'freedom in work' based upon the worker's autonomous problem-solving capabilities (ibid: 167). This directs us to a way of rethinking the relationship between action and work, for if making can be retrieved in politics, then acting can be retrieved in production – provided that labouring, working, and acting are taken to be expressive modes of being rather than exclusive categories (or spaces) for unitary kinds of action. Hinchman & Hinchman (1984) propose that labouring, working, and acting should 'not be understood as empirical generalisations about what most people usually do. As existentials they seek to illuminate what it means to be-in-the-world' (ibid: 197). Lenz (2005) describes Arendt's triad as 'three basic forms of how activity takes place' (ibid: 143), and questions whether activities of labour, work, and action should be 'bound to certain spheres and time periods' (Lenz, 2005: 143). She identifies an Arendtian theme of inter-dependence between the three modes of being so that 'the balance of all three types of activity is necessary for establishing a society grounded in choices and creative abilities' (ibid: 145), arguing that understanding our inter-dependencies across spheres of acting and being allows us to critique the role of gainful employment in our conceptions of the good life. For such a critique to issue in transformatory possibilities for organising and valuing work, then we must create the means for acting in production, such as institutionalised workplace democracy.

If workplaces are imagined, not as spatially bound sites, but as time-spaces intersecting different spheres of human action, and transgressing boundaries which are open, fluid, and contestable, then we can start to see how different expressive modes of being, such as making and acting, exceed the employment relation. Acting in production – that is, exercising existential dimension of political being in the work we do together – enables us to ask what the relevant social needs are which must be met by a system of social cooperation. Conversely, exercising the mode of making – that is, exercising the existential dimension of being a maker in the realm of politics – enables us to answer the question of how we are to meet our own and the needs of others. Indeed, the twin actions of asking and answering constitute in themselves much of the work we do together. This is particularly so if we conceptualise an ethical dimension of work as 'having to do with the needs of others and the common good' (Gurtler, 2005: 120). Indeed, engaging in the identification of needs in our selves and others grounds a general entitlement to being able to make our contribution as actors, makers, and labourers to the work of maintaining a system of social cooperation. Finally, a general entitlement to make our contribution is more likely to be realised when we use the idea of multiple timespaces to acknowledge a wider range of activities as work, and to institute social arrangements where everyone can participate in the roles, practices, and organisations through which individual contributions are coordinated and made productive for the common good.

Interwoven spheres of action

Making creative use of Arendt shows us how differing modes of being can be exercised in a variety of action contexts. But if we think of labouring, working, and acting as modes of being which are instantiated in multiple, overlapping timespaces, then maintaining strictly separate boundaries between action contexts becomes problematic – particularly when separate action contexts fix modes of being and thinking, such as technical reason in the economic realm or emotional expression in the private realm. Habermas's theory of work and interaction is an attempt to illuminate obscured forms of human activity, whilst also maintaining clear distinctions between kinds of actions and spheres of action. But the result is that unpaid work in the realm of the family or community remains obscured, blunting critical evaluation of forms of exploitation and expropriation in the realm of work.

In Habermas's social theory, the sphere of work is opposed to the sphere of interaction. Eyerman and Shipway (1981) identify how Habermas's separation between action contexts originates in his critique of Marx who reduces all relations to economic relations in which 'human emancipation was developed along the single dimension of the interactive relationship between social labor and nature' (ibid: 555). In order to avoid Marx's reductionism, Habermas makes use of Aristotle's distinction between *praxis* (acting) and *poiesis* (making) to raise the status of 'intersubjective understanding as a type of action' (Honneth, 1995a: 45). He distinguishes between work/instrumental and interaction/communicative action, extending communicative action to much of what we would include as social activity, but denies that the experience of work can give rise to anything other than instrumental reasoning. Habermas grounds instrumental action and communicative action in two unchanging and universal human interests of work and symbolic interaction, which are 'analytically separate arenas in which self-conscious human subjects act, thereby transforming themselves and their world' (Keane, 1975: 87). In the realm of work (instrumental action), we satisfy our 'technical cognitive interest' for purposive-rational action which enables us to harness productive forces and gain technical control over the natural world (ibid: 87). In the realm of interaction (communicative action), we satisfy our 'moral-practical cognitive interest' in the development of social norms and subjective formations which underpin the stability and reproduction of the social order (ibid: 88).

Consequently, Habermas's distinction between a technical and practical sphere of action gives rise to an 'almost exclusive concern with developing an emancipatory program in the practical realm of human activity, without the simultaneous development of a program in the technical [realm]' (Eyerman & Shipway, 1981). He strips technical reason of normative content, because: 'the technical interest in control over nature *does not allow for any interpretation*: technical rules are like signs, they point to a direct activity, but neither contain nor generate intrinsic meaning of their own' (ibid: 557). However, the meanings of efficiency or productivity in technical reason are not normatively neutral, nor are they closed off from dissent and difference (ibid: 563; see also Buchanan, 1995). Furthermore, technical and practical reasoning do not take place in separate spheres of action, instead work is '*simultaneously* cultural and technical activity, and is never purely instrumental' (ibid: 558).

In the attempt to illuminate intersubjective communication, but contain it within a separate sphere of action, Habermas diminishes the importance of work as a site for emancipatory social progress: 'work merely designates the action substrate – the development of social forces of production – from which the processes of communicative liberation are then normatively distinguished' (Honneth, 1995a: 50). Although Habermas talks about an 'unforced act of understanding' (ibid: 52) in the realm of communicative action, he has no equivalent concept in the realm of instrumental action. Consequently, Habermas has few resources to offer the diagnosis and cure of the 'moral vulnerability which grows not from the suppression of communicative modes of mutual understanding, but from the expropriation of the workers' own work activity' (ibid: 54). Specifically, by uncoupling or separating 'systems' from 'lifeworld' (Fraser, 1985: 119) Habermas fails to expose the family as a site of unpaid labour, and for failing to recognise the gendered nature of the paid workforce which assigns women to fem-

inised roles of caring and domestic labour, thereby disguising the subordination of women to men (ibid):

> On the one side stand the institutional orders of the modern life-
> world, the socially integrated domains specialising in symbolic
> reproduction, that is, in socialisation, solidarity formation and cul-
> tural transmission. On the other side stand the systems, the system-
> integrated domains specialising in material reproduction. On the
> one side stand the nuclear family and the public sphere; on the
> other side stand the (official) capitalist economy and the modern
> administrative state (Fraser, 1985: 119).

Fraser (1985) ascribes Habermas's inability to take account of gender to
two key distinctions in his social-theoretical categories: firstly, his distinction between 'the symbolic reproduction and the material reproduction of societies' and, secondly, his distinction between 'socially
integrated action contexts' and 'system integrated action contexts'
(ibid: 116). In the first distinction, women's unpaid childcare activities
map onto symbolic reproduction, because they reproduce the norms
and behaviours of social identities through socialisation of the young.
In the second distinction, contexts of intersubjective consensus, such
as the family, are differentiated from contexts of competitive interaction in which 'individual action is determined by self-interested, utility
maximising calculations typically entertained in the idioms [...] of
power and money' (ibid: 117). Two key institutions undertake the
activities of symbolic reproduction – the private sphere of the family
and the public sphere of political participation. By confining consensual normative behaviour to the action context of the private sphere of
family life, and self-interested maximising behaviour to the action
context of the competitive sphere of production, Habermas is unable
to account for how we experience multiple modes of being within the
same spheres of human action. Nor can he account for how consensual
normative behaviour is as likely to arise in a sphere presumed to be
ruled by technical reason as they are to arise in communicative action.

> While it is true that the human need to transform nature requires that
> people turn themselves into instruments, and leads them to act purpo-
> sively as objects rather than communicatively as subjects, this is only
> *one* dimension of the labor process. To this dimension must be added
> another, reflected in the use of imagination and creativity which pre-
> cedes, terminates, and *weaves its way throughout* the instrumental

dimension of the labor process (Eyerman & Shipway, 1981: 558, original emphasis).

By envisaging work as acting and being within multiply interwoven spheres, we broaden the range of imaginative and creative responses when seeking to fulfil our responsibilities towards worthy objects. This will likely give rise to value-generative differences in meaning-making which transcend conventional space/time distinctions. Davies (2001) evaluates the importance of a timespace approach for theorising the everyday experiences of women, which challenges accepted understandings of our relation to the boundaries between home and work, making the separate spheres thesis untenable: 'the ideology of "separate spheres" has obscured the links between work and family' (Ferree, 1990: 871). Not only does it look to be theoretically redundant, but the separate spheres thesis, by invisibilising informal work in the voluntary sector or within the family, fosters social injustice because it fails to explicate how the burdens of work fall disproportionately upon certain groups of people. The diminishing usefulness of maintaining rigid distinctions between action contexts asks us to address the question: 'what are the "normative principles" to guide the structural intersections of institutional spheres?' (Young, 2006) This is a political question for everyday living, as well as a theoretical task, because we must all make ethical decisions about how we fulfil our responsibilities towards worthy objects, necessitating deliberation with those others we seek to involve in our projects, who themselves have projects of their own requiring them to recruit the cooperative effort of their fellows.

The material dimension of intersubjectivity

In his essay, 'Work and Instrumental Action', Honneth (1995a) takes issue with Arendt for separating work into reflexive bodily work, and experiential manual work, resulting in a permanent divide mirroring the Taylorisation of industrial work. He claims that, by purifying the realm of 'true action' of any contact with the production of things, Arendt has removed 'any sort of potential emancipatory significance from the act of working' (ibid: 42). In order to retrieve a normatively positive conception of work out of his critique of Arendt and Habermas, Honneth specifies two levels of action, which can be characterised as work: firstly, at the level of social practice, work includes social reproduction and the construction of the human world 'out of its natural setting' (ibid: 32), and secondly, at the level of action, work includes the release of knowledge in order to 'transform the means of domination and thus also make possible the evolutionary expansion of social freedom' (ibid). In so doing, Honneth directs us towards a critical conception of work in his description of 'an undistorted act of work' (ibid: 45) which is 'complete in itself' (ibid), thereby enabling us to differentiate normatively between different kinds of work. His conception of an undistorted act of work is shaped by the craft ideal which he associates with the pre-mechanisation period of labour, but which has been lost in the modern organisation of work, where whole acts of work have been divided into small, repetitive tasks in order to maximise efficiency and profit: 'most types of work have lost any resemblance to acts of artisanry which are complete in themselves' (ibid: 38). In Honneth's undistorted act of work, work consists in freely expressed action directed towards others and towards objects, which aim at uniting means and ends in the interior content of work as workers act upon objects. By re-uniting means and ends, undistorted acts of work overcome the modern fragmentation of instrumental processes where work has 'been separated from the autonomous control and empirical knowledge of working subjects' (ibid: 46).

Honneth opposes an undistorted act of work to unfree work which subjects workers' actions to imposed bureaucratic rules and norms. But at the moment when work appears to be irredeemably unfree, Honneth turns our attention to an, as yet fully to be realised, emancipatory possibility – that of the intersubjective relation between the worker and the object, which, in order to get the work done, draws from the worker capabilities for judging and thinking in interpreting the needs of the situation. Honneth proposes that workers must engage in a 'process of emancipatory reflection' (ibid: 47), so that work regains the potential to enable 'a morally oriented process of action in the region of social labor which would reclaim the meaningful work content of instrumental action from out of the social forms established through domination' (ibid: 47). As a consequence of encounters with the material realities of working, workers must exercise both instrumental and communicative rationalities, breaking down Habermassian distinctions between instrumental and communicative action. When joined to the political mode of being – of acting in production realised within contexts organised for difference and deliberation – such encounters are capable of bringing to light the values interior to the experience of working, thereby permitting a normative evaluation of worthy and unworthy objects.

But this material dimension of intersubjective relations falls out of Honneth's mature theory of social recognition (Honneth, 1995a), in which action contexts are mediated by three forms of recognitive relations between self and others (confidence, respect, and esteem), but not between self and objects. Honneth reduces the experience of work to struggles for recognition of identity or achievement, without acknowledging the independent value of autonomous action in the interior content of work (Smith, 2009; Moll, 2009). It would be possible, for example, to imagine situations where workers are recognised for their efforts or cultural status, but are still denied the opportunity to exercise their independent agency as they grapple with the ineliminable materiality of work. Consequently, if we are to understand what is normatively significant about work, we need to reconsider how the active agency of workers relates to the material dimension of working life, in addition to the dimensions of positive practical relations to self and others. By retrieving materiality, we reveal workers' irreducible autonomy in their relations to self, others, and objects, specifying the limits of theorising an automatic technical reasoning to explain human action in work. Instead, in undistorted or meaningful work, workers deliberate with others to understand and articulate what is needed to fulfil responsibilities for worthy objects, giving rise to interpretive differences in the meanings of values, such as efficiency, productivity, caring, and needs-meeting. In this way, deliberative evaluation of interactions with materiality surfaces interpretive differences, opening up spaces for temporary agreements over positive values which constitute worthy objects – and furthermore, making the expressive mode of acting in production a worthy object in its own right.

A positive critical conception of meaningful work

To advance the regulative ideal of meaningful work, we need conceptual tools enabling us to judge between desirable and undesirable forms of work. These are provided by a positive critical conception of meaningful work which structures dissent and difference over the meanings of the work we do together. Cooke (2004) says that 'critical social theory is a mode of reflection that looks critically at processes of social development from the point of view of the obstacles they pose for human flourishing' (ibid: 418). Fraser (1985) suggests that Marx's 1843 definition of critical theory as 'the self-clarification of the struggles and wishes of the age' has not been bettered in its implicit call to political action. Hence, to be consistent with critical practice, a positive critical conception of meaningful work will enable a normative inquiry into how the interior content of work adds to or detracts from the meaningfulness of our lives. Smith (2009) puts the motivation for a normative inquiry into work as follows: 'the moral significance of work lies, to put it bluntly, in the contribution it makes (when not distorted) to a meaningful, fulfilled, dignified human life' (ibid: 49). He argues that a conception of work possesses critical power when it: defines a 'standard' by which it is possible to distinguish between different kinds of work; possesses 'normative content' which enables critical evaluation; has empirical validity as a fact about the world; and indicates the direction of social and individual emancipation (Smith, 2009: 47–53). In the end, meaningful work will accrue critical power when the value of meaningfulness is constituted by difference and deliberation in a politics of meaningfulness. In Chapters 4 and 6, I shall argue that a politics of meaningfulness is provided for by a system of workplace democracy which combines democratic authority at the level of the organisation with agonistic participatory practices at the level of the task.

A positive critical conception of meaningful work, operating within a liberal perfectionist framework, will provide us with an enriched, pluralised source of values we can appropriate to the meaning content of our lives, although bounded by deliberative agreement over what constitutes an independent value. This is not an unattainable ideal, but draws upon what we already know about how people value and draw meaning from the work they do together. However, if acting in production is to be successful in securing collective, albeit temporary, agreement on positive values – and hence grounding the objective dimension of the bipartite value of meaningfulness – then we need some standpoint from which to judge between values, as well as to assess how we are doing with respect to fulfilling our responsibilities for worthy objects. To this end, I explore how an ethic of care might provide the basis for objective judging between values, as well as assessment of our acting and being towards worthy objects.

Ethic of care: Fulfilling our responsibilities towards worthy objects

Affective appropriation of worthy objects to the meaning content of our lives entails our being able to understand how we are doing in relation to promoting the good for those worthy objects. This means taking up responsibilities for worthy objects which we fulfil through meaning-making in acting and being across multiple interwoven timespaces. Consequently, we need to establish social arrangements which will enable everyone to engage in sense-making, rather than alienating our meaning-making agency to a managerial or political elite (Tourish, 2013). In any case, such alienation would be inconsistent with a positive critical conception of meaningful work, constituted by freedom, autonomy, and dignity. This is because experiencing the bipartite value of meaningfulness by fulfilling our responsibilities towards worthy objects depends upon our active engagement with the positive values which inhere in those objects. The experience of meaningfulness is diminished, and perhaps thwarted entirely, if we alienate our meaning-making agency by allowing the relevant capabilities to lie idle or be appropriated to empower the meaning-making of others.

The requirement to understand what responsibilities we have towards worthy objects indicates how being responsive to, and engaging with, the particular value of those objects does not mean we can have any kind of orientation we want towards them, just in case such orientations generate strong affective attachments consistent with experiencing the bipartite value of meaningfulness. Instead, what is required is that our appropriation of worthy objects to the meaning content of our lives gives rise to legitimate involvement, where legitimate involvement constrains us to promote the good for the worthy objects – in other words, that we have a care for how well they are doing. I propose that we judge the good for worthy objects, and our actions towards those objects, against an ethic of care. Thus, if they are to contribute to the meaningfulness of our lives, our relations to objects of value must orientate us beyond how worthy objects add to our own welfare, because meaningfulness depends upon, not only the fitting together of the dimensions of subjectivity and objectivity, but also being 'able to do something about it or with it' (Wolf, 2010: 25):

> One must be able to be in some sort of relationship with the valuable object of one's attention – to create it, protect it, promote it, honor it, or more generally to actively affirm it in some way or other (ibid: 9).

Discharging our responsibilities requires a 'proneness' (Wolf, 2010: 33), or a readiness to have our actions guided by reasons of love, which ensures that we are 'acting in a way that positively engages with a worthy object of love [...] even if it does not maximally promote either the agent's welfare or the good of the world, impartially assessed' (ibid). Becoming susceptible to reasons of love means putting ourselves into an active relationship with objects of value, where we develop the capabilities for recognising what is of value and for acting appropriately towards worthy objects. One source of active relations to worthy objects is the numerous social roles which structure the work of complex social cooperation. However, Schumacher (1979) blames the introduction of modern technology into the technical division of labour for creating work without dignity which is 'utterly uninteresting and meaningless' (ibid: 27), resulting in a stunted personality, a corruption of human relations, and fostering 'a spirit of irresponsibility' (ibid: 28). Schumacher is critical of the social complexity which absorbs so much personal time and effort: 'modern industrial society is immensely complicated, immensely involved, making immense claims on man's time and attention' (ibid: 24–5). But I disagree that the complexity of society dissociates people from a sense of responsibility, and therefore from a potential source of personal meaning. Despite the many ways in which work oppresses, degrades, and exposes us to harm, we know from daily experience that people willingly take up complex and important responsibilities:

> Despite the many centrifugal forces of modern societies, despite their materialism and inequalities, despite the currency of ideological or self-serving notions of freedom and autonomy – despite all this it is striking that most of us not only depend upon one another but act in ways that allow others to depend on us. Most people take on extensive and demanding responsibilities, and – to their great moral credit – many of them act responsibly, often across all the roles they play. They thereby sustain a fabric of relationships and institutions that [...] channels immense energies toward meeting one another's needs and wants (Williams, 2008: 466–7).

Each day (and night), cleaners, call centre operatives, labourers, and carers clean, make calls, and care for the sick and elderly – and they do not take up these responsibilities simply because they are paid to do so, but because they want to do good work. Indeed, many seek to extend their roles, excavating meanings from their work, meanings which motivate them to expend discretionary effort in order to meet the needs of fellow human beings. Of course, it is possible for people to train, to take up responsibility, and to go the additional mile without their work having the relevant structure for meaningfulness, but this is to instrumentalise persons with no regard for their fundamental need for meaning.

Meaningful work therefore entails a notion of both our personal responsibility to care for worthy objects and our collective responsibility to aid one another in being able to care. Vitally, an ethic of care provides a moral standpoint from which we equip ourselves to take responsibility when we find ourselves in 'a context for agency based in relationships, developed and borne out intersubjectively or in conjunction with others' (Borgerson, 2007: 479). This means that fulfilling our responsibilities is tied closely to our membership of practices and institutions, and the social roles we inhabit within those institutions (Sciaraffa, 2011; see also Hardimon, 1994). When informed by an ethic of care, appropriate orientations towards worthy objects, consistent with the bipartite value of meaningfulness, are characterised by caring relations, which aim at fulfilling our obligations towards worthy objects.

An ethic of care

An ethic of care provides the standard for evaluating how well we are doing in our actions and in orientations towards the worthy objects we have appropriated to the meaning content of our lives, where an ethic of care is concerned with 'the compelling moral salience of attending to and meeting the needs of the particular others for whom we take responsibility' (Held, 2006: 10; see also Bubeck, 1995; Engster, 2005; Lawson, 2007; Lipman, 1995; Tronto, 1993, 1999). In so doing, we need to acknowledge that taking up our responsibilities of caring for worthy objects may include relations to worthy objects which are not entirely self-chosen: 'we may be given responsibility, assigned it, inherit it and then accept or refuse it' (Card, 1991: 29). Furthermore, adopting the standards set by practices of care demands that we pay attention to how caring for worthy objects points us beyond ourselves to what is required to secure the good of the object in question, including, dialogue with others over what constitutes good care, and defining with those others what the relevant needs are, where needs interpretation is a fundamentally political undertaking (cf. Fraser, 1989a). Thus, in the bipartite value of meaningfulness, fulfilling our responsibilities towards worthy objects means having a care for those objects, that is, acting towards them with the correct orientations for promoting and protecting their welfare. Affective appropriation of worthy objects in the subjective dimension is legitimate when it is consistent with what promotes the good of worthy objects, where our understanding of the good arises from our own and others' judgement as to how we are doing with respect to caring for those objects.

Care as a value and a practice

Fisher and Tronto (1990) define taking care as including 'everything that we do to maintain, continue and repair our world, so that we can live in it as well as possible' (ibid: 40). They identify four dimensions of care which imply four values in an ethic of care: caring about (attentiveness), caring for (responsibility), taking care of (competence), and care receiving (responsiveness). Held (2006) distinguishes an ethics of care from an ethics of justice in what is morally relevant for 'attending to and meeting the needs of the particular others for whom we take responsibility' (ibid: 10). She rejects abstract reasoning as the only way to understand what morality requires, and proposes that practical reasoning, informed by attentiveness, trust, responsiveness to need, narrative sensitivity, and cultivating caring relations, directs us to what is required for satisfying obligations (ibid: 15). For Held, care is both a value and a practice. Care is a *value* because it has critical purchase in enabling us to 'pick out a more specific value to be found in persons' and societies' characteristics than merely finding them good or bad, or morally admirable or not, on the whole' (ibid: 38). It is 'probably the most fundamental value' because 'there can be care without justice' (ibid: 17) – and without care there would be no people or other worthy objects which can be subject to principles of justice. Care is a *practice* because it involves 'the work of care-giving and the standards by which the practices of care can be evaluated' (ibid: 36). Held (2006) points out that activities can be performed without adhering to the values relevant to the practice: 'An activity must be purposive to count as work or labor, but it need not incorporate any values, even efficiency, in the doing of it. Chopping at a tree, however clumsily, to fell it, could be work' (ibid: 37). Hence an ethic of care directs us to a concern for particularities: that is, the distinct projects that constitute the value of meaningfulness, and the particular persons, things, and activities which colour and granulate our individual lives.

Care as a standard

As well as guiding our thinking and acting towards worthy objects, an ethic of care provides a standard against which we can judge how well we are doing in meeting the particular needs of those objects. Sennett (2008) evokes a standard of care in his revival of the craft ideal when he identifies how, through our engagement with things, we learn to 'care about the qualities of cloth, the right way to poach fish; fine cloth or food cooked well' leading us 'to imagine larger categories of "good"'(ibid: 8). Ruddick (1998: 4) suggests that caring practices can become a vantage point from which to evaluate a much wider range of human relations and social practices, so that it 'extends beyond the activities from which it arises, generating a stance (or standpoint) toward "nature", human relationships and social institutions' (ibid). If work which incorporates the ethic and practice of care is meaningful work, we can establish the objective dimension of the value of meaningfulness by evaluating our actions against a standard of care. The requisite standard of care is arrived at by asking: what constitutes caring in relation to the particular worthy objects at which the actions aim and how will we know that caring has brought about good for those worthy objects. And this, I suggest, is a profoundly political question, because it involves disagreement, contestation, and deliberation over what is meant by good care. Weeks, K. (1998) argues for 'intimate citizenship' such that caring forms part of our status as citizens, where the recognition of the human need for intimacy and belonging form part of practices of care in each person's everyday life. In the bipartite value of meaningfulness, meeting the standard required by an ethic of care in our affective orientations and practical actions towards worthy objects provides us with security and reassurance that our lives are worth living.

An infrastructure of care

Caring relations produce people, animals, things, and indeed whole societies. This implies that, rather than being the repetitive reproductions of the Arendtian realm of labour, practices of care are potentially transformative: 'care has the capacity to shape new persons with ever more advanced understandings of culture and society and morality and ever more advanced abilities to live well and cooperatively with others' (Held, 2006: 32). This demands an ethico-political understanding of care as the basis for deliberating over the values and standards necessary to the work we do together. In other words, we require the practice of 'democratic caring' (Sevenhuijsen, 2000: 22) in which all citizens have access to the spheres of social life and the structures of belonging necessary for them to be able to make their contribution to the work of social cooperation and to participate in the interpretation of values inherent to the work they do. Tronto (2010), for example, argues that 'creating caring institutions' (Tronto, 2010) is an unavoidably political process requiring us to evaluate power relations, ensuring that care remains both particular to the worthy objects in question and pluralist in the range of caring values, and that 'care has a clear, legitimate purpose' (ibid: 162). To enable us to orientate ourselves to the needs of worthy objects, caring institutions must provide public space for needs-interpretation, a 'rhetorical space' (Code, 1995) or a 'political space' (Walker, M.U., 1998), in which each person can engage with values, finding them worthy or unworthy, attractive or unattractive, as they seek to satisfy the human need for meaningfulness. In this way, a politics of meaningfulness, grounded in an ethic of care, has the capacity to enable us to evaluate the extent to which social structures support our ability to fulfil our responsibilities towards worthy objects by developing the relevant capabilities for objective valuing and subjective attachment.

Finally, an ethic of care within a positive critical conception of meaningful work is about the lives of ordinary people, their experiences of working and of not working, and of how those experiences shape their practical identities. Specifically, a politics of meaningfulness must be concerned with designing the political, social, and economic institutions which allow for expressive modes of being beyond the commodification of the self, and the expropriation of human capabilities to a rent-seeking financial elite. One route to proliferating meaningful work is to revive and enrich the public good of meaningfulness, by enabling everyone to engage in the co-production of our common stock of positive values through a system of economic democracy. In the political economy of meaningfulness, the individual is not cast out to create meaning alone, but neither is she subsumed into pre-given meanings; instead, the individual, as an equal co-authority, shares responsibility with others for the co-creation of positive values. This requires the establishment of a deliberative society, including widespread workplace democracy, in order to draw people into meaningful encounters across social and economic divisions. Mary Parker Follett characterised the process of group decision-making as 'the inner workshop of democracy' (Follett, 1998[1918]), because it is in the direct experience of deliberating with others that we form the virtues, attitudes, and habits of citizenship. Thus, the promise of a political economy of meaningfulness is that citizenship becomes grounded in the joining of personal meaning-making to public deliberation, supported by an economic architecture in which structures of ownership and control provide everyone with a share of decision-making power. Chapters 3, 4 and 5 will develop the positive critical conception of meaningful work through an exploration of the constitutive values of autonomy as non-alienation, freedom as non-domination, and social recognition as dignified work.

3
Overcoming Alienation: Irreducible Autonomy and *Phronetic Techne* in a Practical Rationality of Caring

Never has work appeared to be so divided, intense, separated from our personal control and divorced from our sense of who we are. From Blauner's (1964) industrial blue collar workers labouring under changes to the division of labour as a consequence of automation to the 'managed hearts' of Hochschild's (1983) airline attendants, the complaint is that the experience of work has been systematically deskilled and subjectified by a capitalist project which aims to increase profit by appropriating and controlling workers' agency in the exercise of their skills and the formation of their identities. The critique that contemporary conditions of work are thoroughly alienating opposes deskilled and subjectified work to the mastery and secure identity of craft work, but, I shall argue, this dualism presents a narrative of work as irretrievably degraded which is not consistent with work as it is experienced by workers. I shall show the limits to the opposition between alienated work and craft work by describing a floor-level of irreducible autonomy in every act of work, which reveals that there is no completely alienated work from which the possibility of autonomous action has been eliminated. I shall propose that the identification of a level of irreducible autonomy enables us to conceptualise personal autonomy in work as fundamentally relational, and the pre-condition for the exercise of political autonomy.

Alienated work and the craft ideal

In the ideal of craftsmanship, work has intrinsic value and is performed not just for the sake of external rewards, such as status or pay, but also for the sake of the actions and processes inherent to the work itself. The ideal act of work is a complete act where completeness stands for a unity of means and ends in which the craftsman is recognised as having mastery over his skills, independence in his way of living, and is respected for his display of the virtues relevant to his practice (see Murphy, 1993). Mills (1951) describes the craft ideal in the following terms:

> Craftsmanship as a fully idealised model of work involves six major features. There is no ulterior motive other than the product being made and the process of creation. The details of daily work are meaningful because they are not detached in the worker's mind from the product of the work. The worker is free to control his own working action. The craftsman is thus able to learn from his work; and to use and develop his skills and capacities in its prosecution. There is no split of work and play, or work and culture. The craftsman's way of livelihood determines and infuses his whole being (Mills, 1951: 220).[1]

Alienated work is the antithesis of craft work. In craft work, the craftsman achieves personal autonomy when he possesses *control* over the work process and its outcomes, and *independence* of self; by possessing skill in his own person and therefore a sense of personhood, the craftsman is able to choose when, how, and for whom he employs his abilities. In alienated work, the worker is divorced from his skills and capabilities, because the content of his work inhibits his sense of autonomy over his actions, resulting in him becoming separated from his own self because the relations and circumstances of work fail to support his sense of identity as an efficacious, distinct person. In his concept of estranged labour in the 'Economic and Philosophic Manuscripts' (1844), Marx identifies four dimensions of alienation: the worker can be alienated, firstly, from his product which appears as 'an alien object exercising power over him' (Marx, 1978 [1844]: 74); secondly, from his activities in the production process which is 'activity as suffering' (ibid: 75); thirdly, from his human and particular self which forces him to turn his capabilities for living a flourishing human life into 'a mere means to his *existence*' (ibid: 76); and fourthly, from others so that he no longer recognises others in their full expressive humanity, but 'views the other in accordance with the standard and the position in which he finds himself as a worker' (ibid: 77). When we are alienated from one another, we value the other person only for their position in the division of labour, making the mutual needs which should be a source of our solidarity 'a source of tactical advantage' (Miller, 2003). Moreover, alienation from our work, from our needs, and from each other renders us vulnerable to exploitation:

> [...] man's relation to himself only becomes *objective* and *real* for him through his relation to the other man. Thus, if the product of his labour, his labour is *objectified*, is for him an *alien*, hostile, powerful object independent of him, then his position towards it is such that someone else is master of this object, someone who is alien, hostile, powerful, and independent of him. If his own activity is to him an unfree activity, then he is treating it as activity performed in the service, under the domination, the coercion and the yoke of another man (Marx, 1978 [1844]: 78).

Thus, alienation is the radical separation of the worker from the *interior content* of her work, structured by purposes, processes, skills, and products, and from the *constitutive social relations* to self, to others, and to material objects which enable the formation of practical identities (Marchand, 2010; Dale, 2005).

In the *interior content* of work, alienated work is deskilled, divided, and objectified: by structuring their activities so that it does not require much initiative or exercise of human capabilities, capitalists can take unfair advantage of the inferior bargaining position of workers, thereby enabling the consolidation of efficiencies and profit-taking through hierarchical coordination (Miller, 2003). In the *constitution of selves*, alienated work under conditions of global capital leaves no dimension of human expressiveness untouched – management strategies encroach upon the formation of subjectivities for the purpose of increasing profit through the production of affects, requiring workers to work upon themselves to create a self-conception and practical identity which aligns them with the interests of the organisation. 'Alienation-as-subjection' (Elster, 1986b: 56) is a conditioning factor for exploitation in which one person extracts benefits from another with no consideration for the welfare of the exploited individual. Alienation reduces the costs of exploitation to the exploiter because it operates in a framework which legitimises the social conditions under which the exploitation takes place: 'Alienation adds to exploitation a belief on the part of the workers that the capitalist has a legitimate claim on the surplus, by virtue of his legitimate ownership of the means of production [...] The efficacy of capitalist exploitation rests on its ability to perpetuate the conditions under which it appears as morally legitimate' (ibid). Hence, alienation and exploitation operate together to condition workers to the organisation of work under capital, interpreting and controlling the meanings of work so that the pre-determined interior content and subjective formations of work appear as necessary and without any alternative. These are heteronomous conditions which impoverish the field of values available for subjective appropriation, with the consequence that autonomy-promoting meanings of work necessary to joint action are marginalised or even extinguished. Thus, heteronomy in one or more of the four dimensions of alienation inhibits our ability to experience the bipartite value of meaningfulness in the work we do together, because such conditions of work reduce the range of values which can be appropriated to the meaning content of our lives or fix the acceptable meanings of values to serve the ideological interests of a dominant group.

Alienated work, according to Elster (1985), consists of both an objective and a subjective condition, where alienation is understood as the loss of meaning consequent upon an organisation of work characterised by heteronomy: 'spiritual alienation may be seen either as a lack of a sense of meaning, or as a sense of a lack of meaning' (ibid: 74; see also Braybrooke, 1998a). When we *lack a sense of meaning* we are objectively alienated because 'the aggregate outcome of individual actions appears as an independent and even hostile power, not as freely and jointly willed' (Elster, 1986b: 49) making the social structures consequent upon the accretion of past actions and power struggles appear unquestionable and unchangeable. The content of work may be objectively alienated, but this does not entail subjective alienation: workers may experience contentment despite the degraded content of work, because the expanding economic product allows greater satisfaction of needs (Braybrooke, 1998a). When we experience a *sense of a lack of meaning*, we are subjectively alienated because we have 'the experience of one's self and life as empty' (Wood, 1981: 9). In his reading of Wood (ibid), Elster (1985: 75) identifies how Wood makes the objective condition of alienation the primary test of the presence of alienation: 'it is a matter of whether my life in fact actualizes the potentialities which are objectively present in my human essence' and not 'a matter of whether my conscious desires are satisfied or how I think about myself or my life' (Wood, 1981: 23–4). However, since objective alienation is naturalised in social structures which appear not only to be insusceptible to individual and collective action, but also beyond critical discernment and reflective evaluation, if we lack the experience of subjective alienation, then it is difficult to see how we will come to realise that we are living out our lives under conditions of objective alienation. Elster asks, in the absence of the subjective condition of alienation, how are we to realise even the minimal expression of autonomy as political and personal self-determination upon which social change depends? If Wood is correct that the objective condition of alienation is the primary mark of alienated work, and individual affective responses to conditions of work cannot be taken as a guide to the presence of alienation in work, then it seems unlikely that alienated work can be a force for individual and social progress, since the objective conditions of alienation operate beyond our subjective perceptions.

I suggest that the way out of this impasse is to acknowledge that there is no realm of purely objective alienation, closed off from subjective affects, in which self-reflexive practices are rendered sterile by the apparently immovable logic of hegemonic social and economic structures, practices, and ideologies. Even in conditions of objective alienation people must act, and to do so they draw upon their meaning-making capabilities to create and promote values. Our unavoidable engagement with others in interpretive meaning-making allows values to become available for individual subjective appropriation. Our capabilities for interpretive meaning-making are part of the general preconditions for autonomous action, enabling us to mobilise our own and others' agency in the work we do together. Ethnographic studies of what people actually do when they are engaged in work provide significant evidence that, even under conditions of extensive objective alienation, workers are motivated to seek autonomous expression in their working activities independent of rewards, such as status or pay (see Marchand, 2010; Dejours, 1998; Hodson et al, 1993; Hodson, 1998). This urge is enacted in forms of subversion, of resistance, of play, and of humour in the workplace: the factory worker who deliberately damages a uniform product in order to mark it as his or her own; the mother who resists the model of full-time employment; the artisan who adapts organisational rules in order to nurture a machine to produce well; the call centre operative who coaxes a bureaucratic system to deliver good customer service; or the care workers who protest at a job description process which renders their emotional labour invisible. Indeed, Elster indicates something of this kind when he says that social change may occur when 'objectively existing alienation at some point comes to be felt subjectively' (Elster, 1985: 76). I argue that objective conditions of alienation cannot be maintained by those who have an interest in doing so without the recruitment of workers' meaning-making capabilities, but the moment of successful recruitment also specifies the limit to the extractive power of some over others. Thus, the recruitment of workers' subjectivities is never total – there is always a surplus, an immanent potential interior to the content of work, allowing for the possibility of interpretive differences which arise when meaning-making produces 'remainders' (Honig, 1993) irreconcilable with the dominant culture's way of life.

But interpretive differences often remain invisible and marginalised, even though they are constitutive of skill development and the renewal of organisational practices. I propose that these 'difference potentials' can be given voice and purchase as the pre-conditions of social change when they are mobilised through a system of workplace democracy which operates both at the level of the organisation and at the level of the task. Braybrooke (1998b) gives democratic participation a role in overcoming the objective and subjective conditions of alienation because democratic participation generates engagement with the values and purposes framing the work people do together. Braybrooke (1998a) says that we experience alienation when we lack 'a purposeful commitment to doing X' (ibid: 40), that is, when our activity lacks the objective condition of an intrinsic purpose and the subjective condition of 'sense of purpose in doing X' (ibid). But even when doing X has an intrinsic purpose, we may not meet the subjective condition of a sense of purpose in two ways: firstly, we may believe there is an intrinsic purpose, but lack the information to confirm our belief (Braybrooke gives the example of somebody occupied in an undercover operation who may not have full knowledge of the context of their work); and secondly, we may have knowledge of an intrinsic purpose, but find the tasks involved subjectively repellent, boring, or in some way dissatisfying (ibid: 40–1).

Democratically organised work may overcome the objective and subjective conditions of alienation because it provides the opportunity to determine whether there are 'socially more useful alternatives to N's doing X' (ibid: 40) and helps 'to develop purposeful commitments' (ibid: 48). Braybrooke points out, however, that, even where there are no democratic practices, people often work very hard to find an intrinsic purpose in their work, and he identifies the stubborn determination of workers to overcome alienation by constructing meaning out of unpromising work: 'men make great efforts to convert themselves. They seek to rationalize their line of work in such a way that they can develop a purposeful commitment in following it. Certainly, it is very common for people to persuade themselves, once they find themselves doing X, that doing X is of great social importance' (ibid: 43). I suggest that the demonstrated determination of workers to find value in their work supports my point that there is no pure objectively alienated work, from which all possibility of self-determination has been eliminated. The efforts that people make to appropriate values through the interpretation of meaning directs us to a floor-level of autonomy in all kinds of work which is not simply about psychological relief, but indicates how meaning-making is necessary to the possibility of any kind of human action at all.

Undoubtedly conditions of objective alienation do enable elites to mobilise the agency of others, stunting the development of workers' capabilities for meaning-making and thwarting their search for meaningfulness. Our normative concern should, therefore, be directed towards ensuring that workers' efforts to appropriate meaning to their lives should be neither futile nor mistaken. Nor that society should force them through necessity 'to take their chance on alienation' (ibid: 46) by making being able to experience the bipartite value of meaningfulness in work a matter of personal taste. Braybrooke (1998a) cites Hegel, that 'The individual has an "infinite right" to find himself "satisfied in [his] activity and labour"' (ibid: 44). This seems to be correct, and not only necessary for every individual, but also an achievable regulative ideal in a society organised to realise the deliberative capabilities of its members in a system of economic democracy. Furthermore, the regulative ideal of meaningful work becomes a pragmatic possibility when workers' meaning-making capacities are enabled by deliberative democratic practices. This is because when interpretive differences over values and purposes become publicly available for evaluation and judgement, they are made susceptible to generalised appropriation to the meaning content of lives through the exercise of the capabilities for objective valuing and subjective attachment. I shall argue that the floor-level of irreducible autonomy in every act of work is the pre-condition for being able to act as an autonomous being, where personal autonomy is understood to be a relational achievement. To begin with, I shall explore the loss of autonomy argument, and challenge the narrative that work is irretrievably degraded and alienated.

The loss of autonomy argument

The principal hypothesis of the loss of autonomy argument is that our modern organisation of work is inhospitable to autonomous action, because owners and managers have succeeded in undermining the independence of workers – seen as a barrier to increasing profitable productive output – by systematically deskilling work through the division of means from ends in the technical division of labour (Braverman, 1974; Wood, 1982). According to this thesis, autonomy, as the exercise of discretion, competence, and initiative, has been subject to two kinds of loss in the contemporary experience of work: firstly, the objective condition of alienation is consequent upon progressive deskilling in the interior content of work and secondly, the subjective condition of alienation is consequent upon organisational control over the formation of subjectivities.

Objective alienation in the interior content of work

Proponents of the loss of autonomy argument claim that progressive deskilling in the modern organisation of work is relentlessly stripping work of its potential for enabling people to develop and exercise their capacities for personal autonomy. Such claims are grounded in the assumption that the autonomous 'hegemonising power of capitalist ideology and instrumental rationality' has 'become internalised by the fragmented individuals as immutably "natural"' (Eyerman & Shipway, 1981: 551). Essentialising the present organisation of work as a natural inevitability constructs the appearance of a unified consensus that the goals of work, and the way that tasks are performed, are best determined, not by workers, but by managers and organisational experts: 'workers are in effect paid for blindly pursuing ends that others have chosen, by means that they judge adequate' (Schwartz, 1982: 635). Using process management practices, such as Taylorism, and its modern manifestations such as business process re-engineering, organisations have been able to break down the craft-based practices which sustained practical identities, disaggregating acts of work into isolated components and integrating them into a system of production which operates beyond the control of workers. Workers no longer exercise autonomy of skill and judgement over the whole process of creating the product, causing them to become dependent upon the coordinating and unifying mechanisms of a hierarchical system of managerial control in order to get their work done. Such dependence eliminates the need for workers to exercise skill, eroding their human capabilities for autonomy. Braverman (1974), for example, characterises a specialised worker carrying out the plans of others as unskilled:

> typists, [...] receptionists [...] and clerks are subjected to routines, more or less mechanized according to current possibilities, that strip

them of their former grasp of even a limited amount of office information, divest them of the need to understand and decide, and make of them so many mechanical eyes, fingers and voices whose functioning is, insofar as possible, predetermined by both the rules and machinery (Braverman, 1974: 34).

In the loss of autonomy argument, objective alienation is exemplified by the use of techniques for the disaggregation and deskilling of work based upon the scientific management principles of Taylorism (Taylor, 2003 [1911]), which Pruijit (2000) defines as 'management strategies which are based upon the separation of conception from execution' (Pruijit, 2000: 440). Taylorism generates standardised tasks which can be distributed among cheaper, unskilled workers, thereby creating a controllable, low cost, undifferentiated work force, and allowing management to claim that a Tayloristic organisation of work is justified by reason of coordinative efficiency. But Taylorism tends to increase indirect labour costs by multiplying administrative and bureaucratic functions, generating additional costs in the form of inflexibility, loss of innovative capacity, poor quality work, and conflict with values such as autonomy (Pruijit, 2000: 442–5). The use of Taylorist principles, characterised by a division of means and ends, lack of trust between workers and managers, reduced worker control over the purpose of the tasks they do or the means they employ to do them, and increased arbitrary interference by managers and organisational experts, entrenches objective alienation into the organisation of work: 'Deskilling is seen as an act of capitalism designed to transfer control over work to management by depriving the worker of his or her skill' (Inkson, 1987: 165). Thus, because Taylorism operates as an ideology to make the administration of work through the division of means and ends seem the natural and inevitable form of modern organisation to which there is no alternative, it meets the definition of objective alienation.

Under Tayloristic techniques of work organisation, an objective loss of worker autonomy is united to a re-interpretation of the meaning of autonomy, which is employed to serve managerial interests: 'In managerial discourse, the clash between Taylorism and autonomy gives rise to a language game in which the meaning of autonomy is emptied out' (Pruijit, 2000: 6). Managerial discourse deploys flexibility, generalised skills, devolved decision-making, and teamwork to manufacture a simulacra of worker autonomy which serves the interests of capital. However, the objective conditions of alienated work remain present, even in forms of working meant to increase workers' autonomy, such as teamworking. The 2001 Skills Survey, for example, showed a sharper decline in task discretion for those who worked in teams (Gallie et al, 2004: 255), depending upon the degree of scope over decision-making afforded to teams. Organisational forms embodying manufactured autonomy attempt to secure existing patterns of power and control by appropriating the irreducible autonomy of workers, but they do so at the cost of increasing objective alienation in the interior content of work. Teamworking, for example, can be used by management to capture the benefits of worker discretion based upon self-directed, semi-independent teams of workers.[2] Despite this, organisational forms are never entirely successful in appropriating workers' autonomy, leaving the objective condition of alienation incomplete and available for the active engagement of workers' meaning-making capabilities. Moreover, the objective condition of alienation cannot operate in isolation of the subjective condition of alienation, meaning that there is always a surplus of subjectivity in objective alienation which cannot be incorporated into the ideological project of management control.

Subjective alienation in the formation of subjectivities

The management of subjectivities thesis claims that, in the contemporary organisation of work, the condition of objective alienation from one's product and from the process of production has been extended by management strategy into alienation from one's sense of self, one's practical identity, and one's relations to others for the purpose of turning subjectivities into new sources of profit. Work is becoming increasingly subjectified, both enabling and obliging workers to be subjects of work through psychotechniques which recruit the subjective potentials of individual workers to further capitalist interests. Subjectivities are formed, managed, and exchanged so that 'the prescription and definition of tasks transforms into a prescription of subjectivities' (Lazzerato, 1996: 135). Appropriation of subjectivities operates through the psychotechnical tools of organisational power where workers' autonomy becomes a disciplinary project of control and extraction. The aim of psychotechniques of subjectification is to form the self according to a fixed set of characteristics, such as the entrepreneurial self (Wee & Brooks, 2011) or the enterprise self (McNay, 2009), which becomes the form for socially acceptable individual self-development in general: 'work's focus on precisely individual accomplishments and obligatory autonomy has changed its character to such an extent that it has been reduced to a tool by which to fulfil the objective of individual competencies, projects and strategies' (Petersen & Willig, 2004: 342; see also Honneth, 2004). Workers are obliged to submit to this psychotechnical project of engineering selves in order to remain economic players, causing them to engage in 'play acting' activities of self-presentation, but leading to dissociation from their identities, rendering them vulnerable to psychological harms of anxiety and fragmentation (Goffman 1959; Sennett 1998; see Garrety, 2008). The conception of autonomy constituting the core of this project of appropriation is a very thin notion of autonomy, whereby autonomy as control over work processes is transformed into a type of 'pseudo autonomy' (Petersen & Willig, 2004: 342), tied to heteronomously given objectives of efficiency and productivity: 'The expectation of individual autonomy is devalued by the individual's need to follow the requirements of efficiency and productivity and her/his exposure to constant efficiency tests' (ibid: 342). As a consequence, an individual's ability to act from normative demands is undermined, and her autonomy in work is reduced to marketing the self as a bundle of exchangeable capacities (ibid).

But against inevitable submission to the forces of self-commodification, Garrety (2008) identifies a dualism in the management of subjectivities argument which opposes the vulnerable fragile self, under pressure from the management project, to the resilient self, resisting imposed formation of her subjectivity by carving out a private identity or using organisational identities for her own purposes. Hochschild (1983), for example, describes a process of 'deep acting', or self-management, where workers try to become the prescribed organisational self. And she advises that workers 'reclaim the managed heart by forging a "healthy" estrangement' in which they 'clearly define for themselves when they are acting and when they are not; they know when their deep or surface acting is "their own" and when it is part of the commercial show' (ibid: 187–8). However, many individuals possess a limited ability to foster a resilient self through healthy estrangement, because such strategies of resistance impose psychological penalties, making a resilient self difficult to maintain. This is because, in cases of 'too much acting' (Garrety, 2008), resistance to manipulation is achieved only through workers offering a public presentation of the self which is not their real inner self, generating psychological costs to the worker in the form of strain, anxiety, and even depression. Consequently, the difficulty of maintaining an inauthentic self produces a 'special kind of alienation from self' (Goffman, 1959: 229), in the form of internal conflicts, as workers are forced to work on themselves to produce and present inauthentic selves for public consumption. In sum, the conditions of subjective alienation support the entrenchment of objective alienation by aligning affective identity and emotional labour with the purposes of the organisation (see Hardt, 1999; Holtgrewe, 2000).

As a consequence of subjective alienation, being able to appropriate meaning content to one's life because of the work one does is increasingly difficult in modern organisations, structured as they are by 'a minimal ontology of a relatively pliable world susceptible to technical domination' (Connolly, 1995: 3). The management of subjectivity is a key feature of contemporary working life which Hancock and Tyler (2001) summarise in the following terms:

> the management of subjectivity has come to be recognised as fundamental to the pursuit of those essentially managerial imperatives of functional flexibility and the pursuit of cultural homogeneity often associated with so-called flexible or post-Fordist modes of workplace organisation (Hancock & Tyler, 2001: 565).

In many economic enterprises, public service organisations, and civil society associations, intersubjective relations and the ways of being they engender are being shaped to an ever greater degree by a management ideology informed by the values of efficiency and profit, thereby excluding other values, such as well-being and environmental sustainability. 'Engineered corporate cultures' (Ezzy, 2001) are management strategies for cultivating consent through self-disciplining practices consequent upon employees internalising corporate-crafted modes of being, rather than compelling obedience through authoritarian mechanisms such as financial rewards and incentives: 'workplaces with engineered cultures are an institutional site for the production of a culture of self-gratificatory narcissistic individualism consistent with more general consumerist social relations' (ibid: 631). Courpasson and Dany (2003) claim that in order to ensure obedience to management authority, 'post-bureaucratic business firms' have become 'individualised and subjectivized forms of organisation' (ibid: 1231). Hancock and Tyler (2001) describe strategies aimed at the management of subjectivity as 'strategic interventions into the perpetual process of *becoming* a subject at work' (ibid: 569) in which intersubjective relations between employees – both managerial and non-managerial – are manipulated to serve organisational interests, and values such as individual autonomy and trust are co-opted for the instrumental purpose of enhancing corporate performance, resulting in 'a hypertrophy of the inner life of the subject' and 'eventually mitigates against their ability to engage in the kinds of social cooperation which remains central to any successful organisational project' (ibid: 575). This means that the organisation of work has increasingly come to rely upon 'the goal of an imposed unity – a false reconciliation ... Difference is thus conflated into an inauthentic and alienated subjectivity' (ibid: 581).

As a result, the experience of autonomy in work has been pushed out by an all-encompassing strategy to recruit capabilities and subjectivities into an organisation of work in which differences are not only suppressed, but made redundant by a closed, 'naturalised' agreement that there is no other way for the work of social cooperation to be organised. If we are to experience autonomy, then we had better look elsewhere to private or political life, for there is no possibility of it in an economic life dominated by the subjective and objective conditions of alienation.

Challenging the loss of autonomy argument

Whilst both objective and subjective conditions of alienation are present in the contemporary experience of work, there is no purely alienated work, because objective alienation itself depends upon harnessing the irreducible autonomy and subjective potentials in every act of work, thereby leaving permanently open the possibility that workers will be able to re-appropriate the meaning and content of the work they do with others, and by so doing alter the objective and subjective content of their work. Studies show that where there are reduced opportunities for decision-making then job satisfaction declines, indicating that workers continue to subjectively value the experience of being able to exercise autonomy in work (Blumberg, 1968; Patchen, 1970; Green, 2004, 2006). But, whilst these studies provide a degree of support for the loss of autonomy argument, they do not provide conclusive evidence for an irreparable loss of autonomy in work, consistent with critical theory's abandonment of work as an arena for emancipatory action. Whilst I agree that contemporary work has multiplied the harmful characteristics of work, I argue also that the loss of autonomy argument presents a narrative of work as irredeemably degraded and devoid of autonomous action which does not stand up to the evidence of what people actually do in work. I propose that it is possible to identify a floor-level of irreducible autonomy in every act of work which, when revealed by workers themselves through engagement in democratic practices of public evaluation, provides the normative pre-condition for realising personal autonomy as constitutive of the meaning content of work.

The loss of autonomy argument is motivated by Marx's theory of estranged labour, but Marx's theory contains a dualism opposing alienated work to craft work – a dualism which has been criticised for tying the concept of work to 'a nostalgic ideal of pre-industrial artisanal work and to an essentialist ontology of labour' (Weeks, 2007: 243; see also Adler, 2004). Consequently, the oppressions and power asymmetries of craft labour, as well as the potentials for autonomy and self-development in industrialised work, are elided from the critical evaluation of work (see Rosser, 1997). Pruijit (2000) points out that because Taylorism is a rule transparent bureaucratic system it was seen as a protection against arbitrary interference, hence the unions' support of Taylorism in the 1920s. Adler (2004) argues that 'Taylorism may well have been negative for craft workers; but just as plausibly it constituted a net improvement for the far greater mass of less skilled labourers and operatives' (ibid: 8). This is because Taylorism increases the need for coordination, interdependence, and a broader understanding of the work process, thereby fostering the pre-conditions for the socialisation of production which workers can appropriate to advance their interests. Adler identifies the ways in which work, organised according to the principle of Taylorism, retains possibilities for autonomous action which workers can appropriate for their own purposes: 'Taylorism was also a progressive step in the socialisation of the forces of production, both objective and subjective' (ibid: 8; see also Sohn-Rethel, 1978). Adler defines socialisation as 'the process whereby people new to a culture internalise its norms' (ibid: 6): thus, forces of production are socialised in an objective sense through an increasingly complex social division of labour, and in a subjective sense through the realisation of innate human capabilities for solidaristic social relations (ibid: 6–7). Through processes of socialisation which aim at the conditions for personal autonomy as a pre-condition for political autonomy, Taylorism has the potential to make a positive contribution to the objective and subjective dimensions of non-alienated, autonomous production by: firstly, creating a body of socialised knowledge which workers can use to secure their interests, secondly, enabling workers to gain access to a wider variety of roles because an increasingly 'differentiated and integrated division of labour' requires specialist planning functions and a range of technical and support roles, and thirdly, requiring workers to engage in intentional coordination with others, thereby gaining a more complete understanding of the object of their work so that 'when mobilised in these tasks, workers find their horizons broadened' (ibid: 8). In sum, whilst there can be no doubt that Taylorism is capable of generating alienated, heteronomous work, it is by no means inevitable that it should do so in all circumstances, for instance, when a democratised coordinating authority employs such techniques with the knowledge and participatory consent of all those who will be subject to them.

In my view, the dualistic opposition of heteronomous work, as divided alienated work, to autonomous work, as complete non-alienated craft work, fails to identify ways in which autonomy operates within even degraded, deskilled work. Instead, identifying a floor-level of irreducible autonomy in every act of work allows us to specify the limits to the ability of some persons to impose the burdens of an unfavourable organisation of work upon others, and provides the grounds for a new organisation of work which meets the terms of a positive critical conception of meaningful work. Work can be more or less alienated, and no work is entirely autonomous or entirely heteronomous. Autonomy itself is never perfectly achieved. If autonomy is conceptualised in terms of the liberal ideal of the independent freely choosing sovereign individual, then the conditions of any work at all must be opposed to autonomy, because all work involves accepting the constraining conditions implicated in joining our actions to those of others. For example, when we take up responsibilities to persons, animals, and objects, we are required to form our decisions and actions according to necessities given by what is good for worthy objects.

But although our experience of autonomy is partial, this does not mean that we fail to be autonomous beings. If autonomy is conceptualised in terms of right actions in relation to the responsibilities of care we have towards worthy objects which we fulfil by engaging with others in acts of joint agency, then what it means to be autonomous becomes constituted by our substantive relations to self, others, activities, and objects in the work we do together. The concept of irreducible autonomy provides the content for the immanent potential of work because, even in conditions of objective alienation, it gives rise to interpretive differences. Many of these interpretive differences remain fallow as political potentials because they are invisible, misrecognised, or appropriated by others. This does not have to be so: instead they could become the material for the exercise of the political mode of being in work when they are brought into public deliberation through democratic practices at the level of the task. To judge interpretive differences within the structure of the bipartite value of meaningfulness demands a kind of reasoning which allows us to evaluate our actions and orientations against the standard of an ethic of caring for the worthy objects one has appropriated to one's life. However, the kind of reasoning we need to employ in interpretive meaning-making includes, but also exceeds, technical rationality, and I consider how a rationality of caring can be described using the concept of *phronetic techne* (Dunne, 1993).

Theorising irreducible autonomy

I argue that there is no work from which autonomy has been entirely eliminated. Instead, following the theoretical work of Dejours (2006), I identify a level of irreducible autonomy in every act of work in order to: firstly, justify the institution of democratic practices in work, and secondly, claim that such practices embody a relational concept of personal autonomy where, to be consistent with a positive critical conception of meaningful work, the relevant intersubjective relations must meet certain normative characteristics. Dejours draws upon the evidence from ethnographic studies which go beyond descriptions of work as given by organisational rules to examine the content of the work that people actually do, and to identify the active agency of workers in all acts of work (see Daniellou, 2005). In addition, Dejours employs Wisner's (1995) conceptual understanding of the experience of work: Wisner (1995) concludes from his evaluation of ethnographies of work that work can be defined as 'the coordinated activity deployed by men and women in order to face that which, in a utilitarian task, cannot be obtained through the strict application of the prescribed organisation' (Wisner, 1995). Dejours (2006) argues that all work requires the overcoming of rules in the confrontation between the agent and material realities, resulting in a struggle which is both a source of suffering and the grounds for the formation of subjectivity. The irreducible autonomy in every act of work overthrows assumptions that hierarchical authority administering impartiality, knowledge, and coordination is the best way of ensuring that work gets done. It shows that the very nature of work is constituted by the actions of workers who seek to reunite means and ends at the level of the task by adapting, subverting, and confounding constraining organisational rules. Even though much of this work is rendered invisible and put beyond deliberative evaluation, it is a potentially rich source of the intersubjective encounters which are constitutive of skill and identity formation. Thus:

> [...] even where work is well conceived, even when the organisation of work is rigorous, even when the instructions and procedures are clear, it is impossible to achieve quality if the orders are scrupulously

respected. Indeed ordinary work situations are rife with unexpected events, breakdowns, incidents, operational anomalies, organisational inconsistency and things that are simply impossible to predict, arising from the materials, tools, and machines as well as from other workers, colleagues, bosses, subordinates, the team, the chain of authority, the clients, and so on. *In short, there is no such thing as purely mechanical work* (Dejours, 2006: 47, emphasis added).

Dejours's argument for the impossibility of 'purely mechanical work' shows us how actual human action in joint coordination supersedes and opposes prescribed human action, indicating an irreducible level of individual autonomy in all acts of work which cannot be controlled or eliminated by rule-based, Taylorised forms of work organisation. Dejours develops a triangular definition of work which integrates the psychological, the technical, and the cultural along three dimensions:

Ego-real: the instrumental moment in which the act of work takes place which involves an encounter between the worker and the real. The real is whatever resists the activity of the worker, engendering a sense of frustration, powerlessness and disappointment.
Real-others: the efficiency of the act which is also social because it is the product of social judgement guided by instrumental constraints and socially formed valuations of what makes an act of work efficient
Ego-others: the cultural moment constituted by the inter-subjective relation within the work collective (however that is structured) which enables the transmission of technique, the formation of judgements of value, and the social integration of the act of work into the division of labour (Deranty, 2009: 71ff).

'The real' element of work consists in 'all elements of the concrete reality of work which cannot be anticipated, regulated or coordinated in advance' (Dejours, 2006: 79), where 'the real' can be social as well as material. The real opens up a gap between the prescribed rules and the constraining conditions of the world, demanding that the active agency of the worker be applied to bridge the gap so that acts of work achieve their purposes. All work is therefore embodied rather than immaterial; simultaneously theoretical and practical, making subjective investment on the part of the agent unavoidable: 'without subjective mobilisation, no production is possible' (Deranty, 2009: 81). This means that, in order to complete tasks – which often involves unifying means and ends divided by the technical division of labour – workers must subvert rules in labours which are rendered invisible by rule-transparent hierarchy (Deranty, 2009). By coming up against the resistance of the real a moment of potential self-formation is created, especially where there is cooperative working and recognition of the worker's efforts, skills, and contributions. In the following sections, I shall examine the intersubjective dimensions of skill and material objects, and of subjectivities and other persons, which allow us to see that intersubjective relations in work are not defined solely by the efficiency of the act, but that efficiency itself is a value which is subject to meaning-making, and therefore interpretive difference, drawing upon other values, such as well-being, caring, solidarity, and usefulness (see Braybrooke, 1998c).

Skill and relations to material objects

In the loss of autonomy argument, conditions of objective alienation are established through progressive deskilling. In Dejours's ego-real encounters, however, workers must acquire and apply skill to overcome social, technological, and material resistances in their environment. Green (2006) characterises skill as distinctively human: 'the utilization of skill is an end in itself, with intrinsic value. Engagement in complex production processes, requiring both conception and execution of tasks in various measures, is the hallmark of distinctively human production activity, and is the means by which people have the potential for self-fulfilment' (ibid: 16). Skill formation relates us to the objects, technology, and social systems which constitute part of the real or the total environment without which 'the properly human cannot exist' (Latour & Venn, 2002: 252). Material objects, bodies, and space form part of a network of social relations, and indeed are constitutive of social relations: 'their active participation in a process of social self-creation in which they are directly constitutive of our understanding of ourselves and others' (Miller, 1987: 115). This means that our practical identities are shaped by our intersubjective encounters with materiality, forming or stunting our capacities to be producers of meaning.

The loss of autonomy argument, based upon perceptions of deskilling, is weakened by alternative interpretations of what people actually do in work, which do not support a dualistic opposition between craft work and alienated work. Attewell (1990) suggests that Braverman's deskilling thesis unfavourably links skill with control, such that lack of control must imply lack of skill, and that, in a rule-bound environment, all that workers require in terms of skills are basic abilities to read, write, and follow instructions: 'Rule-governed work [...] implies that work is completely predictable' (Attewell, 1990: 442). But Attewell (1990) argues that this is to misunderstand the role that rules play in the experience of work: 'rules – however authoritarian and detailed – provide little more than a schematic for work, a guide into which employees insert their abilities in classifying, choosing, interacting, persuading, and so on' (ibid: 443). Workers operating within rule-bound environments are not unskilled, in fact they must employ a wide range of complex skills which are simply hidden from organisational view, undervalued and dismissed by those who believe they are entitled to appropriate the task of planning the organisation of work. Kusterer (1978) suggests that one reason for the devaluation of 'unskilled' work is that, if the work requires general skills which many people possess or can acquire, then the skills involved must be less important than the skills which are practised only by a few. Kusterer recorded the following interview with a machine operator:

'I don't know why you want to interview me. You don't have to know anything to do my job.' Three hours later, too exhausted to keep writing down all she knew, I brought the interview to a close. As I was preparing to leave, she told me something entirely different, and this too is typical. 'This was real interesting. You don't get to stop and think about things like this, usually ... It really makes you think, all the things we do that we don't even realize' (Kusterer, 1978: 187).

Skill is constructed through our relations to material objects, and through our relations to others. Adler (2004), for example, identifies two components to skill: 'mastery of the complexity of the tasks required of workers in their jobs, and mastery of the relations that coordinate activity across these tasks' (ibid: 4–5). Thus, skills are not acquired and exercised in relational isolation, but are socially constructed, making the interpenetration of social relations with task content necessary for skill development (Littler, 1982). Wenger (2000) comments upon claim processors in an insurance company as follows: 'I noticed that their knowing was interwoven in profound ways with their identities as participants in their community of practice' (ibid: 238) in which 'knowing too much or failing to share a crucial piece of knowledge would be a betrayal of their sense of self and of their community' (ibid: 239). Barley and Kunda (2001) characterise communities of practice as networks of practitioners in which knowledge is unevenly distributed, and where practitioners must actively mobilise the resources of the community to solve problems. In contemporary work, rather than deskilling leading to loss of autonomy and objective alienation, the increasing complexity of tasks and the broadening of necessary social relations points towards a general uplift in the content of skills requirements (Adler, 2004: 2; see also Lindkvist, 2005).

In communities of practice, people exercise their meaning-making capabilities intersubjectively through practical encounters with material realities, generating different interpretations of their work, or 'difference potentials', which I argue can be articulated by, and made expressive of, the political mode of being when framed by democratic practices. Orr's (1997) classic study of Xerox's copier repair technicians shows how technicians make little reference to formal programs and documentation, but instead pass on knowledge to one another through 'war stories': 'technical knowledge is encoded in and transferred through the narratives that technicians recount for themselves and one another' (Barley & Kunda, 2001: 88). Commenting upon the continuing importance of Orr's work, Barley (in Orr, 1997) says: 'Orr documents and develops the important and counterintuitive notion that technical knowledge is best viewed as a socially distributed resource that is diffused and stored primarily through an oral culture' (ibid: xiii). Knowledge and skill are constructed from intersubjective meaning-making encounters which are framed by the norms, values, and standards of communities of practice. Bechky (2003) in her ethnographical study of engineers, technicians, and assemblers in high-tech manufacturing shows that the meanings that the work has for the worker shape the knowledge and skill they acquire. Consequently, the most basic means workers require to accomplish their work – their knowledge, skill, and sense of identity – are intersubjectively formed and reproduced through their relations with others in joint working. Marchand (2010) in his review of the literature on embodied cognition suggests that whilst cognition is individual, making knowledge is 'a process entailing coordinated interaction between interlocutors and practitioners with their total environment' (ibid: 2). In the concept of embodied cognition, mind and environment are so inextricably linked that cognition itself is emergent from their interactions: 'our cognitive processes are *constituted* through our embodied engagement in the world and predicated on inter-subjectivity' (Toren, 1993: 467, original emphasis). Ingold's (2000) reflections upon apprenticeship which leads him to conclude that: 'meaning is not the form the mind imposes onto the flow of purely perceptible data, through innate or learned schemas, but that it is continually generated in the relational involvement contexts that people pursue in their surrounding world' (Adenzato & Garbarini, 2006: 753). Communities of practice structure our relations to others in the joint undertakings which require an investment of time, effort, and subjectivity in order to develop the skills relevant to the internal goods embodied in the practice.

In sum, the frustrations and struggles people experience when grappling with material realities stimulates differing interpretations of the meaning of their work. Although these difference potentials are often invisible and unarticulated, they provide a reservoir of knowledge, understanding, and skill development enabling workers to bridge the gap between prescribed and actual work. I conclude, therefore, that such difference potentials are a rich source of values formation, challenging the hegemony of efficiency as the sole value determining action, and providing the material for political self-determination in work, when the conditions for democratic participation pertain.

Subjectivities and relations to others

When people work together, they join their capacities with those of others in the shared production of knowledge and skill, which emerges from active meaning-making between participants embedded in a context, or 'community of practice', including 'artefacts, tools-to-hand, and raw materials; space, place and architecture; paths and boundaries; time-frames and temporal rhythms; light, darkness, and weather' (Marchand, 2010: 2). This is not simply a technical exercise of coordination, but demands intersubjective encounters with other persons, where the marshalling of one's subjectivity through reflecting with others upon the meanings of values interior to the content of work is intrinsic to the work process itself. Such interactions shape our sense of self, making subjective formations vulnerable to recruitment by a management project which seeks to profit from the voluntary cooperation of workers by exploiting subjective affects. For example, networked forms of work organisation lacking a hierarchical structure to enforce involvement attempt to mould subjective formation (cf. Ezzy, 2001), but, in the absence of opportunities for workers to deliberate over the framing rules which structure the terms of their cooperation, the participation of workers under such conditions cannot be considered 'uncoerced'.

Even though such organisations structure forms of compulsion, this does not mean workers' subjectivities are co-opted without remainder into the management project. Indeed, the management of subjectivities argument overemphasises the ability of cultural engineering to align the individual self to organisational goals (Garrety, 2008), because workers seek to exercise agency, and indeed they *must* exercise agency if they are to get the work done. The irreducible autonomy in every act of work challenges the idea that organisational control over the formation of the self can be absolute: organisational controls over the self are more or less effective, providing opportunities for resistance and alternative subjective formations, although I acknowledge that psychological costs and power asymmetries mean that workers cannot always maintain internal autonomy over their true selves. But internal fragmentation, as a result of simultaneous resistance to, and accommodation of, pressures to align self-conception to organisational purposes is not inevitable: Ashforth and Tomiuk (2000), for example, found that occasional acting did not alienate service workers who acknowledged an alignment between the requirement of their job and their sense of self. Rau (2011) proposes that psychotechniques do not necessitate oppression, but can instead form the basis of a psychopolitics of emancipation, where workers not only work on the self using defensive strategies of resistance, but also claim the subjective experience of work as a source of self-realisation. Thus, workers do not accept the management of subjectivity without awareness and protest: 'workers do not simply acquiesce to engineered culture' (Ezzy, 2001: 634): Kunda (1992) highlights how employees see themselves as engaged in a kind of game or role-play; Graham (1995) shows how new recruits manipulate the selection process so that 'over a period of time, team members withdrew their active participation from company rituals and resorted to open acts of defiance and resistance against management and company philosophy' (Graham, 1995: 117); McCabe (2007) identifies the resilience of unionism in an environment of radical restructuring around team-working designed to undermine collective action and the forms of identity upon which such action depends.

In an attempt to break down distinctions between reproductive and productive work, Weeks (2007) suggests that, rather than thinking in terms of a true versus an alienated self, we conceive of a potential self, where 'the self at work could thus be judged in relation to a self that one might wish to become, and both work and non-work then could be accessed in relation to the possibility of becoming different' (ibid: 246). Recognising different subjective formations in the creative process of becoming requires us to acknowledge the dialectical relationship between an inner self and a public self, opening up 'a discursive space' which operates between different action contexts and timespaces of work 'from which individuals can evaluate, resist and adapt' (Garrety, 2008: 25). I suggest that discursive spaces mobilise intersubjective encounters with others from which interpretive differences over meanings, values, and purposes of work arise, but that most of these interpretive differences will remain as pre-political 'difference potentials', invisible, ignored, or perhaps appropriated into a management project of engineered selves, unless they are given a voice through public evaluation structured by democratic practices.

Aronson and Neysmith (2006) describe how the identities of care workers are put under strain by job description processes which render invisible, and therefore difficult to contest, the emotional labour which is central to effective home care. They also explore how displaced care workers who had been made redundant from their not-for-profit employer – which failed to compete in the creation of a new market for home care – were unable to protest effectively because, rather than locating the responsibility for their loss in government policy, they blamed themselves for lacking flexibility and sufficient self-interest. I do not think it is too small a step to imagine how democratic practices might have enabled them to mount a protest, exposing the exploitative character of the structures of meaning governing their work, and thus to collectively sustain their identities based upon the value they placed upon the affective dimensions of their caring labour.

Furthermore, democratic practices are protective of workers' interests in retaining control over the knowledge and skills inherent to difference potentials. Kocyba (2011) warns that making the processes and practices of work activity visible through 'radical transparency' means that workers' efforts become vulnerable to expropriation. In some instances, making work visible can conflict with the internal goods of the practice, for example, caring for others sometimes involves making one's activities invisible in order to secure the cared for person's sense of autonomy. Thus, we should not aim at transparency without also aiming at the participatory consent of workers, upon whose skill, knowledge, and capabilities for meaning-making the work of social cooperation depends. Additionally, when we create difference potentials we are exercising our status and capabilities as valuers, but this does not mean that difference potentials are automatically transformative of the interior content of work. To realise their emancipatory potential, interpretive differences must be brought into public discourse through the exercise of the political mode of being. Difference potentials, or diverse interpretations of the meanings, values, and purposes arising from acts of work, indicate the presence of an imminent core of irreducible autonomy in work. And this core of irreducible autonomy grounds the possibility for personal autonomy at the level of the task, which, when brought into public deliberation at the level of the organisation through democratic practices, makes possible political autonomy as collective self-determination. Difference potentials, however, will remain pre-political until they are visibilised through public discourse at the level of the task and at the level of the organisation.

In sum, autonomy in work is given by control, not only over the material dimensions of work, but also over the meanings of work, that is, the interpretive differences arising from the interactions with self-other-real which occur during the work of social cooperation. But to understand how we promote participatory practices which are productive of difference demands an appreciation of the relational dimensions of personal autonomy, where intersubjective encounters in the work of social cooperation must possess the relevant normative characteristics to encourage the equal participation of all meaning-makers. Interpretive differences indicate that personal autonomy over meaning-making is a fundamentally relational capability – a capability which is a pre-condition for political self-determination in a system of workplace democracy which operates at the level of the task and at the level of the organisation.

However, interpretive differences will remain as pre-political potentials until they are activated by democratic practices at the level of task, and this requires the exercise of the political mode of being. By enabling the political mode of being in work, we reconstitute both the *content of work* so that people gain discursive, embodied and practical control over the tasks they do and the purposes for which they do them, and the *social bases for the constitution of selves* by enriching the sources of identity formation and narrative possibilities which contribute to a life of meaning.

Phronetic Techne in a practical rationality of caring

To discharge our responsibilities of care, and thus to be able to claim that we have legitimately appropriated worthy objects to the meaning content of our lives, requires the exercise of a rationality of caring, which takes the particularity of worthy objects, and how they structure the meaning content of our lives, into account. A practical rationality of caring is one where the ends are not specified in advance, but emerge out of the developing needs of the worthy object in question.

In exercising a practical rationality of caring, we must be able to respond with intelligent feeling to an evolving situation, which demands experience, intuition, practical knowledge, as well as commitment to the standards determined by the relevant practice of care. Furthermore, when the worthy object is a person, a practical rationality of caring requires an engagement with the cared for, such that we do not assume we know in advance what their needs are, but negotiate an understanding of their needs through mutual interaction (cf. Fraser, 1989a). Thus, a capability for intelligent feeling is not based upon obeying automatically rules of care, set out prior to action, but crafts caring relations attentive to the particular needs of worthy objects.

I suggest that a practical rationality of caring useful to realising the bipartite value of meaningfulness can be described using Dunne's (1993) rationality of phronetic techne, which he draws out from Aristotle's distinction between two different kinds of practical knowledge: poiesis (production) and praxis (action) (cf. Breen, 2011; see also Murphy, 1993). In an Aristotelian conception of action, poiesis is the mode of producing or making, in which the goal that is pursued is external to the action itself; and praxis is the mode of acting, in which there is no product and the action is meaningful in itself. Dunne (1993) unites the technical and pragmatic requirements of poiesis to the expressive valuing and judging of praxis in the rationality of *phronetic techne*, where *techne* is a person's knowledge of the principles and techniques inherent to the practice in which they are engaged, and *phronesis* is the way in which that same person acquires understanding of how to live well 'not in the making of any product separate from oneself but rather in one's actions with one's fellows' (ibid: 244). Dunne opposes *'monopolistic reason'*, which he defines as 'masterful, autonomous, technocratic and logocentric' justified by 'materiality, contingency, vulnerability, nature, and embodiment' (ibid: 355), to *'phronetic techne'* where 'responsiveness to the situation is not fully specifiable in advance and which is experiential, charged with perceptiveness, and rooted in the sensory and emotional life' (ibid). Dunne says that production, governed by technical reasoning, has been the dominant rationality in the development of modern capitalist societies, giving rise to ambitions to control and master the contingencies of living through rigid specification of rules and the elimination of individual judgement. A technicist rationality aims 'to construe specific tasks as value neutral and to immunize them [...] against the human condition' (Dunne, 1993: 244). In contrast, the rationality of *phronetic techne* acknowledges the simultaneity of *phronesis* with *techne*, such that to be a person of practical knowledge, uniting the rationalities of *techne* and *phronesis*, is to be a 'feeling, expressing and acting person' whose 'knowledge is inseparable from one as such' (ibid: 358). This means that technical knowledge is not divorced from ethical thinking, but is instead constructed through ethico-political modes of interacting with others and the material world. Dunne says that to act out of *phronetic techne* is to see oneself as immersed in networks of intersubjective relations, and to exercise efficacy as influence, rather than efficacy as efficiency; and especially to recognise one's non-sovereignty in situations requiring us to respond with intelligent feeling (ibid: 359). The necessity for responsive relationality in the successful practice of *phronetic techne* suggests that *phronetic techne* constitutes a pragmatic, everyday capability, which people already exercise in their ordinary activities in order to fulfil their responsibilities towards worthy objects – and is therefore susceptible to inclusion into a rationality of caring. If we conceive of a practical rationality of caring in terms of 'phronetic techne', we are directed beyond rationalities predicated upon an automatic response to pre-given technical determinants to a mode of reasoning requiring responsiveness to the situation, and evaluated against standards inherent to the community of practice in which the action is framed. Moreover, when we exercise *phronetic techne* in the intersubjective relations between self and other, and self and materiality, then interpretive differences arising from encounters with others and with material realities generate values, which are not simply read off from action, but are constitutive of action itself:

> Human behaviour is really human to the extent to which it means acting into the world. This, in turn, implies being motivated by the world. In fact, the world toward which a human being transcends itself is a world replete with meanings that constitute reasons to act and full as well of other human beings to love (Frankl, 2004: 93).

Because *phronetic techne* does not rely upon pre-given technical solutions, but requires open-ended evaluation and judgement crafted to the demands of particular situations, then to exercise *phronetic techne* is to engage in meaning-making, where meanings are created from the interpretive differences which arise from the work people do together to care for worthy objects. This requires, I suggest, a kind of authority in conceiving, speaking, and negotiating which Tirrell (1993) identifies as a form of 'power of naming' (Daly, 1973: 9). An authority which allows us to engage in 'the distinctively human activity of defining, describing, and re-creating ourselves while simultaneously defining, describing and re-creating our social and material world' (Tirrell, 1993: 2). In order to participate in activities of meaning-making which produce the world (including ourselves), then we require 'semantic authority' which is 'a matter of having a say (about something) that others recognize and respect; it is an important, perhaps necessary, element in constructing oneself as fully human' (ibid: 16). Meaning-making is thus a distinctively human activity in which 'I become a person and remain one only as an interlocutor' (Taylor, 1985: 276). In fact, the extent to which I am a free person depends upon the degree to which I am included or excluded from the means to realise my status as a valuer, and to acquire the capabilities for valuing: 'We are fully human only as creators (and inheritors) of values, as beings who make norms and to whom norms apply' (Tirrell, 1993: 7). Tirrell argues that our ability to become valuers depends upon our membership of communities, because 'our past actions and the actions of others establish a structure of significance' (ibid: 13), and we depend upon communities to provide a structure of meaning, which 'give our articulations "uptake"' (ibid: 15). Communities can embody oppressive intersubjective relations, but, as I have already identified in relation to a management ideology which seeks to impose a unilateral interpretation of meaning upon the subjectivities and actions of workers, no oppressive community is entirely successful in closing down on differences in meaning-making (ibid: 10). Interpretive differences can lie fallow, or they can be made part of a public discourse of sense-making and world-building when we join with others in deliberations and disagreements over the value of objects, and the importance they should have in our lives. Such joining together in deliberation over interpretive differences multiplies the range of positive values within a liberal perfectionist framework which can be made available for meaning appropriation, and also makes possible emotional engagement consistent with the subjective dimension of the bipartite value of meaningfulness. Furthermore, when we evaluate, judge, accept, reject, and create meaning out of interpretive differences through the application of a rationality of caring, then we are best placed to realise the bipartite value of meaningfulness in our lives. And being able to exercise a rationality of caring requires us to see ourselves as relationally situated in structures of meaning in which we see ourselves as having the status of co-authorities in the realm of value, and where we possess the capabilities for meaning-making.

Activating a politics of meaningfulness

Simone de Beauvoir said 'It is in the knowledge of the genuine conditions of our life that we must draw strength to live and our reason for acting' (1948: 9). The everyday experience of work provides some of the most important action contexts from which we draw our reasons for acting, and for being. I argue that acts of work are not irretrievably degraded, devoid of the prospects for personal autonomy which is constitutive of meaningfulness, but are replete with interpretive differences, as a consequence of 'the anticipation of the problems by workers, responsibilities that are very difficult to evaluate and supervise' (Sitton, 1998: 76–7; cf. Offe, 1977, 1985). Bringing the difference potentials inherent to the core of agency in every act of work into public discourse requires an understanding of the relational dimensions of autonomy, where each meaning-maker is regarded as a potential or actual carrier of autonomy capabilities. This demands democratic practices at the level of the task. In work, to make such deliberative processes available to everyone requires, I argue, democratic participation at the level of the task and the level of the organisation. The active capacities which workers must employ to get the work done justifies their status as co-authorities able to edit (and revise) the rules and behaviours framing their activities. This means that their status as co-authorities is grounded not only in their human status as ends-in-themselves, but also in their activity which bridges the gap between prescribed and necessary/actual work. In order to make visible encounters with 'the real' – or the material realities and irreducible agency in every act of work – workers need to be able to exercise the political mode of being in work. This requires a form of workplace democracy which acknowledges the realities and the responsibilities of work as they are experienced by workers. I argue that democratic practices with agonistic dimensions have the potential to foster a form of workplace democracy consistent with a positive critical conception of meaningful work. This amounts to a normative claim that 'a just society has an obligation to promote autonomy by ensuring that its basic social, legal, political and economic institutions provide the recognitive basis for its citizens to realize their autonomy' (MacKenzie, 2008: 524), where the basis for the realisation of autonomy in work is given by institutional guarantees of meaningful work for all through a system of widespread economic democracy.

4
Confronting Domination: Freedom and Democratic Authority

I argue that the proliferation of meaningful work requires the institution of a system of workplace democracy with the dimensions of democratic authority and agonistic participatory practices. In this chapter, I will explore the first dimension of democratic authority, arguing for a system grounded in the value of freedom as non-domination.

In the standard economic treatment of work, freedom in work is preserved when we enjoy the negative freedom to enter into or exit from a contract of employment. However, negative freedom fails to account for what we think is worthwhile in the most attractive forms of work; in other words, meaningful work as free expressive activity which creates and reveals the full humanity of the worker. Given this, freedom in work is often explored using ideas based upon positive freedom. However, in my account of meaningful work, we cannot call work free when capabilities meant for the purpose of experiencing the bipartite value of meaningfulness are illegitimately constrained. Examining capability deformation requires an understanding of freedom which takes account of how relations between persons, and particularly authority relations at the level of the organisation, enable or disable our capabilities for meaning-making, and support or undermine our status as co-authorities in the realm of value. I shall explore this concern by applying the republican concept of freedom as non-domination to the action contexts in which we interact with others in the work of social cooperation. In so doing, we shall need to conceive of domination, not only in the neo-republican sense of being subject to the capricious will of another, but also as being excluded from participating in the framing of social structures which shape our subjectivities. I shall show that non-dominating intersubjective relations in the work of social cooperation are secured within coordinating authorities, which are legitimate when they are democratic authorities, and that realising the link between freedom as non-domination and authority as democratic authority is part of what enables us to realise the value of meaningfulness in work.

Non-domination and the value of meaningfulness

In order to experience the bipartite value of meaningfulness, we must develop the two capabilities for objective valuing and subjective attachment, supported by our equal status as co-authorities in the realm of value. By acquiring these capabilities we become valuers, able to make our contribution to the creation and maintenance of positive values within a liberal perfectionist framework. I went on to claim that the constitutive dimension of autonomy as non-alienating work is grounded in the irreducible autonomy in every act of work, where a person's ineliminable encounters with materiality and with others give rise to interpretive differences – replete with productive potential to multiply the range of positive values when they are brought to conscious evaluation in public deliberation. I identified how interpretive differences with the possibility of realising the emancipatory potential of work emerge from applying the rationality of *phronetic techne* to our responsibilities of care for worthy objects. In the midst of fulfilling these responsibilities, we respond to the demands of particular situations requiring the uniting of means and ends, by exercising our capacities for thinking, feeling, and judging. And I proposed that we realise our autonomy in the meaningfulness of work when we act as valuers, as meaning-makers, by bringing interpretive differences into public deliberation through democratic practices at the level of the task, participation in which demands that we be able to experience certain kinds of supportive institutional and intersubjective conditions.

If we are to be secure in our capabilities and status, and thus to have the confidence to bring interpretive differences into public evaluation with others, then we need to experience the personal condition of non-domination in institutional arrangements which are characterised by non-dominating intersubjective relations. Thus the possibility of any particular individual being able to realise freedom in their work does not depend solely upon forms of positive freedom such as experiences of expressive freedom in experiences of 'flow' (Csikszentmihalyi, 1991), or negative freedom such as being able to choose to enter into or exit from employment relations, but also upon his or her ability to resist the arbitrary use of power. In the conceptual analysis of meaningful work, Pettit's (1997) neo-republican concept of freedom as non-domination captures the intersubjective dimensions of freedom more fully than negative and positive freedom alone (Berlin, 1969).

I concentrate upon developing an understanding of freedom as non-domination in my positive critical conception of meaningful work, because, where relations between persons are dominating, then the risk of capability deformation is increased. Under dominating relations, even when institutional procedures for deliberation are in place, it becomes less likely that individuals will have the sense of their worthiness as co-authorities, entitled to bring interpretive differences into public evaluation. In processes of meaning-making which generate interpretive differences, asymmetrical power relations can operate to suppress or distort the interpretations of some to the benefit of others. Pettit (1997) describes 'being dominated' as 'occupying a position where another can interfere on an arbitrary basis in your life' (Pettit, 2002: 341; see also Skinner, 1998), where 'someone has an arbitrary power of interference in the affairs of another so far as they have a power of interference that is not forced to track the avowed or readily avowable interests of the other: they can interfere according to their own *arbitrium* or decision' (ibid: 342). Because the possibility of domination exists in the structure and character of the relations between two or more people, Pettit describes freedom as non-domination as 'social freedom' (Pettit, 2007), such that, 'corresponding to social obstacles – obstacles generated by the power of others – there will be social freedom' (ibid: 711). Furthermore, Pettit says that an individual's personal freedom does not consist in his or her choices, but in the extensiveness of their acquired and exercised capabilities; that is: 'in a standing capacity of some kind and his or her choices will count as free so far as they are exercises or manifestations of such an ability' (ibid: 715). Consequently, the capacity to resist dominating relations depends both upon structural support and individual capacities, requiring equality of capability formation for meaning-making, and equality of status when making claims for one's own interpretations of meaning and value in deliberative encounters with others.

Simone Weil: Yearning for freedom in work

Simone Weil is one of the few theorists of work who combines philosophical reflection with personal experience of everyday working life (Weil, 1977 [1946]). Weil worked in a number of Parisian factories, as a factory hand at Alsthom, a packer with Carnaud, and a line worker at Renault, when the Taylorist technical division of labour was beginning to shape the organisation of work (Ezzy, 1997). Weil observes two aspects of Taylorism which she argues makes work an experience of unfreedom: firstly, 'an unbroken succession of ever-identical movements' (Weil, 1977 [1946]: 57) gives rise to modes of acting and being which distort capabilities for thinking and feeling, and secondly, such distorted modes of acting and being are permitted when there exist oppressive relations between persons, such as those which can occur between manager and worker in hierarchical organisations of work, resulting in the managerial order becoming 'the sole factor making for variety' (ibid).

For Weil, Taylorised work is oppressive because 'the act of working is performed out of fear, rather than within the framework of an awareness of the purpose and value of the task' (Ezzy, 1997). However, despite the unpromising nature of factory labour, Weil seeks to excavate from her experience an emancipatory form of action which is immanent to the interior content of work. Against the oppressions visited upon thought and action by the factory system, Weil sets out an ideal of freedom in work where 'true liberty is not defined by a relationship between desire and its satisfaction, but by a relationship between thought and action; the absolutely free man would be he whose every action proceeded from a preliminary judgement concerning the end which he set himself and the sequence of means suitable for attaining this end' (Weil, 2006 [1955]: 81). Hence, free work engenders an experience of true liberty when a person is able to exercise capabilities for judging and feeling through a social organisation of work which gives 'a proprietary feeling to all men' (Weil, 1977 [1946]: 62); overcomes a sense of homelessness (ibid: 64); and relieves the irritations and anxieties that arise from being subject to 'the boss's unpredictable will' (ibid: 57).

Weil's experience of factory work is characterised by a relationship between manager and worker in which subjection to the will of another in hierarchical authority negatively impacts the worker in two vital dimensions of thinking and being. Firstly, perceptions of a future are eclipsed, and with the loss of time-extended sensibility the possibility of thought and action is extinguished. Secondly, the worker's sense of worth as a person is impaired. For the person engaged in repetitive factory work, the anxieties and humiliations attendant upon having to respond to 'someone else's beck and call' (ibid: 57) are exacerbated by 'being forcibly reminded that the Boss's orders are all that matter' (ibid). In order to protect himself from the harms of domination, the factory worker will avoid imagining the possibility of change; his 'thought draws back from the future' so that 'this perpetual recoil upon the present produces a kind of brutish stupor' (ibid). Consequently, the factory worker's capabilities for judging and feeling are stunted, as he trains himself into unfeeling and loses his time-extended sensibility, of future possibilities and the prospect of purposeful ends (see Truss & Madden, 2013).

However, the factory worker's state is even worse than this because thought cannot remain permanently withdrawn, but 'is obliged to remain in constant readiness not only to follow the monotonous progress of movements indefinitely repeated, but to find within itself resources to cope with the unexpected' (ibid: 59). The possibility of the work process going wrong puts the worker into a permanent state of anxiety, making him vulnerable to dependency upon others for the means to get his work done: 'when, as is so often the case, one has to turn to someone else in order to get on with his work, someone like a foreman, a warehouse keeper, a straw-boss, the feeling of dependency, of impotence, of counting for nothing in the eyes of those upon whom he is dependent, can become painful to the point of making a man cry' (ibid: 58). When the work itself is determined by the thoughts of those who plan the outcomes of the work, without reference to the worker's needs for self-determination, for positive intersubjective relations and for cognitive engagement with the tasks for which he has been made responsible, then the worker's sense of worth, of his status as a person, is undermined.

For Weil, the oppressions of work reduce to conditions of servitude (Weil, 2006 [1955]: 90), which she understands in terms of how the 'existence of other men' press the worker into a relation of dependence, so that 'his own life escapes not only out of his hands, but also out of the control of his intelligence; judging and resolution no longer have anything to which to apply themselves; instead of contriving and acting, one has to stoop to pleading or threatening' (ibid: 91). Finally, she pleads for conditions of work which will 'not render them docile, nor even to make them happy, but quite simply not to force them to abase themselves' (Weil, 1977 [1946]: 72). The basic condition for expressive free and human work is therefore the condition of intersubjective non-domination, not being subject to the arbitrary will of another which humiliates and extinguishes the humanity of one to the benefit of another.

Dominated work

Weil's insights into the experience of work expose the patterns of intersubjective domination in the institutional organisation of work, which allows her to illuminate vividly the extensive harms to human capability formation and a sense of worthiness which such relations of domination engender. In a recent account of the concept of domination, Lovett (2010) identifies both objective and subjective harms which can be mapped onto Weil's capability and status distortions: *objective* material harms of domination give rise to exploitation and insecurity which distort capability formation, and *subjective* relational harms of domination give rise to damaged self-respect which undermines status.

Lovett argues that domination makes a person vulnerable in areas of vital interest to them, either *directly* through forms of exploitation where material benefits are extracted from one person to benefit another without consideration given to the needs and interests of the dominated person in the relationship, or *indirectly* because the dominated person engages in 'strategic anticipation' (ibid: 131) by voluntarily giving up valued goods in order to avoid the anticipated unpleasantness of being on the receiving end of the arbitrary use of power. The possibility that a person may, at any moment, be subject to arbitrary interference generates such a degree of insecurity that her ability to plan her own life is severely restricted. A permanent state of insecurity gives rise to pathological behaviours where an individual attempts to avoid social interaction, or simply becomes resigned to their circumstances.

Objective conditions of *direct* domination – and the harms they engender – are strengthened by subjective conditions of *indirect* domination. This is because the subjective condition of distorted self-respect undermines a person's confidence and ability to defend him or herself from the objective conditions of material exploitation and insecurity. Many strategies, institutionalised in norms, processes, and structures, are available to those who have the power to promote the subjective conditions of domination. For example, Lovett (ibid: 132) refers to Scott's (1990) concept of the 'public transcript', which Scott uses to identify how domination involves symbolic structures of deference on the one side and dishonouring on the other. Public transcripts are used in the structure of ideologies which aim to shape the subjectivity of one person to the advantage of another, thereby making it less costly for the dominant partner to extract the benefits of the relationship.

In the contemporary organisation of work, objective structures and subjective formations are often integrated to form a system of domination. For example, Blaug (2007) identifies how pathologies of cognition and subjective formations arise when dominating organisational structures foster the development of perverse capabilities such as obsequiousness, impression management, and co-dependency. He argues that strategies of objective and subjective domination deliberately exploit meaning-making capacities in order to support managerial ideologies, such as the natural superiority of hierarchical organisations of work, with the result that 'any democratization of organisational life is seen to turn on the capacity of participants to selectively use and manage hierarchy and to minimise its cognitive costs' (ibid: 24).

When the objective conditions of domination are reinforced by subjective conditions of socialisation, adaptive preferences, and predetermined identity formations, a dominating elite is well placed to extract benefits at low cost from others, with no regard for their welfare. For example, McMahon (1994) argues that the directives of managers have the force of orders which are meant to pre-empt an employees' own judgement upon how he or she should employ her time (ibid: 188). Forms of socialisation based upon the internalisation of organisational rules mean that managers do not need to add coercive force to their directives; instead, 'subordinates are expected to be adept at reading the wishes of their bosses and putting them into effect without being told in so many words to do so' (ibid). Such dominating relations are more likely to take root in 'conditions where people have to live at the mercy of another, have to live in such a way that leaves them vulnerable and exposed to the arbitrary interference and imposition of the will of another' (Alexander, 2008: 166). And these conditions pertain when the organisation of work thwarts capability formation by making workers dependent upon the coordinating powers of others in order to get their work done.

Free work

But Weil does not leave matters thus – she goes on to identify the 'joys of work' (Weil, 1977 [1946]: 59), of a 'life spent among machines' (ibid: 55), where 'any series of movements that participates of the beautiful and is accomplished with no loss of dignity, implies moments of pause, as short-lived as lightning flashes, but that are the very stuff of rhythm and give the beholder, even across extremes of rapidity, the impression of leisureliness' (ibid: 61). Meaningful work is not work from which effort and hardship has been eliminated, but is work which presents to workers the possibility of a 'completely free life' as 'one wherein all real difficulties present themselves as kinds of problems, wherein all successes were as solutions carried into actions' (Weil, 2006 [1955]: 82). Free work requires a mode of thought and action combined such that:

> [...] the only mode of production absolutely free would be that in which methodical thought was in operation throughout the course of the work. The difficulties to be overcome would be so varied that it would never be possible to apply ready-made rules; not of course that the part played by acquired knowledge should be nil; but that it is necessary that the worker should be obliged always to bear in mind the guiding principle behind the work in hand, so as to be able to apply it intelligently to ever-new sets of circumstances (ibid: 90).

However, workers are obstructed from being able to develop principles, adapt rules, respond to the variety of problems at hand – and thus, to integrate thought and action – by the specialisation of coordinative functions 'which implies the enslavement of those who execute to those who co-ordinate; and on such a basis one can only organize and perfect oppression, not lighten it' (Weil, 2006 [1955]: 41). Increasing complexity entails increasing needs for coordination (ibid: 62), and therefore presents ever more sophisticated and extended opportunities for the arbitrary interference of some into the actions of others, sanctioned by the relations of authority between management as coordinators, and workers as executors. In Weilian terms, creating work with the requisite structure for free action and freedom in the person will demand attention to the character of work (Dagger, 2006), for work which integrates thought and action, commands the respectful attention of others (Ezzy, 2001), and develops the capabilities and status necessary for resisting domination (Alexander, 2008). And this will require, I argue, subordinating the activity of coordination to a democratically authorised authority at the level of the organisation.

Weil's vision of free work is one which secures a sense of rootedness, of being at home in the world, of usefulness (Weil, 2006 [1955]: 37), of imaginative horizons (Weil, 1977 [1946]: 70), and of ownership. For Weil, freedom of the person depends upon how social structures inhibit or extend freedom of thought and feeling, where freedom of thought and feeling is fundamentally relational and concerned with human dignity (see also Lutz, 1995). She gestures towards the republican understanding of the inter-relatedness between political self-determination and personal freedom when she says 'as long as working men are homeless in their places of work, they will never truly feel at home in their country, never be responsible members of society' (Weil, 1977 [1946]: 64). The free person is one who has a share in the determination of the rules governing society, including those institutions in a system of complex cooperation of which she must be a member, if she is to exercise her entitlement to make her contribution. She must also be a co-authority in the determination of the scope and content of the 'dispensation' or 'common domain of choice' (Pettit, 2007: 715) which determines how she may act, and how others must attend to her status as a free person. Freedom in personal acting and being depends upon political freedom.

In this respect, Weil's concept of freedom diverges radically from Arendt's (1977 [1954]). For Arendt, freedom as 'the sheer capacity to begin' (ibid: 167) is possible only within the sphere of political action; whereas, for Weil, freedom can be found within work which integrates thought and action in relations of attentive respect. My argument is that such work can be made widely available to the many, rather than the few, only when there is co-determination and co-production, through democratic authority, of the principles and rules governing the sphere of action. Modern conditions of work are prone to relations of domination because joint action and cooperative activities necessitate coordination, where coordination involves relations of power in which one person has the capacity to set purposes and give directions to another. But, although complex cooperation requires coordination, this does not mean that the activity of coordination is automatically subject to managerial prerogative. Instead, where freedom as non-domination is taken to be the normative principle, then coordinating authorities become democratic authorities, requiring the rules of coordination to be legitimated through the authorisation and endorsement of those who will be subject to the rules governing their thinking and acting, and the modes of being shaping their intersubjective relations.

Creating freedom as non-domination

Young (1990) defines domination as a social system which constrains self-determination as 'participating in determining one's actions and the conditions of one's actions' (ibid: 38). She argues that a system of domination enables the oppression of individuals by restraining capacities for self-development as 'developing and exercising capabilities expressing one's experience' (ibid: 38).

The neo-republican conception of freedom as non-domination helps us to understand Weil's concern for how unfree work which unites objective and subjective conditions of domination creates a social organisation of work inhibiting feeling and thought, thereby undermining a person's sense of self-worth. Specifically, a social organisation of work structured by domination is bad because, by malforming meaning-making capabilities, it diminishes possibilities for experiencing the bipartite value of meaningfulness. Where our capabilities for meaning-making are exploited, distorted or coerced, then the interpretive differences which arise from our attempts to fulfil our responsibilities of care for worthy objects are prevented from achieving their emancipatory potential, because even where deliberative procedures are in place our interpretations may be ignored, mocked, or otherwise rendered invisible and impotent.

Conversely, establishing 'an infrastructure of non-domination' (Lovett & Pettit, 2009: 11) will require meaningful work because such is needed if citizens are to develop the relevant skills, habits, and virtues for collective self-determination. This entails a system of workplace democracy, where democratic practices at the level of the task are united to democratic authority at the level of the organisation. In such a system, personal freedom and political freedom are mutually implicated, because, in the absence of political freedom, our personal freedom to negotiate and make sense of our encounters with things and beings is constrained to serve purposes determined by others, and in the absence of personal freedom, the sources of pre-political interpretive differences necessary to enrich the political mode of being are impoverished. But when personal freedom and political freedom are united into an infrastructure of non-domination, then we generate fresh sources of objective valuing. When we establish procedures of democratic deliberation in which equally situated participants advance their interpretive differences, and engage with one another in positive value formation, then our collective judgements upon what is worthy yields objectivity, in the form of stable, albeit temporary, agreements. In this sense, objectivity is socially constructed, although at a different level from the subjective constructions of individuals. The independent objective value is not 'out there', free floating, but in our midst, requiring from us that we take responsibility for its care and maintenance.

Personal freedom

We experience personal freedom in the work we do together when we are situated in relations to others which enable us to use meaning-making capabilities to co-create positive values which are then made available for identity formation (which will be explored in more detail in Chapter 5). Stable self-identities depend upon our being able to identify our actions and orientations towards worthy objects as being authentically our own, as well as being legitimate, in the sense that they issue in actions which are centred upon what is good for the worthy objects we have appropriated to the meaning content of our lives. Pettit's concept of personal freedom provides useful support to my argument that free actions constituting the value of meaningfulness are those which are directed towards fulfilling our responsibilities of care for worthy objects. Pettit (2001) says that a free person is one who is 'fully fit to be held responsible' (ibid: 4) – one who sees their actions as essentially their own, so that they are not a 'mere bystander', but 'identify with what is done by their hands' (ibid: 10), and are ready to give public account for their actions. This requires both an attitude and a standard by which to judge whether one has fulfilled one's responsibilities, which is given by what it means to *care for* the worthy object.

Pettit specifies that the capacity for being a free person consists in: first, 'a common domain of choice in which each is said to be free' and second, the recognition by all that each person enjoys a 'protected, empowered status' (Pettit, 2007: 715). Furthermore, he makes our status as free persons dependent upon our having 'discursive control' in which 'when one is actively treated in a discursive manner by others, and thereby is recognised as a free person, one enjoys discursive authorisation or address' (Pettit, 2001: 77). Thus, to be able to enjoy discursive control requires the developed capabilities and status for being a free person in the midst of others, for which we need immunity from domination within a sphere of action where intersubjective relations are normatively characterised by mutual recognition: 'the free person will normally enjoy such protection and empowerment as a matter of common awareness, with everyone aware of the resources available to the person, aware that everyone else is aware of this, and so on' (ibid: 716). Again, being a free person depends upon our political freedom, or our collective self-determination, in the institutions to which we belong.

However, it would be a mistake to conclude that spheres of action providing immunity from domination render us free from any kind of interference whatsoever. Some interferences are legitimate, provided that the interferer tracks the 'common avowable interests' of the interferee (Pettit, 1997), where common avowable interests are interests that the interferee would 'adduce without embarrassment as relevant matters to be taken into account' (Markell, 2008: 15). And it is possible for interferences to be legitimate at both the level of individual inter-relations and at the level of institutional rule-making. Thus laws which we have a share in framing are not dominating, but constitute a sphere of action allowing us to lead a life we have reason to value, provided that sphere of action embodies intersubjective relations supportive of our equal human status. For example, in the case of the newly democratic state, interferences are not dominating when they secure freedom through strong laws, properly constituted institutions, and embody distinctive ideals (Maynor, 2002: 75). And at the level of individual inter-relations, we might allow interferences which support the development of individual capabilities for participating in rule-making, provided that there is an absence of threat in the case of failure to develop such competences. In the case of the benign slave master, for example, a state of domination exists, even when the master is unlikely to exercise his capacity to interfere – it is the state of threat, not the act itself, which constitutes domination as unfreedom: thus, a reduced experience of personal freedom is about 'a life lived under the threat of interference or coercion' (Honohan, 2002: 183; see Wall, 2001). Such a condition is made possible when the subordinated person is constructed as incapable, inferior, a being of diminished human worth, lacking in the relevant capabilities and status to be counted as a member of the category of free persons. In a notorious example of such a strategy, Taylor (2003 [1911]) deconstructs the worker as a being capable of autonomy and independent judgement in order to justify his complete subordination to the will of another:

> Now one of the very first requirements for a man who is fit to handle pig iron as a regular occupation is that he shall be so stupid and so phlegmatic that he more nearly resembles in his mental make-up the ox than any other type. The man who is mentally alert and intelligent is for this reason entirely unsuited to what would, for him, be the grinding monotony of work of this character. Therefore the workman who is best suited to handling the pig iron is unable to understand the real science of doing this class of work. He is so stupid that the word 'percentage' has no meaning to him, and he must consequently be trained by a man more intelligent

than himself into the habit of working in accordance with the laws of this science before he can be successful (Taylor, 2003 [1911]: 41).

Such a radical reduction of capabilities and status renders silent and invisible every autonomous action and human feeling of the worker. Whilst total domination is rare in the contemporary organisation of work, tendencies towards unfreedom are common. However, with a positive critical conception of meaningful work to hand, systems and practices which strip workers of thinking and being can be illuminated and remedied using an analysis of freedom as non-domination.

Political freedom

Political freedom and personal freedom are mutually implicated, and it is one of the key insights of republicanism that the personal freedom of every person depends upon their political freedom because all are subject to common vulnerabilities which can be mitigated only through the participation of each in framing the rules of social engagement (Pettit, 1997; Honohan, 2002). In order to be able to identify with our own actions, to be capable of planning our lives (Wall, 2001), and to be acknowledged as co-authorities with equal social standing, then we must have a share in determining the rules governing our acting and being. Furthermore, being able to make and carry through plans of living depends upon being able to access a range of worthwhile options, supported by adequate resources, where the kind and range of options depend upon the framing rules describing the limits to acting and being in the action contexts in which we participate. This means that the non-dominating *res republica* is 'a shared political system in which there is no direct, personal rule of some people by others, but rather a condition of equal citizenship governed by the rule of law' (Lovett & Pettit, 2009: 12). Honohan (2002) describes the concept of the common good which is central to republican politics as: 'intersubjective recognition in the joint practice of self-government by citizens who share certain concerns deriving from their common vulnerability' (ibid: 156). Consequently, for republicans, to be a free person means to be free under the law, within a state which does not subject citizens to 'arbitrary caprice' (Rogers, 2008: 802), and where the law governing the state and its constituent parts is a common good, which each citizen subject to the law has had a share in producing and maintaining.

So, being a free person depends upon the acknowledgement of others that we are co-authorities in the determination of the rules governing our common lives in a free state which 'promotes citizens' freedom from domination, without dominating them' (Lovett & Pettit, 2009: 12). This means that, in order to allow for inclusive and open-ended deliberation over the framing rules specifying the kinds of interventions we will authorise, non-domination must be structurally embedded both at the constitutional level of the state and at the intersubjective level of individuals. The aim is for each person to become a 'full member of the human commonwealth' (Pettit, 1997: 65) by securing their status as co-authorities and developing their participative capacities – which, in Pettit's terms, are voice, standing, and claims to conversational attention – through an institutional infrastructure of non-domination. In a positive critical conception of meaningful work, political freedom as collective self-determination will require democratic authority at the level of the organisation, as well as democratic practices at the level of the task. Furthermore, that political freedom as participation in rule-making is constitutive of the meaning content of work. This is because political freedom is not merely instrumental to realising personal freedom, but is intrinsically valuable when participation itself constitutes an element of what gives life value: 'one's identity as a republican and as a human being is bound up with realising a distinctive essence that can only be realised through one's participating activities' (Rogers, 2008: 801; see also Maynor, 2002).

The organisation of work

One can argue that the modern organisation of work secures personal and political freedom because the rules of bureaucratic organisation are non-arbitrary, derived from expert knowledge, and available for amendment (Weber, 1970, 1978; Clegg et al, 2006). Hence, at the level of organisational rule-making, a Weberian ideal-type bureaucracy is non-dominating because relations between managers and workers are subject to procedures which expose and prohibit dominating behaviours, requiring managers to track the common avowable interest of their subordinates, so far as their interests consist of being employees of the organisation. The status of managers as technical experts in the coordination upon which cooperation depends is used to justify the bureaucratic form as an integrative system of man, machine, and organisation: 'no longer was managerial power merely the blind, arbitrary, or wilful exercise of authority; it could be depicted as scientifically grounded and rationally, objectively judged' (Miller & Rose, 1995: 432). In this way, the interference of a manager can be deemed to be non-dominating, because the system of rules determining interference derives its authority from impartial scientific principles, and aims at the common interest of efficient production. Workers have exercised their negative freedom and chosen an employment contract. Once inside an organisation operating according to such principles, then, although they must follow instruction, they are not coerced nor are they dominated. The rules apply equally to all.

But at the level of individual inter-relations, such a system may not alleviate an individual's vulnerability to domination because the rules, even when transparent and made known to the employee, may be formulated to secure the self-interests of the interferer, and such rules may be changed without notice or consultation (Wall, 2001). When the activities of rule-making (entitlements, procedures, and capabilities) are appropriated by a managerial elite or even a simple majority, then those rules will be made to suit some to the detriment of others. This is a form of domination, because the ones who are at a disadvantage can never plan their lives with security: 'it reduces their freedom by frustrating their intentions and plans. It obstructs their ability to plan their conduct according to their view of what is worth doing' (ibid: 227), where 'freedom consists in the ability to act in accord with one's plans and intentions' (ibid: 228). Besides, although modern capitalism has produced a variety of new organisational forms, such as networked organisations and soft bureaucracies, in response to criticisms that classic bureaucratic organisations are inflexible, slow to innovate, and stifle the development of human capabilities, these new organisational forms continue to be prone to the temptations of dominated relations (Courpasson, 2000). This is because such organisations institute opaque and shifting procedures for rule-making, which favour those with an insider's knowledge and connections.

Hence, forms of empowerment freedom can be deployed to make workers' capabilities and subjectivities conform to organisationally defined needs for self-discipline and self-mastery – a practice of power which Lukacs described as 'objectified "performance"' (Lukacs, 1971 [1922]: 90). Willmott (1993) traces the efforts of 'corporate culturalists' to 'constitute a self-disciplining form of employee subjectivity' (ibid: 523), where not only does the behaviour of employees become the target of cultural formation, but so do their thoughts and feelings, resulting in practical autonomy being extended to 'colonising the affective domain', and to 'promoting employee commitment to a monolithic structure of feeling and thought' (ibid: 517). When the objects of empowerment freedom – that is, the values constituting the subjectivities of being a good worker – are framed and defined by some, to be imposed upon others, then the category of free persons is reduced to a vanishing minority. In hierarchical authority relations, managerial authority operates to define the good for all, with the result that 'only the natural person or corporate actor at the top of the hierarchy is an undirected source of directives. The organization is thus a tool or instrument by means of which this person can achieve his, her goals' (McMahon, 1994: 189).

Meaningfulness in an infrastructure of non-domination

When a system of domination operates to exclude (from rule-making) and to subjectify (the experience of being), it becomes easier for some to exploit the efforts of others, without having to take the interests of those others in account. Lovett (2010) says: 'Domination is bad because, given the sorts of creatures we are, it presents a serious obstacle to human flourishing' (ibid: 130). Domination inhibits human flourishing by distorting the intersubjective relations upon which we depend to be able to imagine and to act upon life options (Rogers, 2008: 803). The objective and subjective harms of domination lead Lovett to claim that we are all under a moral obligation to reduce domination wherever it occurs.

A system of domination multiplies dominating relations by excluding some from the shaping of social structures, norms, and practices which define options for thinking and being, thereby enabling others to extract benefits without taking their vital interests into account: 'people live within structures of domination if other persons or groups can determine without reciprocation the structure of their lives' (Young, 1990: 38). The result is that the intersubjective relations which ought to be a source of solidarity, community, and fellowship are degraded into exploitative dependence of one person upon another, to which that person is forced to submit in order for her to secure her unavoidable needs, including her fundamental need for meaning. However, in order to understand the means by which systems of domination induce such a state of insecurity and dependency, we must consider both the objective and subjective dimensions of domination – that is, not only the framing rules governing action, but also the rules and norms governing the formation of subjectivities. In an elaboration of Pettit's theory of domination as arbitrary power and dependence upon a master's will, Thompson (2013) proposes a three-fold concept of domination as coercion, authority, and extraction, where Pettit's conception of domination describes the dimension of coercion only. Thompson identifies the other dimensions of domination to be: *authority*, where organisational routines reinforce the perception that the authority relation is legitimate; and *extraction*, where the productive and reproductive activities of one person are secured as a source of benefit to another. In Thompson's more expansive concept, domination does not reduce the arbitrary use of power to coercion, but takes account also of 'the larger, systematic dimensions of domination which frame the actions and relations of particular agents' (ibid: 283). Thus, domination is not described solely by arbitrary interference which fails to track the interests of the interferee, but also identifies how the capacity for domination is enabled by 'the constitution of individuals' (ibid: 279), where domination is a *'logic* rather than the mere arbitrary exercise of authority' (ibid: 292) which shapes a person's life projects, including their work and their subjectivity to the benefit of others.

The shaping of the subjectivities of some to the exclusive benefit of others engenders in the contemporary work of social cooperation a form of coerced participation, where domination is the 'rule by another who is able to prescribe the terms of cooperation' (Bohman, 2007b: 9). Subjects are 'produced in power/knowledge', and subjectivity is 'the experience of being subjected' (Blackman et al, 2008: 6). To become a subject, we must all undergo the experience of being subjected, but prevailing norms and processes of subjectification leave little room for freedom in self-definition: 'If the subject – right down to its most intimate desires, actions and thoughts – is constituted by power, then how can there be a point of independent resistance?' (Feltham & Clemens, 2003: 4). But subjectification is never complete, it is always 'unfinished, partial, non-linear' (Blackman et al, 2008: 16), and grounded in everyday experience and local knowledge (Rose, 1994). Consequently, subjectivity has the potential to be 'an active agent that shapes and is shaped by prevailing social, cultural and political spaces' (Blackman et al, 2008: 14) – provided that an infrastructure of non-domination includes procedures and practices enabling individuals to challenge the structures and norms of social interaction which shape the formation of their subjectivities.

Hence, I take domination to consist both in the individual capacity for the arbitrary use of power, and in the social constitution of selves through structures and practices, where the formation of subjectivity reinforces the capacity of one individual to exercise power over another without reference to their welfare. I propose that an infrastructure of non-domination in work will enable personal and political freedom by securing institutional arrangements in which the norma- tive relation between the value of meaningfulness and non- domination is specified by: *(1) the condition of not being made vulnerable in the affective attachments to the worthy objects which constitute one or more areas of one's vital interests essential to our being able to realise the value of meaningfulness in our lives; (2) where being made vulnerable is a consequence of intersubjective relations in which some have the capacity for arbitrary power over others, supported by the exclusion of those others from participating in framing the social structures which shape subjectivities and practical identities; (3) because a coordinating authority has the power to specify the terms of cooperation, then to be legitimate, such an authority must be a democratic authority.* When one's vital interests are threatened intense emotions can be aroused and adaptive behaviour can result in the withdrawal of affective attachment from worthy objects. Thus, to be affectively secure in our areas of vital interests, we must possess the necessary capabilities to resist domination, and to engage in the unco- erced participation necessary for fulfilling our responsibilities of care for worthy objects. This means that we must be situated in non- dominating intersubjective relations, which to be consistent with the bipartite value of meaningfulness are characterised by: an acknowl- edgement of our mutual dependencies which makes us vulnerable in areas of vital interest; security of affective attachment to worthy objects we have appropriated to the meaning content of our lives; equal status of participation in the social structures and subjective for- mations which frame the circumstances of our inter-relations; being in possession of the capabilities necessary for resisting domination; and participating as a co-authority in defining the rules which frame action. Finally, my strong claim is that, in order for each individual to be defended against the objective and subjective conditions of domina- tion, any coordinating authority must be a democratic authority.

Cooperation, coordination, and authority relations

In the main, we do not question why the work of social cooperation is organised in hierarchical authority relations. Even so, 'since the quality of political and public life is affected by how people spend most of their working hours, the authority structures within which most people live is a matter of serious concern' (Brenkert, 1992). This is because, in order to increase worker effort, many conventional capitalist firms use empowerment freedom to increase individual responsibility, but without instituting collective self-determination in decision-making (Pot & Koningsveld, 2009; Purcell, 2012). Courpasson and Dany (2003) argue that 'where empowerment systems apparently play a central role in the enhancement of cooperation, the issue of obedience to an authoritative centralised power deserves scrutiny' (ibid: 1231). Authority relations can easily become dominated relations, in the absence of checks and balances. The arbitrary use of power displaces the judgement of the subordinated interactant, with the following consequences: her vital interests are ignored, her actions are structured to benefit another, and her identity is shaped by social structures and norms which she has had no share in creating. In sum, dominating authority relations are both morally disturbing and illegitimate because: firstly, any kind of one-sided submission to the will of another (Hsieh, 2008) is inconsistent with autonomy and personhood; secondly, domination in the form of rule-based authority excludes many who are subject to those rules from the co-determination of rules and social structures which shape subjectivities and practical identities; and thirdly, dominating authority relations produce capability deformation, and undermine mutual respect. But mitigating such harms requires, not the extinguishing of all authority relations upon which coordination depends, but a system of workplace democracy which legitimates authority relations when they are democratically authorised (Alvesson & Spicer, 2012).

The need for cooperative relations to secure the value of meaningfulness

Cooperative joint working is both necessary and constitutive of the bipartite value of meaningfulness because cooperation fosters solidaristic relations which are both sources of affective attachment and generative of objective judgements on the content of work. When they are expressive of the 'democratic ethical life' (Honneth & Farrell, 1998: 780), such relations are generative of positive values which can be appropriated to the meaning content of a life. Cooperative interrelations foster acts of solidarity, where 'solidarity requires that one enters into the situation of those with whom one is solidary' (Freire, 1970: 31). In specifying the normative characteristics of cooperative relations in joint activities, Bratman (1992) says that 'shared cooperative activity involves appropriately interlocking and reflexive systems of mutually uncoerced intentions concerning the joint activity' (ibid: 336), where cooperative activity is characterised by: mutual responsiveness, commitment to the joint activity, and commitment to mutual support (ibid: 328). He adds that mutual responsiveness occurs in circumstances where 'I will be trying to be responsive to your intentions and actions, knowing that you will be trying to be responsive to my intentions and actions, and arises out of the commitment each has to the joint activity'. Commitment to the joint activity motivates each person to be mutually supportive of the other in 'playing her role in the joint activity' (ibid: 328).

Bratman's thick conception of cooperative relations demands that individuals have an understanding of, and interest in achieving, the purposes of the organisation. By contrast, Kutz (2000) establishes the non-necessity for joint action of intending the overall goals of a large-scale, hierarchical organisation. His minimalist account of simple participation helps to explain how much joint working takes place in complex and large-scale organisations. However, such minimal conditions for securing joint action are not sufficient for realising the bipartite value of meaningfulness – and, indeed, are not even seen as sufficient by the large hierarchical organisations with which are the object of Kutz's concern. Many such organisations acknowledge the importance of intending the overall outcome for generating employee engagement, and they frequently undertake extensive communications and participation programmes in order to foster employee commitment through enlarging their understanding of, and commitment to, the organisation's purposes and goals (see Cox et al, 2011). Moreover, such organisations may deliberately seek to secure a sense of meaningfulness by promoting a better understanding of, and commitment to, the organisation's purposes and goals, thereby increasing employee engagement and appropriating the consequent discretionary labour.

Just because we cannot do without cooperation does not mean we can achieve such cooperation by any means whatsoever; rather, we must elicit the willing effort of workers in a 'moral way' (Courpasson & Dany, 2003: 1232). In the value of meaningfulness, this means that cooperation must be characterised by substantive normative relations which are voluntary, foster mutual recognition, employ complex capabilities, and directed at worthwhile purposes. Moreover, being cooperative is not just about obeying rules – it is also about joining our actions to others in a manner which enables us to fulfil our responsibilities of care towards worthy objects. Pettit and Schweikard (2006) evaluate the normatively ideal case of joint action in terms of 'unforced cooperation' (ibid: 20) where cooperation means joining our agency to that of others in order to produce a shared outcome: 'There can be nothing underhanded or overbearing involved in unforced joint action; people must voluntarily contribute whatever is required for the desired performance' (ibid: 22). This means that joint action, when it is constituted by unforced cooperation, does not simply produce a joint effect from the sum of individual contributions, but is activity in which all persons involved are 'acting jointly' to produce an outcome for which they are 'responsible together' (Pettit & Schweikard, 2006: 19). Normatively satisfactory joint agency, characterised by the voluntary joining of one person's efforts to another, requires attentive intersubjective relations which exclude treating others as tools to secure our own advantage: 'It might just be that we each thought that others were zombies who would automatically, as if under hypnotism, do what was required of them. It might be, in other words, that we thought of ourselves as the only properly intentional agent involved' (ibid: 22). However, such a nightmare of total domination which thoroughly eliminates thought and feeling in the Weilian sense can never be fully successful, because there are always remainders and differences, giving rise to emancipatory potentials from within the structure of joint action itself. Such emancipatory potentials can be fruitful and productive of the experience of meaningfulness when democratically organised relations bring them to public evaluation and recognition.

The necessity of coordination for normatively satisfactory cooperative relations

Normatively satisfactory cooperative relations depend upon the existence of a coordinative function, governed by a coordinating authority, authorised and entitled to provide the rules and mechanisms for aligning multiple effort. I claim that, in a positive critical conception of meaningful work, this coordinating authority must be a democratic authority, because such is required to secure the legitimacy of the coordinative function. Maintenance of legitimacy obliges the authority to secure each person's capabilities and self-confidence for involvement in the process of collective self-determination. Marx recognised the need for the coordination of individual actions, to make possible an increasingly complex system of cooperation which exceeded the capacities of self-organisation:

> All combined labour on a large scale requires, more or less, a directing authority, in order to secure the harmonious working of the individual activities, and to perform the general functions that have

their origin in the action of the combined organism, as distinguished from the action of its separate organs. A single violin player is his own conductor; an orchestra requires a separate one (Marx, 1978 [1867]).

In the bipartite value of meaningfulness, our basic obligation is to fulfil responsibilities towards the particular worthy objects we have appropriated to the meaning content of our lives. It is the particular demands of the object in question which grounds responsibility, and being able to fulfil such responsibilities depends upon being able to participate in an extensive system of social cooperation, including legitimate authorities which have the capacity to exercise coordination. In order to decide and to act upon our judgements of how responsibilities towards worthy objects are to be satisfied, then we often require the involvement of others – sometimes this involvement is extensive, such as the parents of a disabled child who must rely upon the services of various medical and social agencies. Since cooperation requires coordination, which entails authority relations, a legitimate authority can be regarded as a good when it enables the coordination without which the cooperation necessary to our being able to fulfil our responsibilities towards worthy objects is exceedingly difficult to attain. However, to be consistent with the constitutive dimension of freedom as non-domination in the bipartite value of meaningfulness, then a legitimate authority is constrained to be a democratic authority.

Authority relations

Although hierarchical relations are not essential to the coordination of activities (Marglin, 1974), they remain the desire and object for those who wish to command the instrumental means of organisations. Where hierarchical relations are no longer legitimated or effective, then control shifts to the softer constraints of subjective power and charismatic leadership (Courpasson, 2000). The desire for control over coordinative mechanisms can be understood from inside the structure of joint action: we must all secure the cooperative involvement of others, if we are to make a success of our life plans and see ourselves as autonomous agents. Since persuading and negotiating with others in order to secure their unforced cooperation is costly, shapers of organisational life are motivated to construct conditions of subjective domination in which subjectified workers willingly align their interests and actions to those who seek to command. But coordinative systems which institute control through soft constraints are vulnerable to forms of radical unfreedom which 'distort the worker into a fragment of a man' (Marx, 1978 [1867]), creating heteronomously conceived and imposed work in which the worker is constructed as an extension of the manager's will – an instrumentum vocale, or 'ultimate human tool' (Patterson, 1982). Rather than a system of rational necessity, Young (1979) characterises hierarchical organisation as a 'system of perfect non-self-determination: all members of an organization, with the possible exception of those in top positions, are obliged to obey directives in whose formation they have no part' (ibid: 34). For Young, the only free society is one which engenders 'a situation of cooperation in which no persons have the right to determine the basic conditions of the actions of others without reciprocation' (ibid: 40), although she does allow that some hierarchy may be necessary to ensure coordination and cooperation. In a system of democratic authority, it is only to the extent that authority relations need power over coordinative mechanisms to secure our vital interests that they are allowed to command our acting and being.

The requirement for democratic authority

Warren (1996a: 46) argues that there are many circumstances where authority may be instrumentally valuable. In particular, authority may be functional in complex societies burdened by a vast increase in the number of difficult decisions, giving rise to specialised discourses closed to broad participation. In situations where deliberative decision-making is impossible, then we should prefer authoritative decision-making, but only if such decision-making can be made subject to democratic accountability and authorisation: 'democracy is necessary to chasten authority, to limit its claims and dangers' (Warren, 1996a: 47). Thus democratic authority is one which is open to contestation and difference through the institution of deliberative procedures which produce 'an authoritative background of commitments and beliefs that both sustain and contain democratic challenges' (ibid). This type of authority requires subjects capable of autonomous judgements informed by beliefs and commitments (ibid: 54–5). However, the development of this desirable form of subjectivity is hindered by oppressive structures of obedience: 'democratic authority requires a context of critical challenge that is all too easily damaged by hierarchies of status and inequalities of resource distribution' (ibid: 56). Concern for the harms to personal and political freedom of hierarchical relations leads Young (1979) to make the strong claim that the principle of self-determination must be carried through into a society of democratically organised enterprises and collectivities at an increasing scale (ibid: 42), and that this precludes 'the possibility that persons can form organizations of social cooperation possessing a hierarchical structure of basic decision-making' (ibid: 43). The need to defend individuals against the harms of domination implies widespread subjectivities and capabilities for collective self-determination in a system of democratic authority where all coordinating authorities, whether public or private, small or large, are democratic authorities.

If it is the case that we cannot avoid having some coordinating authorities – and this seems reasonable, given our understanding of how organisations and systems function – then, in order to secure the value of freedom in the interior content of work, that authority must be legitimated by being subjected to processes of collective self-determination. A coordinating authority can be organised more or less hierarchically and more or less cooperatively, but, in my positive critical conception of meaningful work, there can be 'no authority without democracy' (Sevenhuijsen, 2000: 8). In Raz's service conception of authority, for example, an authority is legitimate when, in its coordinative function, its aim is to secure and promote the vital interests of those who are subject to that authority (Raz, 1986). Warren (1996a) identifies how any social order is made up of a diversity of legitimate authorities, variously arising from: the internal goods of a social practice, a substantive identity from membership of a social group, collective self-determination in deliberative contexts, or a coordinative function derived from a role in the division of labour held either by ourselves or another we have jointly authorised. Such authorities are legitimate when they foster democratically determined intersubjective relations which are functional for meaningfulness.[1] In other words, coordinative authorities must be democratic authorities if they are to underwrite the basis for experiencing the value of meaningfulness. Thus to develop the relevant capabilities for meaningfulness, and to be secure in our status as equal co-authorities, we must all have the opportunity to belong to and participate in at least one democratically organised, coordinative authority, such as a role, practice, or institution.

A system of non-domination and the value of meaningfulness

In order for people to realise the capabilities and status for experiencing the value of meaningfulness, a system of non-domination must prevail. This means that all organisations in the system of social cooperation must be governed by a democratic authority, however constituted. To this end, McMahon's (1994) work, *Authority and Democracy: A General Theory of Government and Management,* remains an important and sophisticated account of managerial authority which focuses upon the 'nature of the employment relation' (Hsieh, 2006: 348), and 'the moral limits to relationships that involve the submission of the will on the part of one person to another' (ibid). McMahon (1994) identifies how, in a subordinate relation, one person's actions are controlled to some degree by another's, their will is displaced by another's: 'the subordinate's judgement of what the applicable directive-independent reasons require is displaced from its normal action-inducing relation to his will by a directive' (ibid: 30). He describes governmental and nongovernmental organisations as operating in a single social system of political authority, where government and management make up 'two components of an integrated system of social authority that is essentially political in nature' (ibid: 3). Political authority arises out of circumstances in which fundamental disagreement over the common good is combined with the requirement to coordinate activities in order to promote general well-being. And management is analogous to government in that it is a public authority defined by coercive power where the legal right of some to control access to the resources necessary for leading a decent human life enables them to force others, who have no such legal rights, to do as they demand (McMahon, 1994: 7): 'If disagreement among people holding different substantive moral conceptions is the mark of the political sphere [...] nongovernmental organizations are as political as states' (ibid: 22).

Those persons, such as employees, who are subject to authority relations will judge whether the decisions that guide their actions are legitimate on the grounds of whether these decisions further their vital interests in fairness and welfare maximisation (where McMahon refers to fairness as the chance that one's preferred policy will be chosen at some stage in the voting cycle, and welfare maximisation refers to what the majority would prefer). But, the existence of a plurality of conceptions of the good means that there is a good chance of employees being required to follow directives which conflict with their moral convictions. If we are to demand obedience to directives from those who are in a weak position to resist, then we need to develop persuasive normative reasons for the legitimacy of such directives. Coercive power cannot justify political authority – therefore, we need to find other reasons for why people may submit to the directives of another which does not depend upon any prior legal powers that an authority may possess. McMahon provides such reasons by defining legitimate management authority as democratic 'reflexive authority' (ibid: 12), where directives which carry with them the force of obedience must be generated by those who will be subject to them, on the basis that people have the right to participate in the decisions which will guide their actions.

McMahon therefore proposes a C-authority which enables 'cooperation among people with conflicting views about what constitutes morally acceptable conduct in their working lives' (ibid: 15). In the case of C-authority, the outcomes of cooperating must be more beneficial for those complying with the directives 'than the outcomes from not complying' (McMahon, 1994: 233). A C-authority is therefore 'justified as facilitating mutually beneficial cooperation' in which each person participates in order to realise her own moral aims. McMahon advances C-authority as the form of morally desirable form of managerial authority when it is underpinned by the consent generated by a system of workplace democracy, because 'considerations of fairness and welfare maximisation support the choice of an economic regime in which managers are democratically accountable to workers' (Hsieh, 2006: 351). The legitimate authority which is consistent with the constitutive element of freedom as non-domination in the value of meaningfulness is therefore a C-authority – one which constrains the ability of a few to extract benefits from the many with no regard for their welfare by instituting conditions of political freedom, the freedom of the ancients, in the interior structure of work.

Mill (1994 [1871]) wrote in the *Principles of Political Economy*:

> The form of association, however, which if mankind continues to improve, must be expected in the end, to predominate is not that which can exist between a capitalist as chief and work-people without a voice in the management, but the association of the labourers themselves on terms of equality, collectively owning the capital with which they carry on their operations and working under managers elected and removable by themselves.

In the bipartite value of meaningfulness, affective appropriation of worthy objects is fostered when both the Weilian elements of objectivity and subjectivity are present. In the subjective dimension, of possessing a proprietary sense of being at home in the world, supported by attentive intersubjective relations, and in the objective dimension, of the unity of thought and action bent towards unexpected problems, requiring new solutions or the adaption of rules and principle, which themselves have been subject to co-determination with others. Making freedom as non-domination constitutive of the meaning content of work, equips us to create, and to fulfil our responsibilities towards, worthy objects through joint activities with others. Hence, to be a free person is not about the clearing away of obstacles or even about the expansion of choices, but about being able to act upon those obstacles with one's human capabilities for action/thought in dignified and respectful relations with others. In the final count, freedom exists only in a quality of acting together.

It is this intersubjective dimension of meaningfulness that I will evaluate in the next chapter. There I shall argue that dignity depends upon our having a sense of our value as particular persons with lives of our own to lead.

5
Restoring Dignity: Social Recognition in Practical Identity Formation

As human beings, we are 'obligatorily gregarious' (Cacioppo & Patrick, 2008: 52), implying that we cannot evade our physical, social, and emotional inter-dependences, from which we derive many of our most important relationships, projects, and sources of meaning. To be inescapably social means that, although we are separate individuals, we are not sovereign. We do not pick and choose our life plans from social materials which exist apart from us – instead, we are already constituted by our relations to others with whom we co-produce and co-sustain the meanings, norms, and values of our intersubjective existence. This means that to experience our lives as meaningful, we require positive self-relations of self-respect and self-esteem, which are intersubjectively shaped by our relations to others. But realising positive self-relations becomes problematic when our relations to others are such that our valued identifications are misrecognised, or when institutional norms and values make it difficult to achieve a sense of being a valued person. In the contemporary work of social cooperation, stable positive self-relations are increasingly difficult to experience, making the task of forming a practical self-identity a demanding project. I evaluate the limitations of the concept of self-respect in Rawlsian justice, and of the concept of self-esteem in Honneth's theory of social recognition, both of which mediate recognition through individual achievement. I propose that we need a concept of positive self-relations which is constitutive of the value of meaningfulness. To this end, I shall argue that uniting self-respect and self-esteem to a sense of dignity as particular persons, who bear responsibilities for the worthy objects we have appropriated to our lives, points us beyond the pursuit of individual achievement to worthwhile, if not completely stable, practical self-identities constituted by the values internal to caring for those worthy objects.

Our need for social recognition

Individual subjective formation emerges from a psychological process of increasing individuation through an intersubjective struggle, which arises in infant development and which Benjamin (2002) identifies as 'thirdness', or 'the creation of something that no longer identifiably emanates from one person or the other but mediates between them' (ibid: 49). In critical social theory, most notably in Honneth's (1995a) theory of recognition, this psychological process is translated into the political, cultural, and economic domains in order to provide an explanation for individual motivation and societal change. Honneth (1995a) uses Benjamin's psychological theory of the formative development of the individual to support his ethical claim that individual self-realisation, and thus the possibility of social progress, depends upon the recognitive relations which arise out of the interactions between multiple subjectivities, where subjectivity is 'the experience of being subjected' or 'the experience of the lived multiplicity of positionings' (Blackman et al, 2008: 6). Since our individual subjectivities, or ways of being in the world, are formed through processes of feeling, thinking, and acting (Taylor, 1989) then our subjectivities are implicated with those of significant others, such as parents, colleagues, or fellow members of a community of belonging. In Honneth's account, correctly structured intersubjective relations generate practices of social recognition, resulting in positive self-relations, in the form of self-confidence, self-respect, and self-esteem. Thus, self-realisation, or the development of our human capabilities, depends upon our being able to experience positive self-relations, arising from correctly structured intersubjective recognition (cf. Honneth, 2004).

The inescapable necessity of social inter-relations for positive self-relations means that recognition is 'not just a courtesy we owe people. It is a vital human need' (Taylor, 1992: 26). To be acknowledged, to be seen by others, is essential to human action, and to a stable sense of identity which supports the moral and psychological conditions for well-being: 'We run to be seen, recognised, admired by some subset of the others. If local victories were not possible we would all be in despair long before we were done' (Walzer, 1983: 255). When we lack social recognition, it is difficult to maintain the positive self-relations essential to forming a self-conception of being efficacious and worthy persons to whom it is not legitimate to do certain things, and whose contributions are valued and welcomed by the society to which we belong: 'having both no authority and no intrinsic value in the eyes of others on whose actions and decisions one's life and future depends is a frightening vision for any rational person in any culture' (Ikaheimo, 2007: 40). As a result of being deprived of positive self-relations, individuals experience an insecure sense of belonging and relatedness, and are made vulnerable to the harms of isolation, social exclusion, and dominating, exploitative relations to others. Thus, our need for social recognition grounds political claims that individual flourishing depends upon living in social arrangements which foster positive self-relations of self-confidence, self-respect, and self-esteem.

Our legitimate need for social recognition, however, is increasingly difficult to satisfy in a contemporary organisation of work which mediates recognition through unstable forms of individual merit, thereby causing individuals to become subject to shifting terms in others' valuations of them, thereby undermining the possibility of stable positive self-relations. Following Ikaheimo and Laitinen's (2007) definition of recognition as 'taking someone as a person, the content of which is understood and which is accepted by the other person' (ibid: 42), I argue that the value of meaningfulness provides some remedy to the insecurity of social recognition when intersubjective relations are suitably structured for securing positive self-relations in the form of a sense of one's dignity as a particular person (cf. Noggle, 1999). In the bipartite value of meaningfulness, we advance our claims to recognition based upon our effectiveness in the practices of caring, respecting, or promoting relevant to the worthy objects we have appropriated to the meaning content of our lives. This is because engaging in practices of care for worthy objects removes our attention from seeking social recognition for its own sake to what we must do or become in order to promote the good for worthy objects. But this does not imply that our needs for self-care have no importance relative to caring for others; instead, care of the self becomes part of a constellation of appropriate attitudes towards worthy objects which we form through mutual intersubjective recognition of one another's practical identities. I argue that both self-respect and self-esteem are necessary to a caring self which supports a sense of dignity as a particular person. Massey (1983) identifies that, for self-respect, a person needs both a subjective evaluation of himself, generating a 'certain kind of favourable self-attitude' (ibid: 248), and an objective evaluation of himself, where he does not simply value himself but 'properly' values himself (ibid): 'it is necessary but not sufficient for self-respect that a person believes he acts in ways that he believes are worthy. In addition, the person must have correct views about his worth and act in ways which are objectively worthy' (ibid: 253). By engaging in the numerous practices of care for worthy objects, we satisfy Massey's subjective and objective dimensions of social recognition, simultaneously connecting us with the bipartite value of meaningfulness. This is because the achievement of practice standards requires other-regarding actions which *subjectively* stabilise self-esteem, reassuring us that what we are doing is *objectively* worth our effort.

Wolf (2010) suggests that being involved in the practices framing worthwhile projects can be protective of the damage done to self-esteem consequent upon the failure of our plans, where self-esteem is protected by: mere belonging to communities and practices; subsidiary activities of the practice such as training and mentoring of others; and exercise of the virtues and talents required by the practice (ibid: 106–7). Simply *doing* the activities of a practice containing valuable internal goods can mitigate the personal consequences of failure and be protective of self-esteem, particularly where self-respect – our sense of our value and status as a person – is steady and well-grounded (ibid: 106). In addition, failure is an experience which can be retrieved by the learning and perspective that comes with the unfolding narrative of a whole life: 'Learning from mistakes, failures and disappointments allows us to redeem periods of our lives that would appear as total losses if viewed in isolation' (ibid: 107). Wolf claims that if the failed project has independent, objective value, then we can justifiably appropriate it to the meaning content of our life because putting forth effort to make a contribution, as well as achievement, can enable us to experience the value of meaningfulness:

> *something* of value is achieved in the very commitment to that project and in the striving to pursue it, which can be a sufficiently intentional part of the agent's activities and values to contribute a measure of meaningfulness to that period of the person's life (ibid: 107).

I propose that being able to acquire a sense of our dignity as particular persons through orientations of care, for ourselves and for other worthy objects which constitute our practical identities, meets both the subjective psychological need for esteem recognition and the objective ethical need for respect recognition. This is because seeking the good for worthy objects subjectively reassures us that there is meaning in our lives, that our lives are worth living, and objectively confirms that the value of those objects is worth our effort. In uniting self-respect and self-esteem in a sense of dignity, I address two concerns expressed by critics of the contemporary experience of work who claim that it is no longer possible to secure stable positive relations to the self. Firstly, self-respect is vulnerable to *under-objectivity*, because the modern organisation of work strips collective institutions and practices of their intrinsic goods, thereby removing a source of objective value capable of providing a sense of greater purpose consistent with our need to value ourselves as particular persons. Secondly, self-esteem is vulnerable to *over-subjectivity*, because it can become too dependent upon the opinions of others, with the result that our own evaluations of what is a worthy object, and therefore what our attitudes should be towards those objects, become misdirected, causing us to appropriate to our lives values we would not fully endorse if our subjective evaluations of what is attractively valuable to us were uninfluenced by the need to pursue self-esteem.

I evaluate the problems of over-subjectivity in relation to self-esteem, and under-objectivity in relation to self-respect by drawing upon insights from empirical psychology and moral philosophy. In their well-known exchange, Fraser (in Fraser and Honneth, 2003) critiques Honneth (1995a; Fraser & Honneth, 2003) for grounding his theory of recognition in poorly substantiated and highly contested psychological theory. But Meyers (1995) proposes that we seek a mutual enriching, since each approach is incomplete without the other: 'whereas the moral view insists that only the morally autonomous self and its good qualities can be respected, the psychological theory counters that any self together with its traits can be respected' (ibid: 228). Consequently, each approach contributes to the other in two respects: firstly, moral philosophy remedies an under-objectivity in psychological theory which takes no account of the value of the objects at which esteem recognition aims, and secondly, psychological theory addresses an under-subjectivity in moral philosophy which lacks a complete understanding of how intersubjective relations are constitutive of the formation of positive self-relations.

Self-esteem: The subjective dimension of social recognition

In psychological theory, social recognition secures self-esteem, where self-esteem is necessary for satisfying three fundamental needs for belonging, relatedness, and control (Park & Crocker, 2005). Pyszczynski and Cox (2004a) suggest that the motivation to pursue self-esteem may be hard-wired into human evolutionary psychology, because to lack self-esteem is to be in danger of social exclusion which is threatening to survival. In terror management theory, for example, self-esteem is essential to psychological health, because it protects the self from destructive anxieties and fear of mortality. In modern societies, however, our need for esteem recognition is vulnerable to exploitation: capitalist systems of production mobilise and exacerbate our need for self-esteem in order to secure our acquiescence to organisational controls aimed at pre-determined subjective formations, such as the enterprise self (du Gay, 1996; McNay, 2009; Garetty, 2008). But, over-stimulated hunger for esteem recognition directed towards inauthentic subjective formations is harmful to our ability to satisfy the fundamental human needs which depend upon positive self-relations. Park and Crocker (2005) conclude that fundamental human needs for autonomy, competence and relatedness remain unmet by our pursuit of contingent forms of self-esteem which are dependent upon the approval of others, and therefore of standards and values which are not our own; in turn: *autonomy*, 'the pursuit of self-esteem sacrifices autonomy' (ibid: 399) because self-esteem is heteronomous, and when it becomes a higher order goal it displaces or inhibits other more autonomously conceived goals; *competence*, the pursuit of self-esteem inhibits learning and mastery because failure cannot be tolerated; *relatedness*, the pursuit of self-esteem focuses our attention upon ourselves at the expense of developing care, concern and meaningful relations with others. In the areas of life in which their self-worth is invested, people seek to have their abilities, goals, and achievements validated, and can react to threats to success in destructive ways:

> They interpret events and feedback in terms of what they mean about the self; they view learning as a means to performance outcomes, instead of viewing success and failure as a means to learning; they challenge negative information about the self; they are preoccupied with themselves at the expense of others; and when success is uncertain, they feel anxious and do things that decrease the probability of success, but create excuses for failure, such as self-handicapping or procrastination (Park & Crocker, 2005: 393).

Rather than relieving existential pressures, the frantic pursuit of positive social recognition makes stable self-esteem difficult to achieve – any positive valuations are insecure, forcing individuals to seek continual reassurance of their recognitive status. The result of making individuals responsible for their recognitive condition, whilst simultaneously placing secure self-relations beyond reach, is increased anxiety, and proneness to psychological and physical ill-health (Wilkinson & Pickett, 2009; see also book on health). My proposal is that the search for esteem recognition does not have to be destructive, but that avoiding the excesses of esteem hunger means taking seriously the political project of reconfiguring the bases of social recognition to secure self-respect, as well as self-esteem, within a sense of our dignity as particular persons. For example, Roland and Fox (2003) suggest that psychological approaches to self-esteem, understood as feeling good about oneself, fail to take proper account of self-respect as the 'appreciation of being a person' (ibid). Self-respect operates to mitigate high/low levels of self-esteem, acts as a buffer against failure or excessive self-appreciation, and enables self-regulatory behaviour: 'self-respect is the couch on which the cushion of self-esteem resides' and provides the 'core of one's psychological strength' (ibid: 271). Pyszczynski and Cox (2004a) propose that the pursuit of esteem recognition should be steered towards an autonomous, self-determined life, construed as 'meeting standards of value that have been freely chosen and thoroughly integrated into one's self' (Pyszczynski & Cox, 2004a: 428). And Park and Crocker (2005) suggest that securing stable self-respect is more conducive to autonomy, competence, and relatedness, because it assists in 'shifting from superordinate goals concerned with self-esteem to superordinate goals that are not focused on self-esteem but are larger than the self or are good for others and the self' (ibid: 406). Self-respect draws our attention away from an over-emphasis upon the practices of self-esteem, such as self-presentation: 'monitoring and the ability to alter one's behaviour in order to bring it into line with one's standards [...] self-regulation or self-control is an integral part of a self-respect system' (Roland & Cox, 2003: 273). Thus, self-respect has a vital functional role to play in the development of human capabilities for living a life of meaning: 'the function of self-respect is to protect and nurture the human capacities necessary to know and navigate one's world' (ibid: 279). In sum, to secure a sense of dignity we should concentrate upon developing the social conditions which ground self-respect, rather than seeking to multiply possibilities for self-esteem, thereby fostering a sterile competition for esteem recognition in an economy of esteem in which public attention is an increasingly scarce resource (Brennan & Pettit, 2004).

Self-respect: The objective dimension of social recognition

Moral philosophy makes clearer conceptual distinctions than psychological theory does between different forms of social recognition

(Darwall, 1995; Dillon, 1995). I shall be concerned in this section with how the concept of self-respect is necessary to secure the objective dimension of social recognition which is a more stable form of self-relation than self-esteem, and has a particular role to play in our being able to value objects in the objective dimension of the bipartite value of meaningfulness. The result ought to be the capacity to properly value ourselves by acting in ways which we believe to be worthy, where that judgement is forged by an evaluation of our actions against what is required to have a care for worthy objects.

> Self-respect is something most of us want and need. Few things are as important to our well-being as a secure sense of our own worth, or as debilitating and disempowering as its lack. Deep and enduring shame and self-contempt, unremitting doubts about one's worth, a tendency to see oneself as not quite as good or not quite as valuable as others: such things constrict and deform lives, frustrating the quest for self-fulfillment and self-realisation (Dillon, 1995: 290).

In my formulation, the objective dimension of social recognition is satisfied by: firstly, encounters with objects which we judge to be worthy of our efforts, and secondly, intersubjective relations of the right normative character, which contribute to sustaining a sense of dignity because they confirm we are correct in our evaluations of worthy objects, and give us information on how we are doing with respect to fulfilling our responsibilities of care.

Firstly, encounters with worthy objects: if they are to support self-respect, recognitive encounters must be based upon goods which are worth recognising, because 'to desire recognition is not normally to simply desire to be noticed, but to desire confirmation of the worth excellences independent of recognition. Recognition is parasitic on objective goods' (O'Neill, 1997: 193). This means that social recognition in itself cannot add to the meaning content of a life, unless such recognition is consequent upon our engagement with objects we judge to be worthwhile. So, valuing the social recognition of others depends upon our being able to acknowledge the value of the internal goods upon which recognition depends. Social recognition of goods, values, and identities that we do not endorse is misrecognition, which can occur, for example, when powerful others over-identify us with our social roles, or when institutional rules and social norms promote a personal identity which is at odds with our self-conceptions (cf. Deranty & Renault, 2007). Recognition of one's proficiency in worthless, pointless, or futile practices cannot add to the meaning content of a life, even if we enjoy doing them. Equally, recognition of one's exceptional performance as a doctor or scientist cannot add to the meaning content of one's life if one is yearning to be a potter. I have argued that subjective discounting of an identity-constituting activity, such as one's occupation, may not reduce the *value* of a life, but it does reduce the *meaning* of a life (cf. Arneson, 2000). The goods and the standards may be independently worthwhile in that they add value to the practice or contribute to some social good, but unless they are subjectively endorsed by the agent as valuable according to their conception of living, they cannot add meaning content to the agent's own life.

Second, intersubjective relations: respect recognition must do more than acknowledge us as a universal type. A sense of dignity is supported by being able to experience ourselves as particular persons, giving us confidence that 'one's life has value in all its everyday ordinariness – in the monotony, grime, inadequacy and despair as well as in the shining moments of achievement' (Dillon, 1995: 299). Thus, positive social recognition should enable an individual to arrive at a correct valuation of their particular selves, such that 'the self-respecting person has a keen appreciation of her own worth' (ibid: 292). When we possess positive self-relations, we see ourselves as distinct individuals, able to lay claim to the equal consideration and acknowledgement of others, not only because of our status as co-authorities and our capabilities for being a valuer, but also because we have our own projects and connections to others which constitute our sense of who we are as particular persons. But, to be able to evaluate ourselves in these terms, we need to acknowledge our 'interpersonal reality' (ibid: 300), where positive self-evaluation is based upon 'what we do, on communal activities and achievements, thus moving us toward more integrative and mutually supportive social arrangements' (ibid). This means that, if we are to develop the positive self-relations which secure the conditions for self-realisation, we must encounter one another in our daily activities as *equal* interaction partners, where equality does not mean sameness, but is an equality based upon the particular ways in which we make our contribution to society, including the work of social cooperation, generating an entitlement to the acknowledgement of others because of our efforts to fulfil our responsibilities of care for worthy objects.

I argue that to have a sense of our dignity as particular persons, we need social recognition of our practical identities, where practical identity formation is an intersubjective achievement requiring the appropriation of values through the exercise of meaning-making capabilities (cf. Korsegaard, 2009; see also Roessler, 2012). A stable practical identity acts as a filter through which we make judgements, and in return receive judgements, about how well we are doing in relation to the orientations of care relevant to valuing worthy objects. Consequently, the formation of a self-conception, or practical identity, depends upon our self-attitudes, the beliefs we have about ourselves and the worthiness of the objects and values we have incorporated into our lives: 'self-respect has to do with the structure and attunement of an individual's identity and of her life, and it reverberates throughout the self, affecting the configuration and constitution of the person's thoughts, desires, values, emotions, commitments, dispositions and actions' (Dillon, 2010: 41).[1] When we are affectively engaged with worthy objects, we establish orientations of care which enable us also to experience a sense of dignity as particular persons. Practices of care which develop the relevant orientations support out affective engagement with the values we have appropriated to the meaning content of our lives, consistent with the objective goods which such values embody in worthy objects. In sum, our self-respect is secured through our sense of how we are doing in relation to caring for worthy objects, which I propose provides a richer account of human action than individual achievement or excellence.

Rawls's respect recognition and Honneth's esteem recognition

There are limits to Rawls's self-respect and Honneth's self-esteem as attempts to secure the conditions for self-realisation. I argue that, for different reasons, both theories are tied to a problematic ideal of individual achievement, which is increasingly difficult to realise in modern conditions of work, crowding out alternative values based upon solidarity and collective effort.

The limits of the Rawlsian concept of self-respect

Rawls (1999 [1971]) remains an important theorist of self-respect, because of the central role he gives to self-respect in the organisation of a stable society, in which the development of the individual is secured through a fair share of primary goods and a system of equal political and civil liberties. Rawls claims that self-respect is 'perhaps the main primary good' without which we may lack a sense of life being worth living, where self-respect is of such importance that justice requires 'equality in the social bases of self-respect' (ibid: 440).[2] Rawls's concept of respect depends upon both status and capabilities because, to experience self-respect, we need: firstly, the status which gives us a sense of self-worth and of the worth of our conception of the good (ibid) and, secondly, developed capabilities to give us a sense of confidence that we are able to carry through our intentions (ibid). Thus, Rawlsian respect consists of both an objective status dimension, which relies upon the worth of the person as the 'self-authenticating source of valid claims' (Rawls, 2005: 72) and a subjective individual dimension, where we judge ourselves to be more or less successful against a life plan, which contains activities of sufficient complexity to realise the Aristotelian Principle (cf. Zink, 2007). In Rawlsian self-respect, what social recognition aims at, and how social recognition is mediated, has a particular content which is necessary to Rawls's scheme of justice, but which also exposes the limitations of his concept of self-respect for securing positive self-relations through the work we do together.

The aim of social recognition

In Rawls's theory of justice, social recognition aims at the self-respect necessary for securing a particular political conception of the person, which Rawls defines as 'someone who can be a citizen, that is, a normal and fully cooperating member of society over a complete life' (2005: 18). A fully participating member of the polity is one who is capable of developing the two *moral powers*, or the capacity for a sense of justice and the capacity for a conception of the good, in addition to *developed capabilities* for observing the terms of cooperation and for forming their own particular conception of the good (ibid; see also, Freeman, 2007: 334). For Rawls, self-respect is important for supporting our status as democratic citizens: it does not aim at justifications for securing just socio-economic conditions, such as ensuring that all work in the system of social cooperation is meaningful work. Even so, Rawls acknowledges two obstacles to realising the aims of social recognition: firstly, socio-economic inequalities and secondly, poor quality work. Thus, Rawls recognises that a sense of self-respect may depend upon socio-economic equality, where 'to some extent men's sense of their own worth may hinge upon their institutional position and income share' (ibid). But Doppelt (2009) argues that, by making equality in the social bases of self-respect essential only to democratic citizenship in the political domain, Rawls discounts inequalities in the socio-economic domain in a manner which cannot be justified by our everyday experiences: 'Taken as an empirical claim, the dominance of democratic citizenship over other social positions in shaping the distribution of recognition-respect in modern liberal-democratic society is at best dubious' (Doppelt, 2009: 138). Doppelt (2009) points out that harms to self-respect as a consequence of socio-economic inequalities relate, not only to social status and differences in talent, application, and achievement, but also to the general kind of capability formation taken to be necessary for anyone whatsoever to be able to participate in society:

> [...] certain inequalities of class also impact recognition-respect as well because they are generally taken to signify the presence or absence of powers that *all persons* of sound body and mind are expected to bring to economic life [...] Modern society rests on the presumption that all normal adults possess the capabilities necessary to be productive members of society and gain recognition-respect as such (Doppelt, 2009: 139).

In our everyday lives, social recognition is to be found for most people, not in the experience of political citizenship, but in the experience of socio-economic activity. Consequently, the social bases of self-respect cannot be guaranteed solely by equal democratic citizenship in the political domain. We also need equality in the social bases of self-respect in the economic and social domains, for which we must undertake an evaluation of how socio-economic inequalities undermine self-respect.

Furthermore, self-respect depends, not only upon our socio-economic status, but also upon being able to engage in activities which meet the terms of the Aristotelian Principle (AP), where such activities satisfy our natural inclination for complex tasks enabling increasing mastery and excellence (cf. Moriarty, 2009). In the absence of such activities 'human beings will find their culture and form of life dull and empty. Their vitality and zest will fail as their life becomes a tiresome routine' (Rawls, 1999 [1971]: 377). Work has the requisite structure for realising the AP when it is organised to allow people to 'enjoy the exercise of their realized capacities (and their innate or trained abilities) and this enjoyment increased the more the capacity is realized, or the greater its complexity' (ibid: 426). Moreover, Rawls acknowledges that self-respect is damaged by having to undertake poor quality work when he says: 'Lacking a sense of long term security and the opportunity for meaningful work and occupation is not only destructive of citizen's self-respect but of their sense that they are members of society and not simply caught in it. This leads to self-hatred, bitterness and resentment' (Rawls, 2005: lvii). But what matters in Rawlsian justice is not good quality work for its own sake, but the damage that poor quality work does to the self-respect necessary for securing our status and capabilities as democratic citizens in the political domain (Freeman, 2007: 330). Thus, harms done to self-respect by poor quality work register as a normative concern only to the extent that they manifest as distorted capabilities for exercising the two moral powers in the political domain.

I argue that limiting the social bases of Rawlsian self-respect to those activities which meet the terms of the AP artificially constrains the range of values people may wish to appropriate to the meaning content of their lives because of the work they do. This has the consequence of excluding from the social bases of citizenship forms of contribution essential to the work of social cooperation, such as caring labour. Caring labour is complex and skilled (cf. Bolton, 2009), but the complexity or the skill of the work is not automatically the most subjectively attractive value to practitioners of carework (paid and unpaid), who may instead be motivated by values inherent to the practice of care, such as empathy, concern, and usefulness. Therefore, I agree with Doppelt that making equal the social bases of self-respect will require more than the equalisation of income and status, it will also require a new culture in which we base respect upon 'the capability of persons to perform socially useful work'; and in particular where we recognise that 'the capabilities embodied in love, care, and nurture are reasonable social bases of recognition-respect' (Doppelt, 2009: 145). In particular, this will require a social revaluation of low status work employing practices of care, which I suggest can be provided by extending an ethic of care to institutional maintenance and repair (see Spelman, 2003), thereby allowing us to see how engaging in practices of care underpins every person's capabilities for acting as a participating citizen in the work of social cooperation.

Mediators of social recognition: Achievement and associations

Rawls mediates social recognition through achievement and associations. But I argue that Rawlsian self-respect, by binding self-respect to the recognition of individual performance, narrows the possible range of values against which social recognition can be mediated. Rawls acknowledges the importance of interaction with others for securing self-respect when he says that 'we acquire a sense of that what we do in everyday life is worthwhile' through forms of social recognition in which 'our person and deeds appreciated by others who are likewise esteemed and their association enjoyed' (Rawls, 1999 [1971]: 440). This means that to be in a position to draw the interest and attention of others, we need to belong to a wide range of associations containing activities organised to enable the realisation of the AP: 'what is necessary is that there should be for each person at least one community of shared interests to which he belongs and where he finds his endeavours confirmed by his associates' (ibid: 442). Interaction with others is therefore vital and unavoidable, but interaction in Rawlsian respect is limited to display and response; it does not include an understanding of intersubjectivity where our inter-relations are constitutive of our practical identities, actively shaping our capacities for autonomous action, enabling or disabling our ability to appropriate worthy objects to our lives and to develop the relevant normative orientations towards them. Rawls does acknowledge an intersubjective dimension of shared working when he evokes the importance of cooperation, rather than mere coordination (see Gaus, 1981). But shared working plays a limited part in Rawls concept of respect recognition because, for respect recognition to play the role Rawls gives it in his theory of justice, respect recognition must accrue to the individual, making the relevant dimension of interaction with others the performance of the individual, not the joint outcome for which no individual person alone is responsible.

Rawlsian self-respect is, in essence, transactional: Rawlsian interactive encounters take place through our membership of associations, where other people provide an audience for our individual endeavours. Achieving self-respect depends upon positive relations with others which support the conviction that we and our projects are of worth: 'unless our endeavours are appreciated by our associates it is impossible for us to maintain the conviction that they are worthwhile' (Rawls, 1999 [1971]: 440). Such associations with others encourage us to believe that we are competent to carry through our plans: 'to reduce the likelihood of failure and [...] provide support against the sense of self-doubt when mishaps occur' (ibid: 441). But the worth of our projects, if they are to attract the necessary respect recognition to secure self-respect, must be reduced to their value as vehicles for individual display, rather than for their value as activities of intersubjective co-production, or for the other-regarding care they may provide to worthy objects. With the currency of our individual performance, we trade with others for their recognition of us in an economy of social recognition which cannot properly value joint agency in cooperative work, thereby failing to give a public presence to the intersubjective dimensions of shared working. Other people contract us to fulfil roles in the division of labour which they have not the time, nor the inclination, to undertake themselves; in the process, they become spectators taking pleasure in, or expressing disapproval of, our performance. Thus, our potential partners in social recognition are turned into consumers of the products of our life plan, rather than persons who involve themselves in helping us achieve our life plans, and who are jointly responsible with us for co-production in a system of social cooperation. I would not deny that relating to others as consumers and spectators can be satisfying – the ethical problem lies in reducing all intersubjective relations to their value as mediators of individual achievement, rather than allowing social recognition to be mediated by a wider range of social values, such as cooperation and solidarity.

Our membership of associations provides the arena in which the audience for our performance is gathered. Rawls gives associations a functional role in ensuring that the basic structure embodies plural conceptions of the good, expressing a multiplicity of values. Associations fulfil their functional role – and satisfy the principle of neutrality – when they are allowed to express their 'natural' distinctiveness through their variation from the general principles of justice, provided that they make certain adjustments required by the need to maintain background justice (ibid: 261): for example, 'in a democratic society nonpublic power, as seen, for example, in the authority of churches over their members, is freely accepted' (ibid: 221). Variations within the limits of justice are allowed because we are not bound to an agreement with one another as equals through our different roles in the communities and associations of the basic structure, but through our undifferentiated political status in which we are all assumed to have equal capacities (ibid: 258). Rawls gives two instances of legitimate variations – the authority structure of churches and universities, and the valuing of contributions that people make to associations – but he does not specify what adjustments such organisations are themselves to make in order to preserve background justice. Moreover, Rawls assumes that the internal organisation of such associations is incontestable, and that the basis for evaluating a person's contributions to those associations is their 'marginal usefulness to some particular group' (ibid). I suggest this is a bleak prospect for the majority of people who must compete for the appreciation of significantly placed others in the many associations organised hierarchically, and to the advantage of privileged groups, with the consequence that many forms of work, particularly work performed by undervalued groups, are misrecognised and hidden from public view. The marginal usefulness of low status persons, perceived in terms of how the value of the work they do is mediated through a status hierarchy laden with systemic disadvantage, is not likely to be sufficient for sustaining the positive self-relations upon which the formation of a practical identity depends.

I argue that differences from the general principles of justice must be removed from the presumptive designation of the 'natural and necessary', and made subject to deliberative democratic inquiry. This means that associations claiming that authoritarian leadership is necessary to preserve their character and ensure the widest possible range of values in society, must be subject to public evaluation of how their internal organisation may enhance or inhibit the respect recognition which underpins a person's equal status as a worthy being, and how the measure of a person's value to an association, by virtue of their achievements, contributions, or efforts, enables or disables esteem recognition. This will require the political mode of being to be exercised in all the action contexts of associational life, directed towards on-going deliberations over the terms of cooperation in the associations which make up the basic structure (cf. Young, 2006). And it implies establishing democratic practices, not only in the associations where we work but also, more broadly, in a participatory society to ensure that unpaid family and voluntary work is subject to a similar standard of public scrutiny. Hussain (2007), for example, argues that democratic corporatism is likely to be more stable for a Rawlsian scheme of justice than a property owning democracy, because democratic corporatism expands the sphere of political action by putting within the reach of everyone the possibility of expressing the political dimensions of their personhood, and thereby of achieving the widespread respect recognition necessary to the long-term security of the social order. Furthermore, Hussain makes such participation intrinsic to the content of work:

> [...] work occupies a central role in the lives of individuals in a modern society. And unlike deliberations about laws and policies at the national level, deliberations about the structure of an industry bear directly on the shape of people's work lives. This makes these deliberations *continuous* with the activities and concerns that occupy people at work in a way that national deliberations do not. This continuity suggests that the rate of participation in industry-level rule making will be higher, as people will see these activities as an aspect of their job or career (Hussain, 2007: 17).

The aims of democratic participation in the work of social cooperation are to reveal misrecognised and invisibilised work, to examine the extent to which misrecognition is based upon essentialist and naturalised assumptions of what work is suitable for certain types of people, and to challenge mediators of social recognition such as individualised achievement which narrow the range of contributions which can be made subject to social recognition. In contrast to Rawls, Honneth (1995b) makes social recognition constitutive of the interior content of work, and he takes seriously the need to bring the possibility for social recognition because of the work we do within the reach of every person. But, in reducing struggles over the meaning content of work to claims for recognition, Honneth elides the materiality of the interior content of work (Moll, 2009; Smith, 2009) where, through their struggle with the material conditions of work, workers form identities and ways of being in the world. By so doing, Honneth forgoes the possibility of securing stable positive self-relations based on an organisation of the interior content of work which grounds political self-determination in the immanent potential of work.

The limits of Honneth's concept of self-esteem

In Honneth's (1995b) critical theory of recognition, three dimensions of self-relations – self-confidence, self-respect, and self-esteem – are necessary to the developmental possibilities of self-realisation, which, given our inescapable need for social recognition, also explain the motivations driving social change. For Honneth, esteem-recognition plays a vital role in contemporary liberal egalitarian societies by ensuring that, through the division of labour, each person has access to resources enabling them to experience self-esteem. Esteem-recognition is vital to the possibility of self-realisation, and when structural or psychological distortions disable persons from achieving esteem-recognition for their particular contributions a struggle for recognition ensues, which can result in social change. We achieve esteem through intersubjective recognition of our traits and abilities (ibid: 121), where the bases for recognising traits and abilities are embedded in the norms, beliefs, and institutions of the society in which we are situated. Therefore, to change the bases of esteem-recognition we must alter the norms, beliefs, and structures of our society. Developmental progress in modern social relations, for example, has been directed towards the steady dismantling of hierarchical status structures which value persons according to characteristics fixed by birth, class, social position, and group identity. This is because traditional social structures are unable to provide the symmetrical recognition necessary for enabling each person to be equally esteemed for their abilities and achievements. The virtue of the modern division of labour lies in its capacity to create a progressively individualised, differentiated, and pluralised environment for accruing social esteem to one's person. In the division of labour we find a 'framework of orientation' (ibid: 122) or 'community of value' for social goals and values which 'provides the criteria that orient the social esteem of persons, because their abilities and achievements are judged inter-subjectively according to the degree to which they can help to realise culturally defined values' (ibid). The possibility of symmetrical recognition depends upon the 'pluralization of the socially defined value-horizon' which provides the value diversity necessary for each person to find a measure against which they can be esteem-recognised for their 'personality ideals' (ibid).

Thus, the modern division of labour is a great advance in social relations because, by continually diversifying and pluralising the source of values within an overarching value-horizon, persons have the opportunity to be recognised as individuals, detached from static features defining them by birth or fixed tradition: 'the subject entered the contested field of social esteem as an entity individuated in terms of a particular life-history' (ibid: 125). For Honneth's theory, there is much riding upon the developmental possibilities inherent in the division of labour. It must pluralise to such an extent that all persons can find within it a mode of self-realisation or form of living which will enable them to 'earn' social esteem, but, simultaneously, it must universalise to hold all persons within a cooperative effort that relates them to one another as equal interaction partners. People become distinguished as individual persons against an evolving backdrop of values which allows them to be recognised for their particular capacities developed over the course of a lifetime:

> 'Prestige' or 'standing' signifies only the degree of social recognition the individual earns for his or her form of self-realisation by thus contributing, to a certain extent, to the practical realisation of society's abstract goals. With regard to this new, individualised system of recognition relations, everything now depends, therefore, on the definition of this value-horizon, which is supposed to be open to various forms of self-realization and yet, at the same time, must also serve as an overarching system of esteem (Honneth, 1995b: 126).

The potential for conflict over which values are to be publicly recognised and how they are to be assessed in relation to one another is ever present. The result is a 'permanent struggle' for recognition which cannot be avoided or ameliorated, and is an essential element in the process of turning universalised social goals into recognised forms of self-realisation which express different traits and capacities. 'Secondary interpretative practice[s]' (ibid: 126) mediate the process of recognising and valuing different modes of self-realisation: 'the worth accorded to various forms of self-realization and even the manner in which the relevant traits and abilities are defined fundamentally depend on the dominant interpretations of societal goals' (ibid). Honneth uses the 'seemingly neutral idea of achievement' to mediate 'societal goals' so that they yield up 'criteria of esteem' (ibid: 126). The achievement principle is individualised, available within 'an open horizon of plural values' (ibid: 126), and expressive of many, continuously diversifying forms of self-realisation. And it is dependent upon 'the capacities developed by the individual in the course of his or her life' (ibid: 125). The values against which individual achievements are measured depend upon the 'collective event' of an agreed social goal, which operates to form a value-horizon within which people can earn esteem for their achievements against the values relevant to the activities (or 'shared praxis') necessary for achieving the goal:

> it is the all-dominating agreement on a practical goal that instantly generates an intersubjective value-horizon, in which each participant learns to recognise the significance of the abilities and traits of the others to the same degree (Honneth, 1995b: 128).

The target of symmetrical relations of esteem does not mean, however, that all contributions and achievements are valued equally (ibid: 130), in the sense of being quantitatively equivalent. Honneth defines symmetrical relations as the state where all persons are 'free from being collectively denigrated, so that each is given the chance to experience oneself to be recognised, in the light of one's own accomplishments and abilities, as valuable for society' (ibid). Esteem recognition picks out the distinctiveness of esteem within the realm of work and its relevance to individuated self-realisation, where our inter-dependence with others in the work of social cooperation underpins mutual obligations to give esteem where esteem is due. The modern conditions of work, however, makes individuated self-esteem mediated by the achievement principle an increasingly remote possibility for many people.

The achievement principle

Honneth's optimism that the achievement principle will pluralise the values against which we can secure esteem recognition for all has not gone unchallenged (Smith, 2009; Seglow, 2009; Roessler, 2007; Petersen & Willig, 2004). Smith (2009) critiques Honneth for being 'too sanguine about the integrative potential of social esteem based on individual achievement' (Smith, 2009: 57). In neo-liberal economies, the shackling of achievement to the production paradigm not only reduces the range of activities which can be recognised as socially valuable work, but constrains the variety of ways in which people can exercise their entitlement to make their contribution, leaving much potentially important work undone (cf. Gomberg, 2007). Furthermore, the solidaristic bases for the formation of collective coalitions capable of challenging the terms of recognition are undermined by the individualised allocation of esteem; at the same time, the sources of individual self-esteem are de-stabilised by making the individual responsible for nearly all the risk of failing to accrue esteem recognition (Smith, 2009: 57; cf. Sennett & Cobb, 1972).

> These effects bear on the self, whose capacity for autonomy may seem like a curse in view of the responsibility it brings for non-achievement or failure; and they bear on the social bonds, which are surely just as likely to be undermined as strengthened by the individualized competition for self-esteem (Smith, 2009: 57).

Seglow (2009) identifies how, although Honneth mediates esteem recognition through individual achievement, he makes the challenge to recognitive practices dependent upon collective coalition-building. Honneth relies upon two potentially incommensurable norms: the meritocratic individualistic ethic of achievement and the communitarian, solidarity-based, ethic of contribution (ibid: 70). Seglow argues that, whilst we may applaud contribution and seek it as an ideal, we will struggle to establish contribution as the basis of social recognition because 'there is not the public institutional structure for the matrix of respect to be embedded' (ibid: 73). This means that we cannot multiply esteem based upon contribution whilst the majority of our institutions and structures are framed by the individualistic and competitive principles of merit and achievement, since these principles narrow the range of possible values to those against which we can measure merit-based performance and assign a monetary value for reward. Consequently, making values based upon individual merit-based achievement the basis for public recognition crowds out values based upon collective achievement, such as those eliciting from joining our agency to that of others in order to produce a shared outcome.

When structured by the logic of individual merit-based achievement, our reasonable need for social recognition, instead of being a duty which we owe to one another because of our common willingness to make our contribution and take up our responsibilities for worthy objects, becomes a futile race by each individual alone for the devalued currency of esteem-recognition. In the contemporary organisation of work, the possibility of acquiring esteem-recognition is becoming increasingly elusive, because the pursuit of self-esteem turns 'the individual into a greyhound chasing the rabbit without ever receiving sufficient recognition for the mile sprinted' (Willig, 2009: 351). Economic insecurity, combined with rapid social and technological change, means that workers are finding it increasingly difficult to hold onto a stable sense of esteem-recognition, limiting esteem only to those judged to be the most successful practitioners of a structured activity (Petersen & Willig, 2004: 344). The contemporary organisation of work mobilises and stimulates our need for esteem recognition through performance management practices which make the individual responsible for rendering their actions susceptible to recognitive practices, whilst at the same time reducing the individual's influence over the terms of recognition. Realising stable esteem recognition is put beyond the reach of many individuals by the constantly shifting terms of cooperation, and the restriction of values and meanings which can be mediated by the achievement principle (cf. Willig, 2009). Moreover, meanings of work are appropriated by ideologies of productivity, which aim to recruit the effort of workers into the management project, but, in so doing, subvert those values, making them less employable for the crafting of positive meaning in individual lives. Usefulness becomes superfluousness in the form of unemployment; craftsmanship becomes alienation as autonomy and self-formation are frustrated in the technical division of labour; affective labour becomes commodified by the requirements to extract maximum value from the carer; and solidarity becomes the conscious attempt to use socialisation and the bonds between persons to promote the increase of profit.

The achievement principle has become so constrained under the contemporary organisation of work, that it is 'now too narrow to incorporate types of work which cannot be ascribed recognition value in the reproduction of society' (Petersen & Willig, 2004: 341). But when people seek social recognition through work, they are not searching solely for recognition for their individual achievements as measured by financial reward; in many instances, they also, and perhaps primarily, seek inclusion, membership, belonging, and the recognition that comes through direct relations with colleagues, clients, customers, and patients (ibid; Perrons, 2000: 110; see also Roessler, 2007). The achievement principle fails to describe what is important about unpaid, underappreciated work, such as care work, friendship work, or civic work (Schwarzenbach, 1996). It is a weak instrument for bringing into public view invisibilised dimensions of work, such as emotional labour or the irreducible autonomy in all acts of work. When mediated by the achievement principle, even a substantially diversified and pluralised value horizon cannot plausibly create a sufficiently wide 'esteem-net' to capture all kinds of valuable activities we may wish to count as work, thereby failing to facilitate esteem recognition to as many people as possible, since not all work which contributes to the social product can be readily captured by a metric of 'achievement', however defined. Roessler (2007), for example, claims that family work 'follows a fundamentally different logic, a fundamentally different rationality' (ibid: 141) and therefore family work demands 'a different form of social recognition than paid work; they should not be seen simply as equivalent forms of socially necessary achievements' (ibid: 136). She argues that family work and contractual work must be distinguished because they accrue self-esteem on a different basis due to the differing contribution they make to the good life for the individual (ibid: 153). Each kind of work shapes the development of the self in different ways, and the content of such labours will vary from context to context, such that contractual work with a substantive element of care will offer a different route to self-development than contractual work requiring only interaction with machinery or information technology. In sum, a principle mediating social recognition through an undifferentiating value of achievement will struggle to pick out what is objectively and subjectively worthwhile about each of these forms of labour.

I suggest that a partial way through these difficulties is indicated by acknowledging the value of doing good work, where good work is worth doing because it has the interior structure for autonomy, freedom, and dignified relations to others. Doing work which is worth doing supports a sense of one's dignity as a particular person, independent of the possibility of accruing individual esteem recognition. Thus, our normative concern for the content of work is not simply whether it enables social recognition, but also whether it meets relevant criteria consistent with a positive critical conception of meaningful work – that is, it aims at caring for worthy objects, embodying subjectively attractive values which can be incorporated into a practical identity. Roessler (2007) points out that social recognition measured by achievement and financial reward tells us little about 'whether or not the achievement itself is satisfying' (ibid: 160). An individual in receipt of a large financial reward may still fail to achieve subjective satisfaction if the content of her work misses something fundamental about her deepest value commitments and her understanding of her value as a human being. Work promotes a sense of dignity when it provides persons with 'the opportunity to do something that they can do (well) and in which they have (at least minimal or basic) interest in its achievement, and under conditions that they normatively – at least partly or to a certain extent – want and are able to influence' (Roessler, 2007: 160). I propose that, in a positive critical conception of meaningful work, a sense of dignity depends upon being able to exercise practices of care towards the worthy objects we have appropriated to the meaning content of our lives, which implies that social recognition ought to be aimed at the practical identities we form from the extant values in the roles, practices, and institutions to which we belong. Furthermore, I argue that democratic practices applied to the meaning-making activities in the work we do together allows for the re-interpretation of existing values, and the creation of new values which can be publicly evaluated and made part of our practical identities, supporting a sense of our dignity as particular persons.

A sense of dignity

I would not deny that modern conditions of work, even where democratic participatory practices are widespread, are challenging for securing social recognition for the values and identities which make one's life meaningful. But the difficulties of realising positive self-relations does not mean we should give up on our continuing need to be acknowledged, not just as place-holders in a hierarchy of social functions, but as particular persons (Noggle, 1999). Ikaheimo (2007) identifies two dimensions of personhood we would want to recognise: firstly, 'the interpersonal status of being respected as a co-authority' and 'psychological capacities for norm-administration' (ibid: 36), and secondly, the values, relations, states of affairs such that 'caring about the happiness or good life of oneself/others is a structuring principle' (ibid). In the bipartite value of meaningfulness, to have the status as a co-authority, and the capabilities for objective valuing and subjective attachment, is to have the capacity to become a valuer, and thus to experience a sense of dignity. Personhood is enabled by being a valuer (cf. Tirrell, 1993), because valuing supports the formation of a practical identity, particular to our subjective appropriation of worthy objects. Being able to form a practical identity depends upon the capacity of persons 'to freely constrain themselves to the terms of participation in the many social groups to which they belong' (Davies, 2006: 80–1), implying that each person needs to be a member of at least one social organisation. In order to secure a practical identity which is expressive of our particular personhood, I argue that we need to experience a sense of dignity which combines *self-respect*, as our sense of worthiness and capabilities to undertake right actions towards worthy objects, with *self-esteem*, as our judgements about how well we have engaged in the relevant practices of caring for worthy objects.

Dignity points to something inherently valuable in the subject; in the Kantian formulation of dignity, it is the inviolable worth of our moral rationality: 'a human being regarded as a person, that is, as the subject of morally practical reason, is exalted above all price [...] as an end in himself he possesses *dignity* by which he extracts *respect* for himself from all other beings in the world' (Kant, 1983 [1797]). A sense of dignity is a vital signifier of our recognitive status, where we know ourselves to possess that inviolable worth in our person which specifies the limits upon how we can be treated by others, giving us the confidence that we can legitimately make claims upon others – including our entitlement to contribute to the work of social cooperation, and have that contribution recognised. When we possess a sense of dignity, we understand ourselves to be of equal standing with others, and jointly oblige with them to ensure that each person in the community of belonging is afforded the status to be heard and the capabilities to act and to be. Threats to our dignity through mistreatment or misrecognition are frightening because they render us invisible as a human being with intrinsic value to whom it is illegitimate to do certain things, to humiliate, to ignore, to degrade, to exploit, or whatever. And dignity can be undermined by humiliating institutions which fail to foster intersubjective relations of the right normative character for respect recognition and esteem recognition (Margalit, 1996). A characteristic of humiliating economic institutions is the manner in which they structure intersubjective relations so that it appears to be legitimate for some to treat others solely as the means to fulfilling their plans and projects:

> [...] they must never be treated merely as means, as things that we may use however we want in order to advance our interests, and they must always be treated as the supremely valuable beings that they are. Note that it is not wrong to treat persons as means to our ends; indeed we could not get on in life if we could not make use of the talents, abilities, service, and labor of other people. What we must not do is to treat persons as mere means to our ends, to treat them as if the only value they have is what derives from their usefulness to us. We must always treat them 'at the same time as an end' (Dillon, 2010: 23).

I suggest that establishing our equal status as co-authorities will require: firstly, evaluation of the internal organisation of the associations, practices, and institutions to which we belong and secondly, widespread opportunities to exercise the political mode of being in the work timespaces of social cooperation – both of which require non-humiliating institutions. Non-humiliating institutions enable us to resist acquiescing automatically to another's understanding of who we are, allowing us instead to enter into a relation with the recogniser where we acknowledge their status as a recogniser, approve their competency to recognise us, and respect their judgements accordingly. Moreover, deliberative contestation of the social valuations of others, grounded in our equal status as co-authorities, opens up opportunities to challenge the terms of recognition, enabling us to express differences, ambivalences, incommensurables, and obstacles in our efforts to advance the values we have appropriated to the meaning content of our lives. Furthermore, humiliating institutions are not good for any person who belongs to them: hierarchical authority, for example, undermines managers' own interest in their personhood, because those situated in a favourable position within a hierarchical authority cannot respect workers as co-authorities. In evaluating within a Kantian framework the use multinational companies make of sweatshop labour, Arnold and Bowie (2003) claim:

> [...] managers who encourage or tolerate violations of the rule of law; use coercion; allow unsafe working conditions; and provide below subsistence wages, disavow their own dignity and that of

their workers. In so doing, they disrespect themselves and their workers (ibid: 239; see also Bowie 1998).

Since subordinates in a hierarchy are not in the relevant category of authorisers of norms, they cannot give their superiors esteem-recognition which can only be provided by equal others (peers). Workers can give satisfaction to managers because of their submission or obedience, but they cannot give the satisfaction which comes from the esteem recognition upon which the positive self-relations constituting person-hood depends. Thus, both groups have their potential as valuers distorted, because psychological capacities for valuing and recognising remain under-developed with consequences for all of their 'interpersonal status of being a person' (Ikaheimo, 2007: 13). Humiliating institutions which reduce the value of usefulness to instrumental usage fail to respect both workers and those who employ workers under such conditions, because, by supporting humiliating institutions, employers end up undermining the social conditions for their own recognitive relations.

For a person to lack a sense of her dignity in the work she does with others is for her to be aware that her society does not value her sufficiently highly to afford her the kind of work which is worthy of her human status. Her society regards her potential human contribution as surplus to requirements, or demands only that part of her humanity which can be instrumentalised for profit. Such knowledge, when reinforced through everyday interactive encounters with significant others, erodes positive self-relations in the form of self-respect, self-esteem, and self-confidence. I propose, however, that self-respect and self-esteem can be united in dignified work, which is work capable of supporting us in becoming valuers, and is performed in non-humiliating forms of belonging. Therefore, being able to undertake dignified work in cooperative relations to others, where our intersubjective encounters support the development of positive self-relations, is indispensable for living a life we have good reason to value.

Forming a practical identity

Our sense of dignity depends upon being able to see ourselves as a particular person with a secure practical identity, where practical identities are formed through our intersubjective encounters in the roles, practices, and institutions to which we belong in a system of social cooperation. Korsegaard (2009) defines a 'conception of practical identity' as 'a description under which you value yourself and find your life worth living and your actions to be worth undertaking' (ibid: 20; 1996). We act as individual autonomous agents when we engage in 'an ongoing struggle for integrity, the struggle for psychic unity, the struggle to be, in the face of psychic complexity, a single unified self' (ibid: 7), success in which depends upon our being able to find reasons sufficient to motivate us to act and to be (ibid: 23). Korsegaard says that reasons are derived contingently from the roles and obligations we acquire through living an ordinary human life. Such reasons are contingent because we can choose whether or not to endorse them as part of our practical identity, as sources of meaning and value for us (ibid), but since we cannot choose not to have reasons then we must engage also in the task of 'making the contingent necessary' (ibid). In terms of the bipartite value of meaningfulness, this means we must find some way of subjectively appropriating non-obligatory values to the meaning content of our lives, in the process acquiring obligations of care for worthy objects which embody those values. Indeed, Korsegaard steers close to the bipartite value of meaningfulness when she says 'to have a personal project or ambition is not to desire a special object that you think is good for you privately, but rather to want to stand in a special relationship to something you think is good publicly' (ibid: 211). Our evaluations of how we are doing with respect to our actions and orientations towards worthy objects generates various kinds of self-regard which issue in a positive or negative reinforcement of our self-conception or practical identity: 'you are faced with the task of *making something* of yourself, and you must regard yourself as a success or failure in so far as you succeed or fail at this task' (Korsegaard, 2009: xii).

Furthermore, Korsegaard (2009) says that 'we owe it to ourselves, to our own humanity, to find some roles that we can fill with integrity and dedication' (ibid: 24). Our roles support our dignified status in the midst of equally situated others by providing us with the social bases for positive self-relations. This means that, if we lack certain fundamental positive attitudes towards ourselves, then we will lack the essential conditions for regarding ourselves as the kinds of persons who have projects and plans for living which can legitimately command the attention and support of others. For Korsegaard, our many roles and sources of identity must be brought into a coherent whole in order to establish the basis of a unified self, which enables us to act as autonomous beings – and she makes coherence in our practical identity the marker for autonomy. But I suggest this makes the task of creating a practical identity too demanding, particularly in societies characterised by intersecting social structures of oppression which obstruct the goal of unity and coherence, rendering us vulnerable to heteronomous influence and control (Meyers, 2000: 152). In psychological theory, acquiring recognitive capabilities involves an unavoidable psychological struggle because each of us 'must confront the difficulty that each subject has in recognizing the other as an equivalent center of experience' (Benjamin, 1990: 34), and so there is always the possibility of less than total unity. Identities are always in flux, despite temporary settlements, because 'subject positions are made available in a number of competing discourses [...] identity is thus of necessity always a project rather than an achievement' (Knights & Vurdubakis, 1994). Furthermore, the process of identity formation does not consist only in internal identity formation, but depends also upon the range of 'publicly available "personas" or *social*-identities' (Watson, 2008: 127) – from the definition of which most people have been excluded. So rather than coherence as unity, I suggest we aim at coherence as a constantly adjusting balance of values, meanings, and differences, using the concept of an intersectional self, where an intersectional self is always in the process of becoming:

> To define oneself intersectionally, one must activate competencies that mesh intellect and feeling in order to seek out and assimilate nonstandard interpretive frameworks. One must be introspectively vigilant, attuned to signs of frustration and dissatisfaction, attentive to baffling subjective anomalies, and willing to puzzle out gaps in one's self-understanding (Meyers, 2000: 167).

Meyers (2000) understands an intersectional self to be imperfectly autonomous, but always progressing in self-knowledge and self-definition: 'intersectional identity is constituted in part through a process of self-definition, the authentic self is an evolving self that is not chained to conventional group norms' (ibid: 153). The shifts in an intersectional self contrasts with Korsegaard's basis for self-constitution, which is the independent action of the individual, where a good action is one that constitutes the individual person by moving her towards a unified, coherent self: 'action is self-constitution' (ibid: 25). Korsegaard does not have an intersubjective conception of the joint action essential to the constitution of selves; for her 'action is simply interaction with the self' (ibid: 204), which fails to illuminate the unavoidable social inter-dependency of human beings, particularly

in relation to the work they do together in a system of social cooperation. Korsegaard says that 'a good person is someone who is good at
being a person' (ibid: 26); if this is the case, then a good person is a
social, inter-dependent individual, situated in intersubjective relations,
which enable the formation of capabilities and are constitutive of the
meaning content of our lives. In fact, Korsegaard acknowledges something of this kind when she identifies the effort which is required for
the continual formation and maintenance of practical identity, made
up of many different identities, roles, and forms of belonging, saying
that 'in the course of this process, of falling apart and pulling yourself
back together, you create something new, you constitute something
new: yourself' (ibid: 214).

Capabilities for intersectional identity formation

Meyers (2000) proposes a competency approach to intersectional identity formation which would allow for less demanding criteria of unity
and coherence in creating our practical identities, and which empha-
sises the process rather than the goal of self-constitution, concentrating
instead upon the formation of the relevant skills necessary to engage in
intersectional identity development: 'intersectional subjects analyze
their position in social hierarchies, interpret the psychic impact of
their social experience, and reconfigure their identities as members of
social groups' (ibid: 154). This makes practical identity dependent
upon becoming a valuer, having the status as a co-authority, and the
capabilities for objective valuing and subjective appropriation, which is
achieved by understanding how we create ourselves from intersubjective relations in multiple forms of belonging.

Forming the capabilities necessary for developing the practical identity of an intersectional self depends upon our active engagement with
worthy objects. When we engage with worthy objects, interpretive differences over how to care for worthy objects give rise to a plurality of
meanings. When they are made available for public deliberation, these
meanings have the potential to multiply the range of values within a
liberal perfectionist framework, which can then be made available for
the formation of a practical identity (Korsegaard, 2009; see also
Roessler, 2012) capable of securing a sense of one's life being worth
living. Where the social goal is to widen the bases for experiencing the
bipartite value of meaningfulness, then interpretive differences emerging from the application of *phronetic techne* in a rationality of caring are
particularly productive, because these differences arise from our efforts
to fulfil our responsibilities of care towards worthy objects, where the

worth of the objects are subject to difference and deliberation. Thus, to engage with values through interpretive meaning-making is to have the bases for self-respect and self-esteem, enabling us to form a practical identity which secures a sense of meaning.

> A (thickly) autonomous agent regulates her life on the basis of her values, where a person's values are deep psychological features that ground emotions of esteem and thereby reveal the shape of her self-conception (Copp, 2007: 18).

Meanings of work are understood to be: 'the way in which workers bring significance and order to their experience of labour' (Joyce, 1987: 7). A worker may find meaning in performing hard, menial, or dangerous work well: work such as coalmining, or fishing, for example, is embedded in a rich historical and social context, sustained by dense community relations (Anthony, 1978: 286). Ashforth and Kreiner (1999) found that 'people performing dirty work tend to retain relatively high occupational esteem and pride' (ibid: 413), where dirty work is conceptualised as any kind of work which carries with it some kind of physical, social, or moral taint but which is not regarded by society as unimportant or trivial: for example, undertakers, careworkers, refuse collectors. Workers doing dirty work are aware of the stigma of dirty work, but can obtain identity support through 'strong cultures of meaning making' (ibid: 419) and various strategies of interpretation, the most successful of which is *reframing*. Reframing enables workers to transform the very meaning of the work they do using 'ennobling ideologies' (ibid: 428). Positive interpretive strategies can be encouraged by the organisational environment in which the work is carried out. Salzinger (1991), for example, found that, in one cooperative of domestic services, the work was defined as low skilled and temporary, resulting in no training for staff; in a second cooperative, the work was organised in professional teams which offered training and participation in decisions: 'The result was that members of the first co-op came to regard domestic work as unimportant, whereas members of the second regarded it as an inherently skilled occupation, deserving of respect, fair treatment and decent pay' (Ashforth & Kreiner, 1999: 431).[3]

In sum, it is the formation of an intersectional practical identity which ought to be the target of social recognition where the process of building a practical identity, whilst never complete, nevertheless enables us to experience a sense of dignity as respected and esteemed persons who have a particular life of our own to lead. I do not claim that this resolves the difficulties of securing stable positive self-relations in the contemporary organisation of work, but I do suggest that the experience of work contains positive resources for securing a sense of dignity when interpretive meaning-making is organised along democratic lines. Social recognition is a fundamental human need, which is constitutive of the meaning content of work. In the contemporary organisation of work, however, it is becoming increasingly difficult to sustain the positive self-relations which enable us to experience a sense of meaningfulness. I propose that self-respect and self-esteem be tied to our sense of dignity as particular persons who bear responsibilities towards the worthy objects we have appropriated to the meaning content of our lives. When we evaluate ourselves against the normative orientations relevant to the nature of particular worthy objects, then we find that practices of other-regarding care, which include the importance of self-care, are useful for directing our attention away from the frantic pursuit of self-esteem fostered by the contemporary organisation of work. Hence, a sense of our dignity as particular persons is dependent upon being able to form a practical identity, in which we see ourselves as distinct persons with a life of our own to lead.

6

'The Inner Workshop of Democracy': Agonistic Democratic Practices and the Realisation of Emancipatory Potentials

In Chapter 4, I dealt with the dimension of democratic authority at the level of the organisation necessary for a system of workplace democracy to proliferate meaningful work. In this chapter, I turn to agonistic democratic practices at the level of the task. Despite an extensive literature on economic democracy (Dahl, 1985; Albert & Hahnel, 2002; Boatright, 2004; Blumberg, 1968; Cohen & Rogers, 1992; Cohen, 1989; Cohen & Rogers, 1992; Schweikart, 1980; Strauss, 2006; Williamson, 2004; Bowles & Gintis, 1993; Hirst, 1994)[1] much democratic theory uncritically assumes that the contemporary experience of work is inhospitable to the political mode of being, and therefore devoid of emancipatory potential.[2] Despite this, I have sought to theorise how the active agency of workers can never be entirely eliminated by subjectified and divided work practices, but is, instead, intersubjectively manifested through working with others and upon objects. Furthermore, this intersubjective action gives rise to interpretive differences which will remain as pre-political potentials unless revealed through expressive participatory practices. However, if participatory practices are to be generative of interpretive differences, and capable of mediating those differences into positive meanings, making them available for appropriation to the meaningfulness of people's lives, then they must possess certain characteristics. I shall argue that these characteristics can be specified from an evaluation of agonistic democratic theory. Specifically, when agonistic democratic practices aim at a *differentiated polysensus*, they are able to remedy the difference-suppressing tendencies of deliberative democratic practices. Thus, by eschewing the goal of a unified consensus, agonistic democracy is able to supply participatory practices with vital difference-proliferating features, consistent with realising the emancipatory potential of meaningful work.

Deliberative democracy at work

Deliberative democracy consists of a 'family of views' in which 'the public deliberation of free and equal citizens is the core of legitimate decision making and self-government' (Bohman, 1998: 401). It can be understood as a system of rule, where the 'laws and policies result from processes in which citizens defend solutions to common problems on the basis of what are generally acknowledged as relevant reasons' (Cohen & Fung, 2004: 26). To secure political autonomy as collective self-determination, a deliberative system operates against certain standards, including: respect among members; fairness in procedures; and 'epistemic fruitfulness' (Mansbridge, 2010: 1). Moreover, since citizens learn the standards, habits, and practices of democracy through experience society must provide a diversity of sites enabling people to interact through participation and thereby acquire the norms and values of being a citizen. Pateman (1970) argues that the private sphere of economic association, if organised along participatory lines, stimulates the habit of political involvement beyond the workplace, thereby providing a route to the general revitalisation of political life. My justification for democratic workplaces, however, is based, not upon positive 'spillover' effects,[3] but upon the emancipatory potential for positive meaning-making which makes possible the widespread availability of meaningful work (see also Carter, 2006).

Not all participation is democratic participation: *simple participation*, or having a share in a joint activity, is not the same as *democratic participation*, or having a share in control over decision-making through collective self-determination. Pateman (1970) distinguishes between the full democracy of authority, the partial democracy of influence, and the pseudo democracy of appearance (ibid: 70–3), where full democracy implies a transformation of the authority structure in which each employee has equal decision-making power; partial democracy describes participatory practices which confer influence but not power over decision-making; and pseudo democracy describes management strategies of communication which generate the illusion, rather than the substance, of democratic control. Cathcart (2009) identifies how employee voice is often instituted as consultation rather than a share in decision-making, in order to secure 'harmonious and less conflictual relations with the workforce' (Gollan & Wilkinson, 2007: 1136), where structures designed to represent employee voice are dependent upon the good will of managerial authority. Hence, having a share in participation, as simply taking part in an activity such as consultation, is distinct from having a share in power, as having a degree of influence over an activity (Heller, 2003). I argue that to realise the intrinsic value of the political mode of being in meaningful work requires each person to have a share in power as control over decision-making, because such is required to secure our status as equal co-authorities in non-dominated relations to others, and to develop the capabilities for judging and feeling necessary for uniting the objective and subjective dimensions in the bipartite value of meaningfulness.

In general, deliberative approaches to workplace democracy, such as the Scandinavian model of democratic dialogue, rely upon insights from Habermassian discourse theory to generate dialogue which aims to overcome situated power-laden knowledge in order to encourage self-reflection within an 'ideal speech situation' (Brogger, 2010: 483; cf. Habermas, 2002 [1971]). The conditions necessary for realising the communication of an ideal speech situation are: freedom of entry and exit; equal rights of participants to say what they want; the truthfulness, comprehensibleness, and sincerity of participants' utterances; and 'an absence of coercion' (Habermas, 1993: 56). When such conditions are united to correctly designed procedures, then participants will be brought into an ideal speech situation, where they will more likely recognise the 'forceless force of the better argument' (Habermas 1990: 23). But the need for such pre-conditions, if an ideal speech situation is to pertain, casts doubt over the Scandinavian innovation. Since workplaces lack the pre-conditions of equality, respect, and fairness, then economic life is a sphere of 'norm-free sociality' (Habermas, 1987: 171). This means that Habermassian discourse theory denies the possibility of an ideal speech situation in work from the outset. Technical-instrumental rationality, the imperative to maximise organisational efficiency, and the necessity for hierarchical coordination harnessed towards pre-specified (market-given) goals suffuses relations between workers, managers, and other stakeholders, suppressing differences in the drive to realise a naturalised, uncritical unity. Disagreements may occur over external goods, such as pay, accumulating into interest group politics, but internal goods, such as the organisation of work, are set by market-given goals and practices, and therefore are inevitable and unchallengeable. Consequently, despite an extensive empirical literature exploring participatory practices and worker managed firms, deliberative political theorists have had little to say about workplace democracy. In deliberative democratic theory, the ideals of democratic deliberation – freedom, equality, and the exercise of reason – cannot be realised in workplaces dominated by technical reason, governed by hierarchical authority, and divided by economic inequalities (Estlund, 2003: 131). Indeed, Bowles and Gintis (1993) describe the concept of economic democracy as 'oxymoronic', because 'if the capitalist economy is a sphere of voluntary private interactions, what is there to democratise?' (ibid: 97). Even participatory theorists who support workplace democracy are not immune to the naturalised view of economic organisations, allowing that the hierarchical authority necessary for coordination and efficiency may preclude democratic accountability: 'there is something paradoxical in calling socialisation inside existing organisations and associations, most of which, especially industrial ones, are oligarchical and hierarchical, a training explicitly in *democracy*' (Pateman, 1970: 45).

Consequently, in Habermassian communicative action, the immanent experience of working has been purged of contestation and difference. For deliberative democrats, this may be regrettable, but for proponents of the neo-liberal economic model, this is only how matters ought to be, since the demand for political freedom (the 'freedom of the ancients') is an unnatural intrusion into the affairs of organisations, which are properly understood to be outside the political sphere (Tully, 2002). After the retreat of substantive conceptions of the human good from economic life, we are left with a 'scaled down perspective of the world without intrinsic purpose, indifferent to human concerns, available for human disposition of it through technical organisation' (Connolly, 1995: 3). When imported into deliberative democratic theory, this produces the assumption that, whilst the realm of the political is radically plural, making the harmonisation of interests the inescapable problem of politics, the realm of the economic is radically unified, making politics not only impossible, but unnecessary (Honig, 1993: 201).

For us to experience widespread meaningfulness in work, consistent with the bipartite value of meaningfulness, we need an enriched and expanded stock of positive meanings, created and sustained through our membership of appropriately designed action contexts. However, the contemporary organisation of work diminishes diversity of difference in meaning-making through three key assumptions: firstly, that leaders and managers are the sole source of agency in meaning-making; secondly, that organisations are governed by a naturalised unified consensus; and thirdly, that our economic life is a separate sphere of action, ruled by technical reason, rendering political action redundant. Against these assumptions, I argue that positive meaning-making, and therefore the prospect of widespread meaningful work, depends upon organisations instituting agonistic democratic practices, which aim both at unsettling attempts to create a unity of interests, and at increasing the range of identities describing what it is to be a human being at work. To this aim, I deploy agonistic democratic theory as a corrective to deliberative democratic theories, arguing that instead of consensus, a singular unity from which difference has been eliminated, we aim for *differentiated polysensus*, a multifaceted integration which does not demand permanent closure but maintains interpretive differences as pre-political potentials, securing them as a resource to stimulate the next deliberative moment.

The assumption of elite monopoly over meaning-making

In modern organisations under pressure to demonstrate perpetual change and progress the transformatory leader is a totemic figure, imbued with personal charisma, and extensive capabilities to recreate people and organisations. However, transformational leadership is not an unalloyed good, especially where the leader is afforded the status and means to shape the meanings of work, and the subjectivities of workers (Tourish, 2013). Such concentration of meaning-making power means that agency is 'viewed as totally in the hands of leaders in terms of responsibility for problems' (ibid: 11), giving rise to 'unbridled leadership agency' (ibid: 14). Consequently, according to Fairhurst and Grant (2010), 'when leaders are the primary symbolizing agents, followers putatively surrender their right to make meanings by virtue of their employment contract with the organization' (ibid: 175). This is not only a concern of alienated rights, but also of distorted human capabilities. By abdicating our responsibilities for the co-creation of values, we lose the power of naming (Daly, 1973: 9), and thus of world-making – a fundamental human ability.

Engaging with others in the power of naming is to engage with difference. However, dissent and difference are often suppressed in modern organisations. Tourish (2013) comments that 'an alternative perspective based on the institutionalisation of feedback into organizational decision-making is rarely considered' (ibid: 26). Monovocal meanings are imposed which aim at the project of creating 'designer employees' (Western, 2008: 36), their subjectivities shaped by micro-processes of power against management defined norms and values. The polyvocal potential of human interaction is restricted, inhibited by a self-censored silence, or even, as suggested by Fleming (2012), appropriated to a management project which seeks to colonise the personal life projects of precarious workers, giving rise to a 'post-recognition politics' which 'does not implore to be seen, heard and counted in corporate-sponsored debates' and engages only in the 'struggle to be left alone' (ibid: 490).

Despite his scepticism, Fleming points out the abundant ways in which people seek to redefine the organisation of work, often outside of the employment relation or in diverse corporate forms, such as cooperatives. Inside conventionally organised work, there is considerable evidence that people act upon their meaning-making instincts in order to provide a sense of their work being worthwhile and of value (see Michaelson, 2013; Chalofsky, 2003a, 2003b; Lips-Wiersma & Morris, 2009). If there is a role for leaders in the meaning-making efforts of others, then it is constituted by a 'deliberated authority' (Alvesson & Spicer, 2012), where those who submit themselves to that authority do so only after collective discussion, and for a limited period of time. And where the central leadership task is constituted by 'attempts to negotiate between what are often incommensurable kinds of goods' (ibid: 383) – a negotiation which does not include workers' abdication of their responsibility for wrestling with the meaning-making upon which a decision between irreconcilable values must be made.

How and under what terms such leadership arises depends upon recognition that there are 'multiple modes of authority and leadership is only one of them' (Alvesson & Spicer, 2012: 383). In a system of shared responsibility for meaning-making, relationships between managers and workers will be reconfigured based upon a different concept of power from the power to coerce or 'power over' or the power to influence or 'power to' (Lukes, 2005). Rather, the ideal type of power will be 'power with' or coactive power (Follett, 1930 [1924]). Coactive power is the shared power to work with others to produce just outcomes from which all those affected benefit. And it is the justice of the outcome, through the use of coactive power, which legitimates leadership and organisational form. When people share in power through democratic participation, then they come to appreciate the differences between them, and to use those differences to create new ways of doing things, ways which coordinate the energies and capacities of all those affected for cooperation and meaningfulness (Clegg et al, 2006). The leader of coactive power is one amongst many, temporarily *primus inter pares*, authorised to play an enabling role in orchestrating the deliberative conversations and decisions of the organisation. In this way, deliberated leadership is not only a source of meaning-making authority, but also one which is limited by 'collective deliberation about authority rather than complete democratisation of the process of leadership' (Alversson & Spicer, 2012: 384).

Leadership, by instituting mechanisms for deliberating over delegated authority, has a role to play in the production of a resource of positive meanings in the work we do together. When allied to agonistic democracy, deliberated authority maintains and proliferates difference through reconfigured power relations, thereby promoting the creation of a polysensus. Thus, workplace democracy is justified, not only because of its instrumental efficacy aligning motivations or enhancing information processing capacity, but because democratic practices provide fertile ground for developing and exercising capabilities for meaningfulness.

The assumption of unitary interests

The powers of the transformational leader, gifted with uniquely potent meaning-making capabilities, are supported by the second assumption: that organisational life is characterised by a natural unity of interests between managers and workers, from which dissent, difference, and resistance are aberrations to be legitimately eliminated (Tourish, 2013: 23). Leaders and followers share 'a unitarist interest' such that 'employees, as a relatively undifferentiated mass, should embrace an identifiable set of core values [and] business leaders are well placed to discover, shape and articulate these values' (ibid: 71). This pre-political assumption makes unnecessary any kind of democratic practice, whether these are Pateman's simple participation, Habermassian communicative action, or agonistic democratic practices.

Dismissing political participation from ordinary working life allows economic associations to be characterised as legitimately unfree, closed, and homogeneous. Such assumptions promote arguments that democratic practices are irrelevant, even nonsensical, in economic organisations because technical rationality naturally engenders a unity of interests and a homogenisation of ways of being human. Hence, the expulsion of the political from the economic is justified because the coordination of activities enabling economic functioning depends upon technical reasoning. As a result, economic organisations encourage the flattening out of difference through the use of socialisation practices aimed at aligning workers' subjectivities against ideal characteristics, such as those which make up 'the entrepreneurial self' or the 'flexible personality': 'Likeness is prized because it appears as the primary ingredient of unity' (Wolin, 1996: 32).

Nelson (2003) identifies how, in conventional economic theory, economic organisations are imagined either as '*separative*', that is, as autonomous, rational actors engaged in maximising their self-interest (i.e. profit), or as '*soluble*', that is, subject to economic forces beyond their control (ibid: 81–2). Inside the firm, relations are assumed to be of three types:

a. Separative-separative, when people who make up the firm are themselves considered to be self-interested autonomous agents;
b. Soluble-soluble, when all are assumed to be in pursuit of a common goal;
c. Separative-soluble, when organisational issues are expressed simply as problems of designing the appropriate hierarchies of control (Nelson, 2003: 86).

Unitarist assumptions foster concepts such as 'responsible autonomy' (Friedman, 1977) which attempts 'to meld the interests of workers and their employing organisations' (Hodson, 2002b: 494). Nelson (2003) adds: 'what is missing, clearly, in all these is any notion that firms might be active, connected, evolving organisations, or that they or the people within them have the capacity for acting in engaged, meaningful, and responsible ways' (ibid: 92). According to conventional economic theory, the range of 'motivations and relations' within the unitary firm is narrow (ibid), and of the soluble-soluble type: 'the firm is just thought of as a unit, and it is simply presumed that all parts of it will work smoothly towards the goal of profit maximisation' (ibid: 91). Democratic theorists take up this assumption uncritically, asserting that members of the firm lack the diversity which is a necessary precondition for deliberative democratic practices.

The complex reality of human relations in economic organisations is thereby sidestepped. Capacities for co-creative agency, the need for belonging and a sense of worth, and the desire to exercise moral and political judgement are ignored. Attempts at organisational harmony which aim at the complete integration of individuals can easily reduce to the value of the individual to 'the way he harmoniously functions within his organisation' (Overvold, 1987: 561). This harmonising project ignores how the individual struggle to find meaning in work has the potential to be conflictual, opening up cracks of difference in the presumption of a unified consensus, particularly at the 'lower-levels' of the organisational hierarchy where workers' interests are often characterised as 'soluble', that is indistinguishable from the interests of the organisation. Moreover, as people act within, and move across, different action contexts, they think and feel not simply within the dominant logic of the sphere in which they find themselves, but also actively attempt to link together diverse and conflicting logics across different contexts. Lee (2006) suggests that multiple logics are 'at work simultaneously within the various modes of social life' (ibid: 420), giving rise to a 'struggle to control what is and what is not of value' (ibid: 416). This means that the values inherent in the worthy objects which people may wish to appropriate to the meaning content of their lives do not have to be subject to permanent closure, but can be made available for difference and contestation. Consequently, contestation over values, interpretive differences in meaning-making, and the interweaving of multiple action logics opens out the economic space as 'contingent, historical and thoroughly social', and thus replete with new possibilities, where 'citizens are able not only to freely regulate and redesign existing economic practices, but also to create new ones' (Swanson, 2008: 56).

In sum, work timespaces do not embody a unitary consensus which dissolves the interests of their members into the homogenous goal of maximising shareholder value, profit or national GDP. Rather, they are already loaded with affective relations, a diversity of interests, and ways of being human, thereby providing already extant opportunities for contestation and difference over contingent values. Furthermore, by giving us the resources to claim the involvement of others in helping us to fulfil our responsibilities of care towards worthy objects, work timespaces constitute important webs of relations which contribute to meaning attribution.

The assumption of a separate sphere of economic life

The assumption of a natural unity of interests enables the construction of the economic as a norm-free action context. However, empirical and theoretical literature, such as economic geography and feminist economics, challenges this construction: 'Empirical research indicates that real humans do not simply leave their needs for social relations, their values, their loyalties, and their creativity at the workplace door' (Nelson, 2003: 92). For example, post-structuralist theorists concerned with 'theorising the contingency of social outcomes, rather than the unfolding of structural logics' (Gibson-Graham, 2008: 3) argue persuasively that the economic can no longer be conceived of as a sphere separate from the social and the political. Instead, work timespaces are situated in diverse economies (Gibson-Graham, 2008); riven by conflictual purposes (Noonan, 2005); governed by multiple rationalities (Ettlinger, 2004); and exhibit no natural unitary consensus (England, 2003; Nelson, 2003). This means that, far from being unified and homogenous, the work of social cooperation is already saturated with difference and contestation, obscuring 'not only difference but also the creativity that issues forth an imaginative critique and rejection of existing agreement and in the generation of new and unexpected frameworks for agreement' (Gould, 1996: 173).

Instead, the economic consists of a plurality of overlapping action contexts in which generating and contesting meanings is essential for getting the work done. Rather than being a unified phenomenon, the economic is best conceived of as a patchwork of diverse economic practices, interwoven into the political and the social. By bringing into public view through democratic engagement unacknowledged forms of economic exchange, production, and reproduction, we will be able to 'perform new economic worlds' (Gibson-Graham, 2008: 2) and to 'repopulate the economic landscape as a proliferative space of difference' (ibid: 3). Gibson-Graham claim that such modes of exchange are not marginal economic practices, but are more extensive than conventional capitalist modes of exchange: caring for others, for example, contributes up to 50% of economic activity (ibid: 5).

However, Gibson-Graham (2008) warn against opposing a diverse alternative economics to a monolithic, undifferentiated capitalist economics, arguing instead that we need to understand, not only how 'diversity exists not only in the domain of non-capitalist economic activity' (ibid: 12), but also how 'capitalist enterprise is itself a site of difference' (ibid). They propose that diverse economies are 'openings, to provide a space of freedom and possibility' (ibid: 7), already present in conventional economies, which, if brought into public view, provide a rich field of values for appropriation to the meaning content of a life. Lee (2006) says that the economic is 'an integral part of everyday life, full of the contradictions, ethical dilemmas and multiple values that inform the quotidian business of making a living. In short it is ordinary' (ibid: 414). Ettlinger (2004) defines a context as a symbolic space which is 'present in many localities yet connected across space, through practices, discourses, and networks' (ibid: 32), which usefully identifies how work timespaces cannot be fixed, except temporarily through the meaning-making capacities of those who act in and through them. People who belong to multiple symbolic spaces and networks must knit together the diverse and irreducible 'modes of thought and feeling associated with different spheres of life and different social networks' (ibid: 32).

In the end, there is no separate sphere of the economic. Instead, there is an interlacing of action contexts, between which people move, taking with them the values and practical identities they have formed from their experiences of production and reproduction, and through which they engage with others in the co-creation of meanings. Movement between action contexts and encounters with others gives rise to 'cognitive dissonance' which 'reflects multiple logics that derive from experiences in different contexts, challenging presumptions of ultimate or inevitable conformity' (Ettlinger, 2004: 29). Such cognitive dissonance constitutes an already available source of the interpretive differences, which will remain as pre-political differences unless brought into public evaluation by democratic practices.

Irreducible agency

The three assumptions outlined above are challenged by our understanding of the intersubjective dimensions of getting the work done, which include relations of self to others and relations of self to objects. Our interactions with others and with objects give rise to interpretive struggles over how to overcome organisational rules and get the work done, which in a positive critical conception of meaningful work requires us to wrestle with how to fulfil our responsibilities of care for worthy objects. The impossibility of 'purely mechanical work' (Dejours, 2006: 47) reveals the essential agency in every act of work – an agency which escapes hierarchical control, but which remains obscured by assumptions of leadership as the sole source of meaning-making, a natural unified consensus and the economic as a separate sphere of action. However, simply identifying the irreducible normative agency of workers in every act of work will not overturn the assumptions of a naturalised consensus unless workers are: firstly, recognised as end-in-themselves, that is as having independent moral status in the midst of the act of work, and secondly, allowed to express their active agency in action, and in speech. This suggests a performative approach to new possibilities for the organisation of work which establishes institutional practices in which people are potentially diverse subjects, not simply interest-bearing individuals inserted into deliberative processes which aim to reduce the range of their differences in order to achieve a practical consensus (Wingenbach, 2011).

The conditions for the practical recognition of status and agency include: common frameworks of understanding and widespread access to communicative practices. Deranty suggests:

> [...] since the work process requires cooperation between workers, it functions best if the individualised forms of subjective investment that allow for the mastering of the task are confronted and discussed in a public forum, where a consensus can hopefully be found on the best way to realize the production (Deranty, 2009: 83).

The active capacities which workers must employ to get the work done justifies their status as co-authorities able to edit (and revise) the rules and behaviours framing their activities. Their status as co-authorities is therefore grounded not only in their human status as ends-in-themselves but also in their activity – that is: the content of the work they do, the contribution their work makes to a system of social cooperation, and the extensive responsibilities of decision-making and coordination with others that even the most ordinary and mundane of activities demands. These are responsibilities which cannot be controlled or eliminated by techniques of Taylorism in a technical division of labour, but are even multiplied by attempts to do so, because this simply increases the necessity for workers to subvert the rules in order to secure the achievement of ends. This ineliminable agency gives rise to remainders and surpluses which will remain as pre-political potentials unless given voice through democratic practices which not only reveal, but proliferate, difference.

The invisibility of what workers actually do puts the agency of workers beyond deliberative evaluation. But if workers' agency can be made part of the public – a public which opens out within ordinary acts of work and is not a sphere separate from it – then work becomes a potentially rich source of intersubjective encounter, solidarity, and subjective meaning. In order to make visible encounters with the material realities and irreducible agency in every act of work – workers need to be able to exercise the political mode of being in work. This would require some kind of workplace democracy which acknowledges the realities and the responsibilities of work as they are experienced by workers. We may, however, need something different from the consensus that Deranty (2009) is hopeful of; we may require also a new vocality or means of expressions, which would enable: disagreement over the meaning of efficiency and productivity; challenging of rules and practices; a plurality of perspectives and subjective formations; confrontation of managerial hierarchy based upon status and control over decision-making. Alvesson and Spicer (2012) argue for a critical performativity which will affirm ambiguities, work with mysteries, apply communicative action, explore heterotopias, and engage micro-emancipations. This is an agenda for unsettling difference in the experience of working which is susceptible to agonistic democratic practices, and fruitful for enabling people to develop the capabilities for meaning-making upon which the meaningfulness of work depends. Full autonomy requires workers to be involved in defining the social purposes at which such acts aim. For this, they need to be afforded the status of co-authorities, which acknowledges: first, their ability to exercise active agency and human capabilities, and second, the recognition of workers as ends-in-themselves. Active agency and status are both necessary for acknowledging that workers have a life of their own to lead which is expressive of the human capacity for self-determination.

Agonistic workplace democracy

Workplace democracy is usually theorised within corporatist or deliberative democratic frameworks where it is justified because it increases business efficiency or equips workers for the duties of citizenship. It is rare for workplace democracy to be theorised as having intrinsic value – so that it is justified on its own terms, irrespective of its outcomes – but this can be done if we use an agonistic perspective to acknowledge the irreducible agency in every act of work. According to Schaap (2009), the agon is 'celebrated as a never-ending play of differences which resists the homogenising drive for social unity, enabling plurality to flourish' (ibid: 1). The assumptions of a unitary consensus can be disturbed through the unfolding of difference and contestation over organisational purposes, and the rules which frame action within the experience of working. I argue that where workplace democracy takes the form of agonistic practices, divergences and differences are made visible, consequently encouraging ontological diversity and the pluralisation of values in the work of social cooperation. This is because, whereas deliberative democratic theory starts with the assumption of dissensus and aims at consensus, agonistic workplace democracy challenges assumptions of a pre-existing consensus by setting out to reveal submerged differences, using them to create spaces for acting in production.

In specifying agonistic dimensions to workplace democracy, I begin with Knops's (2012) proposal for integrating agonistic and deliberative democracy. Knops (2012) identifies Mouffe's rejection of the possibility of a universal rational consensus as the core claim dividing agonism and deliberation (ibid: 157). Against irreconcilable division, he argues that agonism and deliberation share essential dimensions of 'recognition, respect and contestation of difference grounded in context and subjectivity, acting against domination, and the avoidance of premature closure in political agreement that marginalises' (ibid: 159), where 'agonism represents a theory of the moment of difference or contest within a wider deliberative dialectic' (ibid: 162).

Deliberation aims at the ideal of a universal consensus, but Connolly argues that 'the presence of consensus is read as a sign of danger' (Connolly, 1995: 103). Accordingly, the deliberative ideal must be adjusted if agonistic dimensions of democratic practice in dialectical movement are to unsettle powerful forces driving assumptions of naturalised unity in workplaces, to account for the permanence of difference, and to make interpretive differences productive. Drawing upon Follett (1998 [1918]), who advocates a difference-begetting process of deliberative dialogue resulting in a polyvocal integration, I propose an ideal of a differentiated polysensus. In a polysensus, thinking and feeling together with others gives rise to a multifaceted integration which both contains and transcends difference. In this way, interpretive differences are not eliminated but are retained as fertile cultivators of the next dialectical moment in deliberative contestation and decision-making.

Thus democratic practices are most likely to realise the immanent potential of work when they possess agonistic dimensions. This is because, by bringing into public view pre-political interpretive differences, deliberation aims, not at a unified consensus, but at a generative differentiation and pluralisation of values. Connolly describes agonic democracy as:

> a practice that affirms the indispensability of identity to life, disturbs the dogmatisation of identity, and folds care for the protean diversity of human life into the strife and interdependence of identity\difference (Connolly, 1991: x).

Connolly (1991) does not claim that agonic democracy constitutes a programmatic priority for society, but suggests, instead, that it works with existing democratic forms by 'folding agonistic respect into identity\difference relations in a democratic state' (ibid: xxv). Consequently, agonistic democratic practices are not opposed to deliberative democratic practices, as a different form of democracy, but are the means for bringing into being the already existing emancipatory potential of deliberative practices (cf. Baechtiger, 2010).

Agonistic democracy and meaningful work

I identify two ways in which agonistic democracy has the potential to multiply the range of positive meanings in a critical conception of meaningful work which is structured by Wolf's bipartite value of meaningfulness: firstly, by challenging technical rationality in deliberative procedures, and secondly, by proliferating the modes of being in work timespaces. Firstly, agonistic democratic practices challenge the assumption that technical rationality governs acts of work. Agonistic democracy advances a critique of deliberative democracy as the class of theories which assume that consensus on political questions can be attained by reasonable persons utilising a fair procedural system of decision-making, where rationality determines the legitimacy of the outcome. But agonistic democracy refuses 'to equate concern for human dignity with a quest for rational consensus' (Connolly, 1991: x). Agonistic theorists take deliberative democrats to task for generating rule-bound democratic practices which are 'overly rationalist' (Barnett, 2004: 5), and for failing to take account of how 'the very essence of democratic politics lies in the constant contestation of the boundaries of the political' (ibid: 4). The deliberative emphasis upon defining fair procedures generates exclusions and assimilations (Tully, 2002), which obscure the inescapably pluralist reality of political life; proceduralist liberalism, for example, leaves 'precious little space for initiatory or expressive modes of political action' (Villa, 1999: 108). Secondly, participating in agonistic practices enables people to express varieties of being and acting. Keenan (2003) claims that the central dilemma facing democratic societies is 'how to create a vibrant sense of democratic community able to generate widespread and active identifications while also recognising and respecting the radical openness of any shared collective identity' (ibid: 71). What modern circumstances demand, therefore, is a practice of democracy which both recognises the existing diversity of identities, and acts as midwife to emergent identities as they struggle to raise themselves from 'below the register' (Connolly, 1995) of dominant practices of exclusion.

Of course, the management of subjectivity does not make every person identical since 'everyone does not become the same in a normalising society' (Connolly, 1995: 90). However, subjectification in the contemporary organisation of work does confine legitimate ways of being to a narrow range of categories, thereby crowding out and rendering invisible the many ways in which people are human at work: 'normalising societies subjugate and deploy otherness without eliminating difference' (ibid: 91). But since the formation of subjectivity is too important to be handed over without critical evaluation of management ideologies, we ought not to leave the development of ontological diversity to a vacated public sphere, and a politically cleansed and homogenised economic sphere. Bowles (1998) identifies the importance of the economic sphere for the learning of general behaviours and competences: 'preferences learned under one set of circumstances become generalised reasons for behaviour. Thus economic institutions may induce specific behaviours – self-regarding, opportunistic, or cooperative, say – which then become part of the behavioural repertoire of the individual' (ibid: 80). Not only are many ways of being de-legitimated, but the ones that remain are treated as essentialised ways of being human: 'a normalising society treats the small set of identities it endorses as if they were intrinsically true' (Connolly, 1995: 89). Organisational hierarchies mediate the management of subjectivity, resulting in framing rules which are alienating, dominating and misrecognising, where experiences of self and other are 'arrested by meanings which are imposed rather than mutually arrived at' (Allen, 2006: 576).

My point is not that, even were it possible, we eliminate social formation of subjectivities, but that we should think who defines, and how they define, the structures and social processes through which the experience of subjectification takes place. Fossen (2008) says that 'the proliferation of identities' is a social good because it is 'a necessary condition of human flourishing' (ibid: 383), but that the range and kind of identities must be made susceptible to democratic evaluation. Kioupkiolis proposes that expressive freedom as 'agonistic and creative self-definition' (Kioupkiolis, 2009: 480) provides another dimension to the production of the subject (du Gay, 1995b) through techniques of ideology and self-evaluation. Following Connolly's exhortation that we need to 'strive to create more room for difference' (Connolly, 1991: 33), agonistic democracy is committed to emancipation which 'involves an expansion of the acceptable range of identities and social practices available to human beings' (Wingenbach, 2011). This requires, according to Wingenbach, 'attentiveness to the opening of horizons of meaning' where 'the fundamental goal of democracy is the preservation of social ambiguity and openness to a proliferation of differences' (ibid: 111).

Hence, agonistic democratic practices do not remove subjectification, but instead resist the reduction of modes of being to existing norms and rules by providing participants with the means to challenge and modify the rules framing action and the extant modes of being. This does not mean that we aim for unlimited ontological diversity since not every kind of difference is valuable in itself, and agonistic democracy 'does not entail the celebration of any and every identity' (Connolly, 1991: 14). Instead, expanding ontological possibilities within limits becomes a political task, facilitated by an agonic politics of meaningfulness which sustains and facilitates a 'social pluralism' as an 'achievement to be protected' (Connolly, 1995: xiv). In the action contexts of work timespaces, such a politics will take account of the social pluralism already immanent within the multiple economic practices which make up the work we do together. This is because agonic workplace democracy exposes the closures we impose upon one another, ostensibly because they are necessary for the coordination of the work of social cooperation, rendering them available for disagreement and renegotiation. Agonistic practices help us to acknowledge 'our deep interdependence and commonalities, yet without seeing each as *identical* parts of a homogeneous whole' (Keenan, 2003: 188). They promote an understanding of our selves as distinct persons, thereby supporting our sense of dignity in a positive critical conception of meaningful work.

Instituting a politics of meaningfulness

I make use of agonistic democratic practices to disturb assumptions of a naturalised unity through the unfolding of difference and contestation over organisational purposes and the rules which frame action. In work timespaces, agonistic practices have the potential to challenge permanent closures by keeping open the possibility of contestation over goals and means, thereby engendering a politics of becoming through the fostering of an ontological diversity which is capable of challenging the management of subjectivities. By forging a politics of meaningfulness as 'a struggle around the very process of constructing and contesting identity' (Smith, 1994: 228), agonistic practices make the prospect of practical identity formation dependent upon being able to participate in the interpretation and formation of the objectively worthwhile values which are available for affective appropriation. This enables agonistic practices to expose value-deprived work timespaces, opening them up to challenge and contestation over means and purposes, advancing new ways of organising the work around different values, and enriching ontological diversity. White (2000), in advocating a weak ontology which combines the generosity of Connolly's agonistic ethos with the respect of standard liberalism (ibid: 220), suggests that what distinguishes human beings is their capacity for 'coherence-making' (ibid: 224) and for natality, or new beginnings, through political action (cf. Arendt, 1958). Coherence-making emerges out of agonistic activity between human beings who are 'constitutively engaged with difference' (White, 2000: 224). Thus, workplace democracy with agonistic dimensions has the capacity to resist the assumption of a natural unity of interests through a coherence-making 'politics of becoming', thereby cultivating the use of different rationalities and fostering different modes of being within the multiple work timespaces to which we belong.

The inner workshop of democracy

If work is to be reconstituted as a site of meaningful work which embodies emancipatory action, then a different kind of group life must be fostered – one in which the public expression of difference gives rise to new interpretive meanings, generating a pluralisation of positive values as a consequence of acting and being together. Follett (1998 [1918]) argues that the processes of a fully human group life are forged out of 'the creative agonies of fellowship' (ibid: 89) in the 'inner workshop of democracy' (ibid: 48). She claims that 'democratic associations on which democracy should be based can maintain difference within unity, conflict within integration' (Mansbridge, 1998: xxvii), where a group is 'a community formed through the interpenetration and integration of ideas, and emphatically not through the suppression of individuality and difference' (ibid: xxvii). For Follett, this constitutes a moral, as well as a pragmatic, imperative to make the democratic group life an everyday experience in work and politics: 'without this activity, both political and industrial democracy must be a chaotic, stagnating, self-stultifying assemblage' (Follett, 1998 [1918]: 48). This moribund condition is revived by a politics of meaningfulness in work, enabled by agonistic democratic practices in multiple and overlapping work timespaces.

Employee engagement

One potential source of a politics of meaningfulness is the current interest in the practices of employee engagement. Meaningful work and employee engagement are closely related (Kahn, 1990). For example, in distinguishing between job and organisational engagement, Saks (2006) finds that:

> Job engagement is associated with a sustainable workload, feelings of choice and control, appropriate recognition and reward, a supportive work community, fairness and justice, and meaningful and valued work (ibid: 603).

Although this is promising for the generation of positive values and difference in a politics of meaningfulness, in reality, engagement practices for the promotion of meaningfulness are invariably tied to management interests and organisation defined purposes. Increasingly, people are being asked to bring the 'psychological capabilities' associated with engagement to bear in order to 'thrive and make organizations survive' (Schaufeli, 2013). Such capabilities include adaptation, assertiveness, communication skills, initiative, self-control, and mental and emotional resilience (ibid), and when harnessed to organisational goals are sources of elevated organisational effectiveness. Indeed, such is the potential contribution from psychological capabilities, that 'companies have no choice, but to try to engage not only the body, but also the mind and the soul of every employee' (Ulrich, 1997: 125). Not surprisingly, much practitioner interest in the concept of employee engagement is therefore concerned with how to foster the formation and application of desirable psychological capabilities, including the sense that one's work is meaningful. Consequently, given the hypothesised empirical connection between meaningfulness and engagement (Kahn, 1990; May et al, 2004), there is a great temptation for organisations to pass onto employees the obligation to find their work to be meaningful by making the right kind of psychological adjustment.

In the bipartite value of meaningfulness, such a project would be normatively, if not empirically, unsound. Normatively, the concept of engagement lacks equity (Welbourne, 2011) and critical bite (Purcell, 2012), leading Welbourne (2011) to ask 'what do employees get for being engaged?' Empirically, engagement is inconsistently defined and conceptualised, and moreover may be redundant because it overlaps with established concepts such as commitment and job satisfaction (see Rigg, 2013 for an overview). Despite this, the promise of high engagement continues to resonate with practitioners, which in itself makes the concept and practice of engagement an important object of inquiry. Indeed, consistent with positive meaning-making in the bipartite value of meaningfulness, a potential mode of critical investigation would be to treat engagement as a value, exploring the positive and negative meanings it has for workers, whilst being attentive to how the conceptualisation of engagement is power-laden and vulnerable to managerial techniques of domination and subjectification, unless legitimated through democratic authorisation. For example, Shuck et al (2010) find that employees identify experiences of personal engagement with a sense of feeling at home, of close connections and relationships with workers, of trust and shared interests, of being involved in learning, and of feeling safe in their relationship to their manager. Following Purcell (2012), engagement as a value might conceivably be legitimated through processes which aim at establishing the preconditions of trust and perceptions of fairness and organisational justice.

Kahn's (1990) research on engagement and disengagement identifies the importance of meaningfulness for how we experience our work, including the judgements we make on its worth. He shows how our evaluations of work are intersubjectively achieved, shaping the ebb and flow of our engagement and disengagement in the midst of our daily experience of working. In most of the literature on engagement, disengagement is cast in pejorative terms, issuing in individual and organisational bads such as burnout, poor health outcomes, and diminished role performance (Macey & Schneider, 2008; Welbourne, 2011), resulting in human energy becoming focused upon simply 'surviving each day' (Shuck et al, 2010: 310). However, rather than simple oppositions, there may be a more complicated relationship between engagement/ disengagement which mediates possibilities for developing psychological capabilities and for experiencing meaningfulness in work. The starting point for recognising the complexity of engagement/ disengagement is to acknowledge that not all kinds of disengagement are the same. Some kinds of disengagement are more harmful than others when the objective content of work is characterised by heteronomy, repetitiveness, and futility in tasks demanding unrelenting vigilance and a state of high alert (Thackray, 1981) – that is, work structured to engender a perpetual condition of boredom and stress. Such chronic disengagement is more likely to be manifested in low trust organisations; for instance, Purcell et al (2009) find that high trust is associated with high commitment organisations. Purcell (2012) argues that 'the engagement gap' is really the growing 'trust deficit'

(Arkin, 2011) which is generated by 'engagement strategies rooted in a discourse of compliance' (Francis et al, 2013: 2715).

This kind of chronic disengagement – systematic, enduring, and alienating – may lead more surely to exhaustion, passivity, and poor performance than the kind of disengagement which is part of the natural cycle of everyday living. This means that negative emotions, such as boredom, may need to be reconsidered. Indeed, where boredom leads to ordinary disengagement, it may have a positive psychological function because it promotes learning and the pursuit of new goals where 'exploring alternative goals and experiences allows the attainment of goals which might be missed' (Bench & Lench, 2013: 459). Moreover, in the interchange between engagement/disengagement, emotional states such as boredom may open out the interior reflexive space for interpretive differences in meaning-making. Indeed, Kahn (1990) hints at such a possibility when he says that we should seek to understand 'the complexities of possible mixtures of personal engagement and disengagement' (ibid: 719) such that 'an individual might [...] express and defend, employ and withdraw simultaneously' (ibid).

Rather than oscillating between (good) states of engagement and (bad) states of disengagement, an individual may experience a simultaneity of being both psychologically present and absent in the midst of working – such a condition, although uncomfortable, may be highly productive of differences in meaning-making which, in a stable system of workplace democracy, people can bring to deliberative inquiry over the interpretation of values upon which the possibility of meaningfulness depends. This condition of the worker will be experienced as alienating if the worker is situated in a context of working where there is a presumption of unitary interests (Tourish, 2013; Morrison, 2011), giving rise to employee silence arising from 'shared beliefs about the danger and/or futility of speaking up through processes of information sharing, social contagion and collective sense-making' (Milliken et al, 2003: 1456–7). Overcoming the alienating effects of suppression, silence and risk requires settings structured to encourage 'dialogic conversational practice' which is non-episodic, non-prescriptive, plurivocal, and constructive (Francis et al, 2013: 2718), and where language is understood to be 'interwoven with action in context' (Francis et al, 2013: 14). According to Francis et al (2013), settings inhospitable to interpretive meaning-making are characterised by compliance, premature closure and consent, monovocal communication, instrumental rationality, and passivity on the part of employees. Conversely, dialogic conversation practice allows the process of engagement itself to be understood as 'socially negotiated and an expression of employee agency' (ibid: 2716). In the conduct of dialogic conversational practice, Francis et al (2013) privilege the role of line managers, making them uniquely responsible for engaging people 'in a type of generative conversation that can creatively address the tension between actualities (what is) and potentialities (what could or ought to be)' (ibid: 2718). However, in a system of workplace democracy – and particularly in forms of co-ownership, such as cooperatives, mutuals, and employee-owned businesses – managers are not the sole guardians of voice. Instead, in a system of workplace democracy structured by the principle of justice, 'conversational responsibility' (Ford, 1999) is invested in all those affected by the activities of the organisation. Thus, within a justice-based system of power-sharing, Follett's command to 'give me your difference!' represents a duty placed upon all those who count themselves as members and participants (Follett, 1998 [1918]).

An institutionalised and embedded voice system will create separations of power around collectivised voice, thereby distributing responsibility for taking care of participation in decision-making and becoming involved in interpretive sense-making. Townsend et al (2014) argue for 'an architecture of collaboration' (ibid: 922) combining collectivised and individualised partnerships between managers and workers which are underpinned by the values and principles of mutuality, dignity and respect, fairness, competitiveness, flexibility, communication, and consultation (ibid: 917). Finally, engagement/disengagement can be theorised as an interior process which generates positive meaning-making when it is enacted in an organisational context of dialectical change and flux – that is, where there are social processes 'imbued with conflict, tensions and contradiction' (Langley & Sloan, 2012: 261). Langley and Sloan (2012) identify how dialectical thought is both *pluralistic*, that is generative of multiple values, ideas, goals, and paradigms, and *processual*, that is emerging, evolving, and dissolving out of the crucible of on-going social interactions (ibid: 262). Potentially, everyday engagement/disengagement is an internal engine for generating dialectical thinking in a system of deliberative inquiry leading to 'possible shifts in individual actions and understandings and in social, organizational and inter-organizational arrangements' (Langley & Sloan, 2012: 262). This internal engine constitutes an 'inner workshop of democracy' (Follett, 1998 [1918]), out of which is forged the differences to be made productive through inter-subjective encounter. With these possibilities in mind, I go on to explore the application of agonistic democratic theory to processes and practices of positive meaning-making which are generative of dissent and difference in the bipartite value of meaningfulness.

Characteristics of agonistic practices

Baechtiger (2010) proposes that agonistic practices, rather than being an alternative and opposing model of democracy, are the means to realising the potential of deliberative democracy – and I apply his insight to the micro-level of the task in a system of workplace democracy. I propose that the already existing potentiality of work to exhibit the characteristics of the democratic group life is realised by democratic practices of agonistic inquiry, which Baechtiger (2010) identifies as questioning, disputing, and insisting: 'agonistic inquiry is a key deliberative technique which helps to unleash essential parts of deliberation's normative potential (epistemic, ethical, inclusionary, and reflective-transformative) while simultaneously counteracting unwanted aspects of deliberation' (ibid: 3). The ideal deliberative process is characterised by 'reasoned, respectful, impartial, impassionate and truthful (or sincere) discussion' (ibid: 2). This leads to the marginalisation and exclusion of the inarticulate, and the intuitive, or the 'remainders' (Honig, 1993) which lie outside deliberative discourse as reason-giving aimed at rational consensus formation. An agonic politics of meaningfulness remedies the exclusions and epistemic limitations of classical deliberation by fostering 'cognitive diversity' (Landemore, 2010; see also Manin, 2005), and bringing into public evaluation interpretive differences, excesses, remainders, and incommensurabilities. Baechtiger (2010) suggests that agonistic practices permit 'tough questioning and radical argument' (ibid: 21) when they are situated within a system committed both to 'deliberative capacity building' (Dryzek, 2009), and are guided by an ethic of respect, attention, and care towards those advancing new and challenging perspectives, sometimes in modes of articulation which are at odds with the emotion-free ideal of reasoned deliberative discourse. Moreover, such practices answer the search for meaningfulness which generate a demand to participate in the democratic group life (Braybrooke, 1998b), because of our desire 'to play a recognised role in a joint human activity' (ibid: 55) – a desire stimulated by feelings of alienation (ibid: 73), a need to be heard (ibid: 80), and the need to occupy worthwhile roles constituted by relations of mutual recognition (ibid: 74; ibid: 77). Thus, agonic democratic practices of questioning, disputing, and insisting in work timespaces address the demand to have an equal share in the decision-making necessary to create and reproduce the common life in the work of social cooperation, where such a demand arises from our fundamental human need for meaningfulness.

In order to create a differentiated polysensus, the interior content of work must be transformed by public spaces for the political mode of being in everyday acts of work, where 'the capacities for judgement necessary for participatory democracy then are always already a developmental potential of social interaction' (Warren, 1993: 218). Follett (1998 [1918]) makes political dialogue a 'community process', characterised by several features conducive to the opening out of public spaces expressive of the political mode of being. The dynamics of correctly structured group action, in Follett's understanding of politics as community process, constitutes a kind of 'governance from the ground up' (Elias, 2008), where conflict and difference is revealed, deliberated, evaluated, and integrated into enriched knowledge or creative decision. And as the cycle is repeated, it becomes a habit, changing each person's understanding of the other, developing the skills for acting together, and providing for the development of political consciousness. Importantly, such a process depends upon local knowledge and practices, making it conducive to revealing the interpretive differences arising from our encounters with others and with materiality when we work together. I suggest there are four characteristics of distinctly agonic work timespaces which frame Baechtiger's (2010) practices of agonistic inquiry in Follett's democratic group life: *association* to create an inclusionary public; *contestation* to foster the generation of difference; an *ethos of enlargement* to support normative orientation; and *decision* to secure temporary closure. Agonistic work timespaces with these characteristics are capable of challenging assimilation of subjectivities by contesting the narrow range of legitimate identities for the purpose of promoting ontological diversity; and challenging exclusion from democratic processes by opening out the spaces in which participants in the work of social cooperation can come together for contestation and decision-making (Tully, 2002).

Association

I propose that we conceive of work timespaces not as distinctly public or private spheres of action separate from the political but as arenas which, at any moment, have the potential to become spaces for expressing the political mode of being. Estlund (2003) suggests that workplaces have a unique capacity to encourage cooperative relations, social ties, and a sense of connectedness that transcends boundaries and social cleavages; the workplace is an action context in which 'people find it necessary to get along and get things done with others with whom they would not otherwise choose to associate. They foster the connectedness which forms the background to a healthy democracy by constructing a 'layer of public discourse' (ibid: 123) from the multitude of everyday conversations. Workplaces supply 'a place for the informal exchange of experiences and opinions and knowledge among people who are both *connected* with each other, so that they are inclined to listen, and *different* from each other, so that they are exposed to diverse ideas and experiences' (ibid: 123). Estlund (2003) identifies two features of workplace discourse which resonate with the values of democratic practices: firstly, conversations have a non-particularist, public dimension, because they take place between people who are not family members or friends; and secondly, they cut across lines of social, ethnic, and gender divisions. Such features of everyday talk potentially enable people to not only explore their own needs and interests, but also to find the common ground upon which they can establish solidarity with others: 'citizens deliberate with each other at work far more than in the fabled public square and far more than through voluntary civic organisations' (ibid: 119). Economic necessity requires people to take up work and then keeps them in relations with others in order to satisfy the need to earn a living (ibid: 103–4), and Warren (1993) suggests that the non-voluntary character of work lends it a particular virtue in holding us to the requirement to engage with others not necessarily like ourselves:

> In workplaces individuals are likely to be thrown together out of need, selected by their skills, and related to one another through the division of labor. Here individuals are not necessarily drawn together by common identities or causes, so that a single organisation might be quite diverse in terms of lifestyle, gender, race, ethnicity, religious orientation and class, or at least more so than in a self-selected group (Warren, 1993: 228).

The voluntary character and ease of exit which characterises self-interested groups make them too homogenous, self-selecting, and therefore strategic in their decision-making, for them to be effective discursive forums – and thus less likely to produce the autonomous selves which are valued by democracies (Warren, 1993: 227). Workplaces, on the other hand, are relatively diverse, focus on common goals, and are part of the daily experience of most people: 'as workplaces democratise, the structure of interests and identities is likely to produce imperatives for critique and discourse of a kind absent in most self-organised groups' (ibid: 228). This means that workplaces play a vital role in providing the background conditions to associational life: they are sites of discourse and deliberation, they build interpersonal connectedness, cultivate civic skills, and generate a sentiment of connection and of a common fate (ibid: 106). Importantly, by enabling the recognition of individuals through everyday cooperative relations which allow 'individuals to get to know each other and to care about each other' (ibid: 108), they are a vital source of the worthy objects and subjective attachments which are necessary to being able to experience the value of meaningfulness. This 'fertile territory' for association provides an enriched social setting for fostering the group life in which agonistic democratic practices can become productive of difference, increasing the possibility of the political mode of being breaking out into everyday work timespaces, and resulting in the proliferation of positive values which can be appropriated to the meaning content of a life.

Contestation

The extent to which agonistic associations enable a politics of meaningfulness depends upon how such associations encourage or inhibit contestation and difference arising from the pre-political potentials brought into public evaluation. Agonic democratic practices in work timespaces foster interpretive differences by preventing a premature consensus which is 'not based on the autonomy of participants' (Warren, 1993: 229). Moreover, they allow workers to resist 'identities that undermine cognitive competence' (ibid), because involvement in democratic discourse places greater cognitive demands upon employees through increasing work complexity, thereby protecting their interests in developing capabilities for reasoning and deliberation. Correctly structured association enables intersubjective contestation through which we 'think together' (Follett, 1998 [1918]: 29). And when we experience intersubjective encounters permitting difference and disagreement, we also generate the possibility for agonic group activity, which is 'an acting and reacting in a single and identical process which brings out differences and integrates them into a unity' (Follett, 1998 [1918]: 33). Follett says: 'Each must discover and contribute that which distinguishes him from others, his difference. The only use for my difference is to join it with other differences' (ibid: 29). Indeed, for Follett, producing and expressing our difference is almost a duty laid upon those who find themselves involved in joint activity: 'Give me your difference' (ibid: 33). She adds 'no member of a group which is to create can be passive. All must be active and constructively active' (ibid: 29), and that in order to 'think together' then 'each man must contribute what is in him to contribute' (ibid).

But applying such an approach to the social organisation of work timespaces may be too risky, because the interjection of dissensus could undermine the coordination and decision-making necessary for the maintenance of a complex economic order. In the tightly bound webs of cooperation that constitute our modern economies, increased democratic freedom of the kind advocated by agonistic practices will surely lead to a dangerous disunity: 'the standard account is that increased democratic freedom over the rules of recognition and distribution is the cause of disunity' (Tully, 2002). But disunity is more likely to arise as a consequence of relations of exclusion and assimilation because the kind of solidarity required in modern societies is undermined when citizens are not afforded deliberative experiences of rule-making which in turn underpin democratic self-formation (Tully, 2002: 225). Conflict need not be destructive and damaging, provided it can be turned into a productive dissensus within the context of an agonic workplace democracy shaped by an ethos of pluralisation. Follett says in relation to conflict and diversity:

> What people often mean by getting rid of conflict is getting rid of diversity, and it is of the utmost importance that these should not be considered the same. We may wish to abolish conflict, but we cannot get rid of diversity. We must face life as it is and understand that diversity is its most essential feature [...] Fear of difference is dread of life itself. It is possible to conceive conflict as not necessarily a wasteful outbreak of incompatibilities, but as a normal process by which socially valuable differences register themselves for the enrichment of all concerned (Follett, 1930 [1924]: 300).

Ethos of enlargement

Contestation which is productive of difference, rather than degenerating into conflict, depends upon an ethos of imaginative enlargement, supported by the virtue of agonistic respect: 'the virtue of agonistic respect requires openness to those who are excluded; and this ethos itself is predicated on the idea that such boundaries are never fixed, but contingent and revisable' (Howarth, 2008: 188). Connolly suggests that pluralistic democracy requires two civic virtues: firstly, 'agonistic respect' between opponents who radically disagree, and secondly, 'critical responsiveness' – an attitude of careful, attentive listening to the demands and claims of others. *Agonistic respect* recognises 'already crystallised' identities, whereas *critical responsiveness* operates where identities are emerging 'from an obscure or negated place below the register of legitimate identity' (Connolly, 1991: xxviii). These virtues underpin the possibility of maintaining a permanently open-ended agreement which retains awareness of the alternatives not chosen, of continued dissent, and of the possibility of revision. The struggle for emergence entails a 'politics of becoming' which Connolly expresses as 'that recurrent, fugitive politics by which a new constituency or event surges into being from below the threshold of tolerance, justice or legitimacy' (ibid). Keenan (2003) suggest that the compassion and generosity for an ethos of pluralisation might draw upon our 'shared suffering' as:

> [...] fluid, open, internally complex beings inevitably trapped (although to different degrees) in more or less fixed identity 'scripts' or self-images. It recognises that suffering comes both from the constraints of identity and from our being radically open and indebted to each other even in our mutual otherness. We depend upon each other, both materially and for the stories that tell us who we are – even as we don't naturally fit together and are constantly called into question by each other's differences (ibid: 188).

Therefore the practice of agonic workplace democracy involves a politics of becoming which fosters emergent ways of being, where workers and managers recognise one another as 'fellow sufferers' in which the management of subjectivity is not only recognised to be a necessity, but also subjects organisational processes of self-formation to permanent openness and contestability. Our stance towards co-workers becomes one reflexive evaluation of the ways in which our working identities are managed through mechanisms of exclusion and difference, and compassionate generosity towards our own and one another's limitations generated by the understanding that we require one another to adopt constricted forms of identification which are incapable of fully expressing our multifaceted individuality. Thus, the inescapability and necessity of difference for identity requires an ethical orientation of agonistic respect towards others which generates a particular kind of bond, based upon gratitude and wonder at the diversity of human being between those who would generally be thought of as locked into irreconcilable conflict, where this ethical bond forms between contending constituents 'engaged in intensive relations of interdependence and strife' (Connolly, 1995: xviii).

To create social roles which will allow individuals to take up their responsibilities of care for the worthy objects they have appropriated to the meaning content of their lives requires not only participating in existing structures but also participating in reframing the rules of engagement in which participants call 'something into being which did not exist before, which was not given, not even as cognition or imagination, and which therefore, strictly speaking, could not be known' (Arendt, 1977 [1954]: 151). In order to do the best we can towards worthy objects, we must all have a share of political autonomy: that is, the participation in the collective self-determination necessary to bringing pre-political interpretive differences into public deliberation, and thereby to shape the framing rules governing our orientations to worthy objects. Inkeles and Smith (1974) observe that factory work 'increases the tendency to hold opinions and the tendency to tolerate or even value the opinions of others' (ibid: 24): to both hold an opinion and to value the different opinions of others is the essence of 'agonistic respect', and to be able to collaborate under conditions of contingency is to learn to appreciate the abundance of life which cannot be constrained within totalising identities which deny the differences upon which they depend. It is also to be in possession of the resources for dissensus and debate which, if enabled within a practice of agonistic democracy, would facilitate the conditions for ontological expressiveness.

Decision

To critics of agonism, it can sometimes seem that agonistic democracy is fixated upon endless disagreement in which nothing can actually get done, therefore not taking us much beyond simple conflict. This means that room must be made for the temporary closures of decision. For Villa (1999), agonism, centres too much around 'incessant contestation and resistance', making it too constricted and reactive. Follett (1998 [1918]), commenting upon democratic decision-making in the group process, talked about integration or interpenetration, rather than 'aggregation, compromise or concession' (Mansbridge, 1998: xxiii), where her idea of interpenetration is a deeply intersubjective, Hegelian-inspired ideal for a process of 'related difference' (Follett, 1998 [1918]: 33). Follett says that 'unity, not conformity, must be our aim. We attain unity only through variety. Differences must be integrated, not assimilated, nor absorbed' (ibid: 39), where purposes are not pre-determined but created through intersubjective encounters, framed by the aim of 'coadaptation' or 'creating ever new values though the interplay of all the forces of life' (ibid: 93). Thus, 'it is man's part to create purpose and to actualize it' (ibid: 58). Moreover, we relate to one another through our differences, and in the act of relating, we initiate acts of creation (ibid: 63). Although the moment of decision describes the closures around purpose and identity which enable cooperative action to take place, in an agonistic framework these can never be permanent closures, but must always be available for contestation and revision. The political mode of being remains an ever present potential, where expressive political agency is permanently available for activation, depending upon the nature of the decision to be made. Follett (1998 [1918]) suggests there is an alternative to both domination, and consensus in collective life, and that is a dialectical impermanent integration which is:

> a harmonious marriage of difference which, like the nut and the screw or the parts of a watch, come together in a way that produces a new form, a new entity, a new result, made out of old differences and yet different from any of them (ibid).

Decision describes the closures around purpose and identity which enable cooperative action to take place. In an agonistic framework where decision is based upon a polysensus these closures can never be permanent, but must be always available for contestation and revision. But this should not be mistaken for a simple unity of interests: the result is not a balance of power or aggregation of interests or elite domination, but the creation of new values, the introduction of something expressively original from the old materials. In sum, the aim of agonistic practices in work timespaces is to forge a particular kind of decision from within the inner workshop of democracy, a decision in which all can be satisfied, but from which differences are not eliminated, excluded, or dissolved because they remain ever present, if dormant, seeds, already available to stimulate the next political moment.

Finally, agonistic democracy applied to economic associations opens out public spaces in spheres of human activity which have been presumed to be legitimately excluded from representative or deliberative democratic practices, and certainly from claims to plurality. A political mode of being structured by agonistic democratic practices aims at overcoming exclusion and assimilation in intersubjective relations – enabling workers to reveal and to articulate their acts of agency and develop the relevant capabilities for meaningfulness and sense of their status as co-authorities in the realm of value. Workplace democracy becomes constitutive of the meaning content of work because it situates individuals in a setting which is rich in potential encounters with worthy objects and for forming the relevant capabilities, where being able to exercise the political mode of being is in and of itself one of the worthy objects. Consensus-based democratic practices which fail to allow for the contestation of ultimate purposes, the revision of rules, or the expression of difference are perhaps particularly susceptible to being used in this fashion. But workplace democracy structured by agonistic practices which aim at a polysensus might offer us something rather different. By situating deliberated difference in the interior experience of working, work has the potential to become valuable for its own sake, because, by making visible the essential agency of workers, it first, establishes the status of workers as ends-in-themselves and as co-authorities, and second, enables learning and freedom by giving voice to experiences which have been rendered speechless by the assumptions of a unified consensus. Thus the individual worker is re-presented as an irreplaceable contributor, situated in cooperative relations with others, and imbued with expressive political agency.

7
Capability Justice and a Politics of Meaningfulness

In structuring meaningful work using the bipartite value of meaning-fulness, I have drawn attention to how experiencing meaningfulness depends upon our being able to exercise the capabilities and status for meaningfulness, which are formed through our participation in action contexts with agonistic dimensions. By re-conceiving work in this way, we can begin to see the outlines of a programme of social and political action aimed at proliferating meaningfulness in the organisation of work. Of course, meaningful work has always existed, but in most societies it has been an ideal which aims at elite meaning or the maximal degree of meaningfulness for a few. However, a system which institutionalises elite meaning transgresses any scheme of justice which is concerned to meet fundamental human needs, including goods such as meaningful work. Hence, I argue that we should aim at egalitarian meaning or a satisficing level of meaningfulness for all. In this case, the goal is not to guarantee that everyone will find their lives to be actually meaningful, but to secure social arrangements that will provide the relevant capabilities for the functioning of meaningfulness, consistent with the demands of justice (Muirhead, 2004).

Capability justice

I make use of Nussbaum's theory of capability justice to outline the principles and measures required to promote the formation and exercise of the capabilities for meaningfulness. A theory of justice is specified by *principles* (what values should guide the institution of justice), *rules* (how the goods relevant to realising the principles of justice are allocated), and *metrics* (what goods are subject to the rules of allocation) (Anderson, 2010). Our concern is the importance of the value of meaningfulness to each individual, generating an equality of need which is difficult to satisfy in contemporary society when our work lacks the requisite structure for meaningfulness. Therefore, I propose that a scheme of justice in work which addresses the fundamental human need for meaning must aim at the regulatory ideal of meaningful work for all through the application of two principles: the *principle of egalitarian meaning*, where all persons are equally entitled to work which has the requisite structure for meaningfulness, up to the *threshold of sufficient meaning*, where the threshold is specified by freedom as non-dominated work, autonomy as non-alienated work, and social recognition as dignified work.

Firstly, *a principle of egalitarian meaning* requires that each person possesses, in equal measure, the capabilities to appropriate meaning to their lives and to realise the functioning of meaningfulness. In order to satisfy the principle of egalitarian meaning, the range of activities recognised as work in a system of social cooperation must be broadened so that society is expanding rather than limiting opportunities for capability development. Gomberg (2007) argues that market societies limit artificially the opportunities for capability development, constraining the efforts of some individuals and groups to participate in worthwhile activities which contribute to sustaining a cooperative social order. Many are excluded from making their contribution; certain groups are favoured with the most desirable forms of participation; and other groups are socialised to accept poor quality work. As a matter of justice, we should not limit opportunity, but instead should make it possible for everyone to make their contribution: 'it is unfair to deprive so many of the opportunity to contribute complex abilities' (Gomberg, 2007: 42). It is important to note that, in the contributory society which aims to promote meaningful work, contribution is rooted in the individual's need for meaning and the trajectory of meaningfulness which makes sense to them, rather than binding the individual to contributions pre-determined by economic necessity.

Consequently, Gomberg argues that a theory of contributive justice will require an adjustment to the capabilities approach where 'a good society should distribute widely the contribution of complex abilities' (ibid: 130), by promoting a general complex functioning consisting of 'participation in the economic life of one's society in a way that confers dignity' (ibid: 131). If a schema of capability justice is to be able to make provision for all persons to form and exercise the relevant capabilities, these contributive activities must be structured by the bipartite value of meaningfulness, so that whilst 'the *capability* to engage in good human activities should be provided to all; the individual is free to decide which activities to pursue' (ibid: 46). In the regulatory ideal of meaningful work, this general complex functioning is expressed in terms of a capability for the functioning of meaningfulness in work, which is constituted by the capabilities for objective valuing and subjective attachment, supported by our status as co-authorities. In a practical politics of meaningfulness, I suggest that these capabilities for meaningfulness can be guaranteed indirectly by securing the Capability for Voice through the conversion factors of a basic income and a system of workplace democracy.

Secondly, *a threshold of sufficient meaning* is provided by the constitutive values of meaningful work, which are autonomy as non-alienation, freedom as non-domination, and social recognition as dignified work. I claim that the threshold of sufficient meaning is a modest standard, based upon the contribution that ordinary activities make to a life of meaning. It does not require that lives as a whole be fully meaningful, but simply that important aspects of our lives, such as the work we do, are structured so that they contain goods and values sufficient to give us good reason to find our lives worth living. Huseby (2009) defines the threshold of sufficiency as follows: 'the maximal sufficiency threshold equals a level of welfare with which a person is content' (ibid: 181), where being content means 'not the absence of any desire to further improve one's lot, but rather satisfaction with the overall quality of one's life' (ibid). When applied to the value of meaningfulness, I suggest this yields a threshold of sufficiency where one is not merely *satisfied*, but *convinced* that one's life contains objects of value giving one a compelling reason to live. I use the term 'convinced' in order to capture the sense in which the value of meaningfulness integrates objective reason-giving with affective attachment to objects of value – reason and feeling work together to create a security of attachment to worthy objects which is supported by social as well as individual endorsement.

The principle of individual development

In Nussbaum's theory of capability justice, the moral object of justice is the individual who needs to experience her life as worth living, rather than collectives such as groups, organisations, or states: 'the flourishing of individuals taken one by one is both analytically and normatively prior to the flourishing of groups' (Nussbaum, 1999: 62). For Nussbaum, the individual is the fundamental unit of concern, thus requiring that, in any schema of capability justice, every individual person be brought over the threshold. The equal value of each person is upheld in the *'principle of each person as end*, articulating it as a *principle of each person's capability* [...] the ultimate political goal is always the promotion of the capabilities of *each person'* (Nussbaum, 2000: 74). Nussbaum's central human capabilities for functioning, by describing what is sufficient for living a worthwhile human life specify 'a threshold below which a human person could not be considered as living in a truly human way' (Alexander, 2003: 9). Moreover, they indicate what is needed to satisfy the political objective of bringing everyone over the threshold into secure functionings.

Under the governing principle of individual development, individual flourishing establishes each person's entitlement to the central human capabilities for functioning. Nussbaum's capability justice is grounded in a conception of the person as an individual possessed of interior potentialities, situated within a social reality which operates to suppress or support the development of those potentialities. Her principle of individual human development in capability justice draws upon an ontological ideal of what it means to be a distinct person which is grounded, not only upon diversity between individuals, but also upon the interior diversity within the individual, such that all human beings are 'pluralistic entities' characterised by 'an internal multidimensionality and plurality which intrinsically characterises each person and that every society should guarantee or at least promote' (Giovanola, 2005: 250). Since the 'constitutive plurality' (ibid: 261) and 'human richness' (ibid: 264) of complex persons cannot be reduced to one kind of functioning, capability justice must therefore be concerned with flourishing in 'different life-dimensions' (ibid: 260), including the plurality of work timespaces. However, although Nussbaum's concern is for the individual, individual capability development is not just about striving to become a fully realised individual, it is also about being related to others through continuing and mutually beneficial bonds: 'the highest richness for each human being is *other human beings* and such a richness is felt in the form of a *need'* (Marx, 1978 [1844]). Consequently, relations which simply secure respect are not sufficient but must include those based upon a strong normative relationality and meaningful connection.

Capabilities Approach and the need for meaningful work

Nussbaum's Capabilities Approach (CA) draws upon Marx's proposition that advancing social conditions bring people to an awareness of their inner potentialities, resulting in the proliferation of human needs, and stimulating demands that society be organised to enable the realisation of those potentialities. Marx says:

> It will be seen how in place of the *wealth* and *poverty* of political economy come the *rich human being* and the rich human need. The *rich* human being is simultaneously the human being *in need of* a totality of human-life activities – the man in whom his own realization exists as an inner necessity, as *need* (Marx, 1844, in Nussbaum, 1987: 45).

It is clear that Nussbaum's principle of individual development is grounded in Marx's maxim of individual self-realisation in association with others where 'the free development of each is the condition of the free development of all' (Marx, Communist Manifesto, Chapt 2). She acknowledges her closeness to Marx when she argues that 'the basic intuitive idea of my version of the capabilities approach is [...] a life that has available to it "truly human functioning" in the sense described by Marx' (Nussbaum, 2006: 74–5). For Nussbaum, the task of societies is not simply to keep people alive by providing enough food, shelter, or paid work, but to secure their capabilities for living a life worthy of a human being, where human needs are expressed and fulfilled in ways consistent with their humanity. Consequently, we do not fulfil 'perceptual needs in a mechanical way, producing a seeing eye, a hearing ear, etc' but rather 'make it possible for people to use their bodies and their senses in a truly human way' (Nussbaum, 1987: 183). When individuals experience the plurality of their human potential to be an urgent need, then a politics of meaningfulness emerges which stimulates the development of society by bringing to public awareness the human need for meaning, and fostering democratic deliberation over what institutional forms and what human capabilities are required to satisfy this need.

Indeed, the very presence of needs indicates what is required to be fully human. Braybrooke (1998d) says that to experience a richness of need is evidence of an advanced condition of human development, which obliges society to secure the development of human capabilities for all: 'the multiplication of desire needs in the successor society will accompany an expansion of human powers' (ibid: 22). As more individuals experience the need for meaningfulness as an interior, urgent, and fundamental need to live a fully human life, then the desire for interesting work becomes, not just an elite preoccupation, but an indication of normal functioning: 'Functioning with normal health and alertness as a citizen and worker may require in the successor society that people have interesting work' (ibid: 26). It is important to note, however, that there are limits to any one person's capability development which are set by the egalitarian principle that all be able to experience the development necessary for achieving human flourishing to a satisfying level. This means that no one should be living a meaningful life through the unfair acquisition of capabilities for meaningfulness, such as: exploiting the capabilities of others to enable one's own functioning; or valuing only those capabilities of others which serve the meaning content of one's own life; or stunting the development of the capabilities of others through disproportionate command over the resources and means to realise functionings.

When meaningful work is construed as a fundamental human need, a general and unavoidable need which is felt as an interior lack, then individuals are more likely to suffer harm as a consequence of impediments to their human flourishing: 'Without food, human beings perish. Without labor, they falter in development; and in functioning, once development has proceeded that far' (ibid: 25). Although human beings have always suffered from the lack of meaningful work, its scarcity in contemporary societies constitutes a peculiarly modern kind of deprivation. This is because, whilst contemporary societies demand that all persons acquire advanced capabilities for normal functioning, participation, and belonging – capabilities which are formed and exercised through work with the requisite content – the organisation of work acts to constrain the variety and complexity of action contexts in which such capabilities can be formed. In other words, the demand to acquire and to exercise advanced capabilities as a condition of social and economic participation has not been matched by the supply of work with the necessary structure.

So, if meaningful work is a need, then it is an unmet need. I argue that the need for meaningful work meets Wiggins's criteria for a basic need which is both absolute and entrenched (Wiggins, 1998): it is *absolute* because it is an invariant fact about human beings that they need freedom, autonomy, and social recognition, needs which if they remain unmet mean that a person will suffer harm, and it is *entrenched* because the centrality of work in contemporary societies means that it is difficult for people to avoid the harmful consequences of being deprived of meaningful work. Wiggins (1998) says 'freedom, choice and autonomy are themselves vital human needs, and are candidates for precisely the kind of protection that is accorded qua needs to other real needs' (ibid: 327). The presence of inescapable human interests in autonomy, freedom, and social recognition implies, in modern societies, a fundamental human need for meaningful work, which is no longer solely an elite concern, but is necessary for each person to lead a human life of equivalent functioning to every other individual. The basic need for meaningfulness in work is met through the formation and exercise of the relevant capabilities (cf. Alkire, 2005) for objective valuing and subjective attachment – although constrained by a functioning politics of meaningfulness which sets limits upon what each person is justified in doing to others in order to promote their own interests in meaningful work.

The central human capabilities

Nussbaum's list of central human capabilities consists of: living a life of normal length; being in good health and receiving adequate nourishment; freedom of movement and freedom from physical assault; being able to use one's senses, imagination, and thought in a 'truly human way'; being able to have emotional relationships with people and attachments to things, including loving and grieving, and freedom from excessive fear or anxiety; being able to form one's own conception of the good (practical reason); being able to live in cooperative relations with others which include being treated in ways which are non-humiliating and which afford self-respect (affiliation); being able to play and engage in recreational activities; and being able to participate in forms of political and property relations which promote autonomy (Nussbaum, 2000: 78–80). Nussbaum specifies two thresholds, one for basic functioning and another for good human functioning: 'a threshold of capability to function, beneath which a life will be so impoverished that it will not be human at all, and a somewhat higher threshold, beneath which those characteristic functions are available in such a reduced way that although we judge the form of life a human one, we will not think it a *good* human life' (Nussbaum, 1992: 221). The different elements of the central capabilities are irreducibly plural (Nussbaum, 2000: 81), because we 'cannot satisfy the need for one of them by giving a larger amount of another' (ibid).

Nussbaum specifies further features of her CA (Nussbaum, 2000: 84–5). Firstly, the realisation of central capabilities depends upon the progressive combination of three kinds of capabilities – basic, internal, and external. *Basic* capabilities are those we are born with – they are innate but rudimentary and consist of capabilities such as being able to see or hear. *Internal* capabilities are the trained, developed, and mature capacities and powers which place a person in a position of readiness to convert capabilities into functionings. *Combined* capabilities are internal capabilities united to the external conditions which allow the actual exercise of a human functioning, where Nussbaum's central human capabilities are a list of combined functionings. Secondly, Nussbaum gives two capabilities – practical reason and affiliation – a particular place of importance: they are architechtonic (Nussbaum, 1992: 222) because they 'organise and suffuse all the others, making their pursuit truly human' (Nussbaum, 2000: 82). This means, for example, that 'the functioning of performing a job becomes a truly human activity only when the employee is given the opportunity to exercise her practical reason and to form it with and towards others' (Alexander, 2003: 12). The architechtonic capabilities are not, however, ends which reduce other capabilities to means, but special capabilities which make the exercise of all the others distinctively human: 'all items should be available in a manner which involves reason and affiliation' (Nussbaum, 2000: 82). All the central capabilities have the potential to be exercised with human distinctiveness, underpinning the normative claim that the object of political action and public policy ought to be the development of these capabilities for every person, including the social conditions for their exercise: 'The basic intuition from which the capability approach begins, in the political arena, is that certain human abilities exert a moral claim that they should be developed' (Nussbaum, 2000: 83).

Work in the capability for control over our environment

Nussbaum (1995) situates work in the central human capability of being in control over our own environment (ibid: 42; Nussbaum, 2000: 79–80), which she describes as follows:

> A. Political – being able to participate effectively in political choices that govern one's life; having the right of political participation, protections of free speech and association.
> B. Material – being able to hold property (both land and moveable goods), and having property rights on an equal basis with others; having the right to seek employment on an equal basis with others; having the freedom from unwarranted search and seizure. In work, being able to work as a human being, exercising practical reason and entering into meaningful relationships of mutual recognition with other workers (Nussbaum, 1995: 42).

The architectonic capabilities for practical reasoning and affiliation imply that work must be activity of the requisite content, if it is to support cooperative relations, afford social recognition, and enable the exercise of practical judgement. Taken together, this suggests work must consist of humanising activities since 'some forms of labor simply are mindless and exhausting enough to make it impossible for the worker to lead a fully human life and the worker himself becomes a commodity' (Radin, 1996: 74). Furthermore, in order to secure work of the requisite content for all persons, then the institutional arrangements and resources of the polity must be structured so that 'everyone can cross the threshold into capability to choose well' (Radin, 1996: 72–3). But such a conclusion renders unsatisfactory Nussbaum's specification of work in the material requirement of 'being in control of our environment' because she does not specify the interior content of the work people do together, consistent with a positive critical conception of meaningful work.

Moreover, by maintaining the distinction between the material and the political, Nussbaum separates work from its political basis, thereby limiting the means available to workers to contest the organisation and structure of work. For work to be meaningful, we need to belong to a wide variety of structures containing roles, practices, and institutions which Williams (2008) describes as the 'self-reflexive web of institutions' (ibid: 465), making up the overlapping practices of social cooperation in complex modern societies. Moreover, Sciaraffa (2011) argues that we have an obligation not merely to belong but to participate in institutional maintenance (ibid: 122), in order to ensure that institutions embody social roles which are 'sufficiently rich and complex to sustain the goods of meaning and self-determination' (ibid: 123). A rich plurality of goods, in the form of positive meanings and values, are more likely to be maintained in work organised along democratic lines, that is, in enterprises governed by democratic authority which encourages affective attachments to worthy objects, because, by having a share in the rules shaping ways of being and acting, we increase our sense of responsible ownership and worthiness to act with others. In order to make this experience available to as many people as possible, we must encourage a plurality of democratic associations, from cooperatives, employee-owned businesses, mutuals, and social enterprises to charities, civic associations, and conventional economic organisations (see Restakis, 2010).

Thus the material and political are not separate spheres, but implicated within one another, where the political basis of work is established through a system of workplace democracy. Indeed, Nussbaum links the content of work to the need for social transformation when she says that 'some forms of labor are incompatible with good human functioning' (Nussbaum, in Radin, 1996: 73), and calls for 'a searching examination of the forms of labor and the relations of production, and for the construction of fully human and sociable forms of labor for all citizens with an eye to all forms of human functioning' (ibid: 74). Nussbaum proposes:

> The idea is that the entire structure of the polity will be designed with a view to these functions. Not only programs of allocation but also the division of land, the arrangements of forms of ownership, the structure of labor relations, institutional support for forms of family and social affiliation, ecological policy and policy towards animals, institutions of political participation, recreational institutions – all these, as well as more concrete programs within these areas, will be chosen with a view to good human functioning (Nussbaum, in Radin, 1996: 240).

Hence, Nussbaum's theory of capability justice supports the transformation of the institutional and economic arrangements which structure work. Consequently, the object of justice, informed by a politics of meaningfulness in work, must be to ensure 'work regimes' which 'enlarge and assure particular human capacities that can be seen as universally essential for those who labour in a civilized society' (Pocock, 2006: 1). In short, we are led to consider the prospects for a socialised economy, where democratically organised enterprises able to support the development and exercise of the Capability for Voice are instituted through an appropriate regulatory framework (Hall & Purcell, 2012).

A politics of meaningfulness and the Capability for Voice

Voice is needed for an individual to have a share in the co-decision necessary for functioning as an equal co-authority in the creation and maintenance of positive values which inhere in worthy objects. In a politics of meaningfulness, a Capability for Voice supports the development of the capabilities for objective valuing and subjective attachment, helping us to become valuers capable of evaluating what is worth doing and being, and of incorporating these valuations into practical identities which give our lives a sense of meaning. Drawing upon Sen's Capability Approach, a Capability for Voice consists of both an individual and social dimension (cf. Bonvin & Farvaque, 2006). The *individual* dimension of the Capability for Voice is constitutively inter-subjective, that is, dependent for its formation and exercise upon our inter-relations to others in the groups to which we belong. The *social* dimension of the Capability for Voice is provided by a diverse associa-tional landscape of economic, social, and political organisations embodying a plurality of positive values. Thus, the Capability for Voice depends upon personal characteristics, such as self-confidence and dis-cursive abilities, and upon the responsiveness of the institutional envi-ronment to expressed concerns (Bonvin & Farvaque, 2006). Bonvin & Farvaque (2006) describe a capability for work as 'the real freedom to choose the work one has reason to value' (ibid: 126), implying that since there are some forms of work which we do not have reason to value, then a capability for work depends upon being able to distin-guish between valuable and non-valuable work – and moreover, being able to do something about non-valuable work:

> The capability approach requires that all people be adequately equipped to escape from the constraint of valueless work, either through the real possibility of refusing such a job (with a valuable alternative, be it a financial compensation or another job), or through the possibility of transforming it into something else one 'has reason to value'. Thus capability for work implies either a) capa-bility not to work if one chooses (via a valuable *exit* option); or b) capability to participate effectively in the definition of work content, organisation, conditions, modes of remuneration, etc. (the *voice* option) (Bonvin & Farvaque, 2006: 126, original emphasis).

Since most people cannot readily shake off the work upon which they are dependent for an income, then the 'capability for work' is not simply about being employable, it is also about being able to parti-cipate in the 'shaping of the social context in order to make it more professionally and socially inclusive' (Bonvin & Farvaque, 2006: 127). Democratic participation which aims at involving people in shaping the framing rules which construct their subjectivities and action con-texts is inherent to a capability for work which is worth doing, and which supports the development of human capabilities relevant to eco-nomic participation over the life course. This requires the Capability for Voice in the work one does with others, thereby integrating the material and political dimensions of Nussbaum's capability for control over one's environment.

The Capability for Voice is 'the ability to express one's opinions and thoughts, and to make them count in the course of public discussion' (Bonvin & Farvaque, 2006: 127), where the concept of capability combines individual agency or 'what the individual is able to do' with social agency or 'what opportunities are open to him' (Bonvin, 2003). De Munck (de Munck & Ferreras, 2004) specifies three aspects to the Capability for Voice: firstly, it is a constitutive element of 'Freedom of Choice', because, in a fair society, each person ought to have the opportunity to publicly deliberate over the opportunities for acting and for being which society makes available to her; secondly, it is grounded in the plurality of individual abilities, but enabled by social conditions, such as information, collective support, communication, being listened to, and understood by others; and thirdly, it is dependent upon social institutions, such as rights (freedom of speech) and social conversion factors to convert the capability into valuable functionings. Bohman (1996) specifies three conditions for achieving a genuine Capability for Voice: firstly, equality of access must be guaranteed, which goes beyond formal equality to the real ability to access public debate, to express one's views and to be listened to; secondly, the publicity of the debate avoids the discretionary use of decision-making power, including access to independent courts of appeal; and thirdly, freedom of speech for all involved.

In Sen's Capability Approach, the Capability for Voice requires both individual abilities and social agency: *individual* abilities to express rational arguments, to influence, and to persuade others, and *social* agency, such as a supportive legislative framework, including avenues of appeal. This means that a full and equal Capability for Voice requires a transformation of the interior content of work, such that the capability for work itself must be reformed, if it is to be consistent with the bipartite value of meaningfulness. As I have already discussed, there is a difference between having a share in participation, as taking part in an activity, and having a share in power, as having a degree of influence over an activity (Heller, 2003). And in order for the Capability for Voice to be realised as having a share of power in decision-making, then the structure of the Capability for Voice must follow Sen's Capability Approach in having both an opportunity dimension and a process dimension.

Opportunity is 'the extent to which the actors possess the means, instruments or permissions to pursue what they would like to do; and are *actually* able to do things they would value doing' (Sen, 2005: 153, my emphasis). It is concerned with the equity and efficiency of the means, instruments, and resources the institutional framework provides to workers to pursue what they consider to be valuable, and the extent to which it enables them to actually pursue what they value. Having a share in power or 'influence-sharing' depends practically upon both social and individual agency. *Social agency* is concerned with the institutional mechanisms at the micro, meso, and macro levels of economic democracy which address the workers' interest in the actual means they have to pursue what they value, and how they make use of such means (Deakin & Koukiadaki, 2009: 25; see also Koukiadaki, 2010). *Individual agency* combines the basic ableness of the individual with social agency to produce: personal competence in handling information, cooperating and influencing others, a democratic consciousness, trust and confidence in others. When individual ableness is combined with social mechanisms and opportunities for participation in decision-making, then we have to hand the opportunity dimension of the Capability for Voice.

Process identifies what procedures exist to structure decisions and create the conditions for consultation, negotiation, and decision-making. In a system of workplace democracy, process specifies how social dialogue between management and workers takes place (ibid: 30). People define, *in situ*, the criteria for decision-making processes and collective choices, requiring the development of institutional mechanisms and cultural support for collective decision-making (Deakin & Koukiadaki, 2009: 6). The extent of decision-making capability is defined by the degree of control workers enjoy over decision-making, the range of issues over which they exercise control, and the organisation level at which control is exercised. This demands procedures for decision-making, given by consultation, deliberation, negotiation, and agreement. Furthermore, full equality of participation requires the group life to be organised to make visible the agonistic dimensions of the discursive interactions between individuals. Gustavsen (1992) suggests that a process of 'democratic dialogue' will have the following characteristics: it must be possible for all concerned to participate; not only must everybody participate, but each person must be active; everybody has an obligation, not only to put forward his or her own ideas, but also to help others to contribute theirs; each participant must accept that other participants can have better arguments; and finally the dialogue must continuously produce agreements that can provide platforms for practical action (see also Gustavsen, 1985).

Conversion factors for the Capability for Voice

I identify two institutional guarantees which are required to satisfy the principle of egalitarian meaning and the threshold of sufficient meaning: a basic income guarantee and a workplace democracy guarantee. A *basic income guarantee* operates to promote the principle of egalitarian meaning by ensuring the social recognition of a wide range of activities in a system of social cooperation. A *workplace democracy guarantee* operates to promote the threshold of sufficient meaning by enabling a plurality of mediating institutions organised along democratic lines which are conducive to fostering agonic democratic practices at the level of the task, and democratic authority at the level of the organisation. Together, a basic income and workplace democracy constitute the conversion factors for realising the Capability for Voice.

The conversion of capabilities into functionings depends upon resources, favourable background conditions, and human activity. Robeyns (2003) identifies three kinds of conversion factors influencing the transformation of resources into capabilities – personal, social, and environmental. Conversion factors are both context- and individual-dependent: for example, the ability to participate in training opportunities for any particular individual may depend upon company policies (environmental), individual ability to use informal organisational resources (personal), and access to childcare (social) (Bartelheimer et al, 2009): 'this concept of situatedness is at the very centre of the capability approach' (Bonvin & Thelen, 2003). For successful conversion and development of capabilities for conversion, individuals need to be situated in a 'capability-friendly social context' which enables the individual to 'enjoy the real freedom to convert her command over commodities into valuable beings and doings' (Bonvin & Farvaque, 2006: 124). This means that for any particular individual to be able to experience the functioning of a Capability for Voice two kinds of conversion factors are required: a system of workplace democracy and a basic income.

Workplace democracy

In order to secure the internal conditions for stable organisation-based democracy a society-wide infrastructure to support deliberative engagement is required. In his evaluation of societal systems of economic democracy, Brogger (2010) identifies two forms of participatory engagement: firstly, social dialogue, or collective bargaining between employees and management, and secondly, human resource management practices (HRM) which aim at raising the involvement of the individual employee. However, Brogger (2010) suggests that the Scandinavian tradition of 'democratic dialogue' is distinctive because it steers a course between collective bargaining and HRM approaches, where democratic dialogue is 'a praxis informed by sociotechnical, psychosocial and discourse perspectives, developed along with the national systems of industrial relations' (ibid).[1] Moreover, Brogger argues that, although arenas and procedures for participative decision-making are necessary, they are not sufficient – what is also required is a 'consolidated, independent source of influence of continuity' (ibid: 491), or an institutional support system which provides employees with autonomy from the hierarchy and a basis for collective action (see also Frege, 2005; Crouch, 1993; Wiedermann, 1980).

In the UK, recent legislation in the form of the 2004 Information and Consultation of Employees (ICE) regulations represent an attempt to provide the necessary institutional support for employee voice. These regulations were established in response to the EU Directive on *Informing and Consulting Employees*. They were applicable after 2008 to enterprises with more than 50 employees, and were anticipated as a 'realignment of institutional arrangements to enable workers to have a voice' (Dundon & Gollan, 2007: 1183; see also Dundon et al, 2004). However, case studies of attempts to implement the regulations show that the dimension of 'voice' is often constrained to influence and appearance, rather than joint authority over decision-making: 'responsibility for decision-making ultimately remains with management' (Gollan & Wilkinson, 2007: 1138; see also Wilkinson et al, 2007; Hall & Purcell, 2012). Such forms of pseudo-participation fuel criticisms of 'participation as a gloss on the biased structures of capitalism' (Beirne, 2008: 679), where the objective of participation initiatives is to promote the aims of management, rather than to realise the transformation of authority relations (Harley et al, 2005), or the creation of decent work (Ghai, 2003).

Voluntary regulations ensure that the institutionalisation of workplace democracy remains in the gift of management, rather than entitlement due to all those who make their contribution to the work of social cooperation. The capacity of management to withdraw, at any time, the opportunity structure necessary to a Capability for Voice, undermines the institutional stability and civic trust on which voice depends, and is a form of domination as arbitrary interference. Wegge et al (2010, also 2008) identify the importance of 'structurally anchored organisational democracy' including 'broad-based and institutionalised employee influence processes that are not ad hoc or occasional in nature' (ibid: 162). Such processes involve moving away from the leader-subordinate dyad to 'the constructive participation of all organisational members in the creation and implementation of organisational values, norms and rules' (Verdofer et al, 2012). Wegge et al (2010: 154) show that employee involvement in organisational leadership (EIOL) occurs where there is a 'division of leadership tasks between different people at several levels of the organization' (Avolio et al, 2009; Gronn, 2002; Pearce & Conger, 2003). They identify three forms of EIOL: organisational participation instituting processes where power and influence, as well as decision-making and responsibility, are shared; shared leadership which is a collaborative, emergent process of group interaction (Pearce & Sims, 2002); and organisational democracy where there is an 'organisational climate of ongoing, broad-based and institutionalised employee participation which also includes self-governed enterprises' (Wegge et al, 2010: 155). In my argument for the relationship between democratic practices and meaningfulness in work, the emancipatory potential of many different kinds of work is more likely to be realised where there is a broad-based system of organisational democracy. Under such a regime, the full Capability for Voice is secured through a system of organisational democracy and supported by an appropriate regulatory framework. Moreover, it becomes an entitlement which places obligations upon management to institute and maintain. A robust system of workplace democracy will unite a formal representative system with an informal, direct participatory system. However, it also requires the further condition of a background civic culture of meanings and norms which support participation and involvement. Verdofer et al (2012) identify the important relation between organisational democracy and an appropriate socio-moral climate for generating democratic orientations. In Weber et al (2008), such a socio-moral climate is characterised by: open confrontation of employees with conflicts, reliable and constant appreciation, care and support by supervisors and colleagues, open communication and participative cooperation, trust-based assignment and allocation of responsibility according to capabilities, and organisational concern for the individual.

In sum, the Capability for Voice needs, in addition to opportunity and process which are internal to the organisation of work, external conversion factors. These are provided for by, at a minimum, a regulatory framework, which obliges management to create and sustain an organisational democracy. I argue below that these external conversion factors imply further a diversity of mediating institutions and a basic income for all within a socialised economic system.

Institutional variety

Institutions are accumulations of the roles and practices which are sources of internal goods and the means for self-development. Hodgson (2006) defines institutions as 'systems of established and prevalent social rules that structure social relations' (ibid: 2). They operate to enable and to constrain what people can do through established rules and habits: 'institutions work only because the rules involved are embedded in shared habits of thought and behaviour' (ibid: 6), where habits are 'the constitutive material of institutions, providing them with enhanced durability, power, and normative authority' (ibid: 7). Hodgson identifies how habits are the key mechanism for transforming individual behaviour, because they influence the range and extent of human ambition, both as individuals and as members of a collective (ibid: 7). Moreover, Hodgson identifies how institutions are dependent upon individuals for their continued existence and renewal, both through the dispositions of individual persons and through the structured interactions between persons: 'institutions are simultaneously both objective structures "out there" and subjective springs of human agency "in the human head"' (ibid: 8). Thus, persons and institutional structures are 'connected in a circle of mutual interaction and interdependence' (ibid).

In a capability framework, institutions, because they structure our practices and roles (Williams, 2006: 210) determine the opportunity dimension of the capabilities for objective valuing and subjective attachment in a politics of meaningfulness. They are accumulations of the positive values which society makes available for appropriation to the meaning content of our lives. And they enable us to fulfil our responsibilities towards the things we value (Williams, 2006: 209), because they distribute resources, provide us roles through which we can claim the involvement of others, and constitute the public arenas where we can deliberate with others over standards of care. In institutions, we encounter worthy objects, and form the on-going commitments and attachments which structure our lives as a whole: 'people live their lives amid complex, networks of overlapping institutions' (Williams, 2006: 207). Williams identifies how 'technologies of organisation' (ibid: 2008) have produced varied roles in a system of social cooperation which give us 'the freedom to participate in ways that are meaningful by one's own lights' (ibid: 209), and which enable our deliberations over values to become reflexively related to our affiliations and activities. Institutions provide vital resources for the development of attachments which enable meaning attribution because, firstly, the roles generated by institutions structure our activities and our evaluation of our activities in morally important ways (ibid: 210); secondly, institutions provide for the legitimate allocation of power and responsibility by enabling a 'background working consensus to mediate disagreement' (ibid: 212), and, by mirroring the liberal notion of 'divided powers', facilitating accountability and trust; and thirdly, institutions provide sites for individual recognition and a minimal level of social solidarity which are vital to the development of personal identity: 'our interactions are structured in ways that lead us to recognise others as fellow participants in many different spheres of life' (ibid: 215).

Furthermore, Williams (2006) identifies the importance of institutional variety in providing for the individual recognition which is a 'crucial condition for moral agency' (ibid: 215). A 'plurality of institutions' engenders 'infrastructures of responsibility' (Scheffler, in Williams, 2006: 214); they enable us to express the various roles which form the vital basis of our self-conception. Much of the work we do is therefore concerned with the maintenance and development of the social institutions constituting our common life, which reflects Arendt's exhortation that we should have a 'care for the world' (Arendt, 1958), or the fabricated world of structured relations which enable us to lead a fully human life. Out of our experiences of belonging to institutions structured by common activities, we form the particular attachments to worthy objects; and having access to institutional membership enables us to fulfil our responsibilities towards those worthy objects, thereby imbuing our acts of work with expressive meaning and purpose.

But not all institutions contain normatively positive arrangements of roles, practices, and common activities, making it necessary for us to specify the democratic character of institutions which are conducive to realising the value of meaningfulness. Democratic organisations are a reliable social conversion factor for the Capability for Voice, activating individual agency by providing people with the opportunity to participate in collective decision-making. Bernstein (1976) distinguishes participatory mechanisms along three dimensions: degree of control employees enjoy over decision-making; range of issues over which they exercise control; organisational level at which control is exercised.

These are necessary, but not sufficient, for 'the bare structure of participation to become an on-going self-reinforcing system of employee power' (ibid: 497), and he adds several additional components: employee access to and sharing of management information; guaranteed protection of the employee from reprisals for voicing criticisms (plus other rights); an independent board of appeals to settle disputes between managers and those being managed (separation of powers), a particular set of attitudes and values (political consciousness); 'frequent return to participating employees of at least a portion of the surplus they produce' (above their regular wage). Moreover, 'for maximum benefit to the collective there is a particular mix of management authority and democratic control, the precise proportions of which have to be found by each case through its own experience' (ibid: 498). Thus democratically organised enterprises possess identifiable and coherent features which foster the Capability for Voice. Most importantly, democratically organised enterprises change the basis of ownership and governance, underpinning our sense of worthiness to act and to speak which secures our equal status as co-authorities in the realm of value.

Basic income

A basic income (BI) guarantee supports autonomy, freedom, and social recognition in the interior content of work, because, when it is at a sufficient level to secure material independence, people are more likely to possess the real 'capacity for making choices in all domains of life with the security that [...] nobody will have the remotest chance of arbitrarily interfering in their individual life plan decisions' (Casassas, 2007). An unconditional BI grants individuals 'bargaining power' (ibid: 4) in their intersubjective encounters which supports the Capability for Voice, as people bring interpretive differences into public deliberation through democratic practices at the level of the task, and seek to recruit each other in the fulfilment of the responsibilities to the worthy objects which they have appropriated to the meaning content of their lives.

Van Parijs (1997) defends 'real libertarianism' which he proposes is realised in a social order 'that could afford, and would actually implement, the highest sustainable unconditional income, subject to the constraint that everyone's formal freedom should be protected' (ibid: 1). The Principle of Egalitarian Meaning is satisfied when there is the widest range values which people can choose to appropriate to the meaning content of their lives. In the work of social cooperation, this requires an expansion of the activities which are recognised as work, in the sense that there are a plurality of activities, both paid and unpaid, which contribute to the reproduction of society. In a politics of meaningfulness, an unconditional basic income helps to secure a plurality of values in the work of social cooperation, bringing to light values and meanings of work which have been rendered invisible by the standard economic model. Standard arguments for a basic income are grounded in the value of reciprocity, but a BI which is established to secure meaningful work is the means to multiplying the range of recognised activities and the values they embody. For example, those engaged in caring work are not motivated by an 'immediate reciprocal contribution', but by affective attachments (Pateman, 2007: 3). Pateman suggests that the importance of a BI lies, not in the value of immediate mutual reciprocity, but in the opportunity it affords citizens '*not to be employed*' (ibid: 5) because 'employment is undemocratic, a vast area of hierarchy and subordination within supposedly democratic societies' (ibid: 4). Furthermore, the pluralisation of values is encouraged by the role basic income plays in capability security, which directs public policy to what is required to ensure that people can rely upon their capabilities into the future. A basic income means that no person need be forced to neglect or pass up on chosen functionings, or be forced by necessity to pursue functionings they do not value. Where there is an unconditional basic income up to the highest sustainable level, no person need do degraded work in order to avoid immiseration; it also affords society as a whole an opportunity to evaluate the 'undemocratic character of employment' and 'the meaning of work' (Pateman, 2007: 5).

Securing the material basis for the requisite content of work through a basic income guarantee ought not to be implemented in the absence of a critical evaluation and reform of the present organisation of work, in particular, the gendered division of labour. Robeyns (2001) warns that simply applying a basic income with no regard for the position of individuals may do more harm than good. She argues that paying some women a basic income, without altering systemic disadvantage and discrimination in the division of labour, would end up 'sending women back home and tempering emancipation' (ibid: 103). The unequal distribution of labour in the home, replicated in the structure of the labour market, is unlikely to be altered through an increase in women's bargaining power without a corresponding change in the structure of paid and unpaid work. Robeyns' critique implies that a basic income must operate within a system of capability justice, where the position of the individual with respect to her ability to convert innate capabilities into combined capabilities, and then into the functionings of her choice, is what counts in considerations of justice. Where the purpose of a basic income is individual self-determination (Pateman, 2004), then a basic income is a means to 'the creation of a more democratic society in which individual freedom and citizenship are of equal worth for everyone' and to expanding women's freedom (ibid: 90). Pateman says that 'individual self-government depends not only on the opportunities available but also on the form of authority structure within which individuals interact with one another in their daily lives' (ibid: 91). Some commentators are concerned that a basic income would undermine participation in paid work, which they see as formative for cultivating the virtues of citizenship (Dagger, 2006): 'basic income, according to this view, is a direct subsidy of civic vice' (White, 2008: 5). This would imply that a just society must be concerned with the boundaries between different kinds of work (Young, 2006) – who does what, when, and where. In this way, a basic income guarantee can secure the Principle of Egalitarian Meaning only in combination with the Threshold of Sufficient Meaning, where the threshold is specified by democratic equality in the interior content of work.

Finally, some commentators have suggested that the capability approach does not directly address the relations of production and domination which stunt human capabilities (Bagchi, 2000). However, this critique can be countered by recognising in work both the political and the material basis of control over our environment, which, to ensure equal capabilities for the functioning of meaningfulness in work, implies a reordering of social and economic arrangements. Enhancing human capabilities will strengthen the resistance of individuals to domination, provided that the basic structure of society contains non-dominating, capability-enhancing work timespaces, thus enabling the widespread availability of work structured by the value of meaningfulness. A society based upon respecting equal human worth requires that market efficiency be defined by the extent to which the economic system supports the development of central human capabilities, including the capability for meaning attribution. Work with the correct structure for meaningfulness will be established through a plurality of democratically organised actions contexts, where such work is enabled by positive promotion of human capabilities (Gould, 1990), and negative protection from arbitrary interference (Hsieh, 2008). In sum, by requiring the end to de-humanising, unfree, and alienating work, capability justice addresses how we will secure the social and political institution of meaningful work for all.

Conclusion

I have sought to identify the philosophical basis of a political agenda which attends to the importance of meaningfulness in work. In order to diversify and expand the range of work which is conducive to meaningfulness, I have argued for a set of institutional guarantees, including an entitlement to democratic participation in determining the purposes, means, and circumstances of the work one does through the Capability for Voice. Moreover, specifying institutional guarantees implies a public policy suite designed to secure meaningful work for all, including: a good work index; a basic income guarantee; an entitlement to individual capability development through institutional belonging; a regulatory framework establishing direct and representative employee voice, which includes the collective voice of union representation; an equal playing field for different organisational forms, such as mutuals, cooperatives, and employee-owned enterprises – and a general dismantling of hierarchies or networks which foster the arbitrary use of power through non-democratic authority.

In proposing that institutional guarantees are necessary to ensure that the principle of egalitarian meaning and the threshold of sufficient meaning are secured in all the work we do together, some further comments are warranted: firstly, I am not suggesting we attempt to guarantee that all persons should actually find their lives to be meaningful; secondly, neither am I suggesting that we try to guarantee meaningfulness in every dimension of human living, at every moment in time and across the whole of a lifespan; thirdly, the threshold does not guarantee that any particular individual will find any particular work activity or social role meaningful; but I do claim that, fourthly, the inescapable interests met by the fundamental human need for meaningful work entails that all persons are equally entitled to find their lives to be meaningful because of the work that they do – and that social and political arrangements should not impede their search for meaning.

I have described a politics of meaningfulness which has the realisation of a positive critical conception of meaningful work in its sights. Furthermore, I have established that, in contemporary societies where work is a central activity, meaningful work is not a preference in the market, but a fundamental human need. In my positive critical conception of meaningful work, the conceptual content of meaningfulness is given by Wolf's distinct bipartite value of meaningfulness, which unites objective valuing to subjective attachment. In her construction of the value of meaningfulness, Wolf is seeking to respond to Frankfurt's (1982) question of what we should care about; to which his reply is that what you should care about is 'what it is *possible* for you to care about' (Wolf, 2002: 227). Having things we can care about is vital to a flourishing life, but since 'it is not so easy for most of us to find things that we are capable of loving' (Frankfurt, 2004: 94), Frankfurt suggests that we choose the objects of our care according to our ability to undertake the relevant activities of care. And moreover, we must choose something to care about because otherwise we will lack the motivational sources for any kind of acting at all:

> It seems that it must be the fact that it is possible for him to care about the one and not the other, to care about the one in a way which is more important to him than the way in which it is possible for him to care about the other [...] The person does not care about the object because its worthiness commands that he do so. On the other hand, the worthiness of the activity of caring commands that he choose an object that he will be able to care about (ibid).

Wolf is concerned that to simply care 'about what you can' (ibid) fails to take account of what is *worth* caring about (Wolf, 2002: 227). Instead, she seeks to establish an inescapable relationship between the objective and subjective dimensions of meaningfulness, such that when something is worthy of love or affinity then our involvement with those objects contributes to the meaningfulness of our lives. She does not allow that this implies we should care about persons, or even objects, only if they possess worthy qualities, such as intelligence or beauty (ibid: 230). Instead, she argues that we should simply not ignore the connection between care and worthiness: 'worth figures in, somehow, to what is desirable to care about, but not exclusively or

perhaps decisively' (ibid: 231). We want our lives to have positive connections to objects which are independently valuable, so that
'meaning in life arises when affinity and worth meet' (ibid: 237), and
when the focus of our efforts lacks worth, then our lives also lack
meaning. Responding to Wolf's critique, Frankfurt replies that his
concern is to establish the importance of the activity of loving to a
person's life (Frankfurt, 2002: 245), and that 'since loving as such is
valuable, it is reasonable to desire it for its own sake' (ibid). Thus, no
matter the worthiness of the object, a person's life is made better for
him or her, just so long as he or she is engaged in practices of care.
Hitler, for example, cared deeply about the success of Nazism, and his
life was enhanced by having such profound concerns (ibid: 246): 'an
enthusiastically meaningful life need not be connected to anything
that is objectively valuable, nor need it include any thought that the
things to which it is devoted are good' (ibid: 250). Frankfurt makes the
important point that it is the activity of caring, itself, which creates
value and meaning: 'meaning in life is created by loving' (ibid). The
activity of care, itself, generates worthy objects, and forms us as
creators of value – in the process, rescuing us from the frustrations of
having to find sources of independent value: 'locating the source of
meaning in the activity of loving renders opportunities for meaningful
life much more readily accessible' (ibid: 250). Rather than starting out
from worthy objects to which we attach ourselves, we start by engaging in acts of care towards whatever objects it is possible for us to care
about, acts which establish the value of the objects of our attention,
because we make them worth caring about through the exercise of our
meaning-making capabilities – and in the process, we form ourselves as
worthy objects by becoming creators of value.

There is much to be sympathetic with in this account, and I have
made use of it in my incorporation of an ethic of care into the value of
meaningfulness, arguing that meaning in life depends upon our
becoming valuers with the status for being co-authorities, and the
capabilities for objective valuing and subjective attachment. But
Frankfurt's concern centres too much upon the caring person whose
life is made better by engaging in care, taking insufficient account of
the effect that person's concerns or actions may have upon the object
of care, or upon the wider society in which that person is situated. So,
Hitler's caring may have been of benefit to his own life, but he transferred the terrible costs of his caring onto the lives of others, and this
transgresses the commitments of an ethic of care which focuses our

attention upon what is good for the worthy object, and how our activities of care impact others and society at large.

This means that others have an interest in, not only what we care about, but also what we do about our caring. And these interests are given voice through public meaning-making in the form of deliberative democratic evaluation of the worthiness of objects and the place they ought to have in our lives. At this point, Wolf provides us with a useful corrective to Frankfurt's concentration upon the caring person, because she situates her objective valuing in a pluralistic framework 'against the background assumption that the facts about our value are likely to be highly pluralistic and complex and that in consequence our approach to questions of objective value should be tolerant and open-minded' (Wolf, 2002: 237). The presence of background assumptions opens up the possibility for contestation and challenge as to what constitutes such values, and what impact they have upon the objects of care and society at large. So, securing the dimension of objectivity in the value of meaningfulness does not mean a narrowing of the range of values, but instead requires a broadening out of what it means to be a valuer, because objectivity demands an active engagement with the background assumptions and a shifting of perspective from the carer to the cared for. In this sense, establishing objectivity is a practical and intersubjective process, requiring moral judgement including both reason and emotion, and is concerned with relevance rather than impartiality (Wallace, 1993): 'objectivity in morality has to do with identification and assessment of what is relevant to a moral (or legal) verdict' (ibid: 63). I suggest that this approach to establishing the content of objectivity allows us to use an ethic of care to determine what is relevant to a situation requiring objective judgement, because an ethic of care requires us to consider, not only the carer, but also the cared for, where all the worthy objects in a situation must be given proper attention, not just those which are relevant to the caring person. And this demands an intersubjective, deliberative engagement with differences in needs and values interpretation – an essentially political process, requiring the exercise of the political mode of being. Bringing the formation of objectivity into the hustle of everyday life, and uniting it to each person's experience of subjectivity in the bipartite value of meaningfulness, requires capabilities for a particular kind of rationality. I have begun to explore this rationality in terms of *phronetic techne*, opposing it to the pre-giveness of technical rationality, which simply does not stand up to what we know about the ordinary experience of 'lay normativity' (Sayer, 2011). I argued that a rationality of care based upon *phronetic techne* is key to realising the transformative potential of interpretive differences which arise from intersubjective encounters between self, others, and materiality at the level of the task.

To be able to engage in, and become proficient in, agonistic democratic practices at the level of the task requires us to have an understanding of ourselves as capable valuers: that is, possessing an equal status as co-authorities in the realm of value. Effective participation depends upon our having a sense of our worth as co-authorities, entitled to generate interpretive differences and to bring them into public deliberation. This begs the question of the nature of authority in democratic participation. I have argued that a system of workplace democracy will combine democratic participation at the level of the organisation with participatory practices at the level of the task, and that at the level of the organisation this requires an authority which is a democratic authority. An important argument in favour of management authority is its epistemic superiority – managers are best placed to make decisions because they possess the expert knowledge and information necessary to resolving complex situations; the local knowledge of workers may make a useful contribution to management decision-making, but their partial understanding can never place them in the position of epistemic equality necessary for effective democratic participation. So, for efficient and effective decision-making we ought to accept a 'technocratic model of expert authority' (Moore, 2011), even though this must require from workers a surrender of their judgement, because technocratic expert authority, by its nature, excludes workers from independently evaluating and forming judgements upon the information and criteria for decision-making. By contrast, democratic authority demands the taking up, not the surrender, of judgement, which submits expert authority to wider practices of scrutiny and accountability. Fraser (1990), for example, proposes that we open up public spaces based upon 'subaltern counter-publics' which 'invent and circulate counter-discourses' and 'formulate oppositional interpretations of their identities, interests and needs' (ibid: 57). Bringing out the agonistic dimensions of interpretive differences which arise from the work we do together links our status as co-authorities at the level of the task with mechanisms for democratic authority at the level of the organisation.

The concept of meaningful work deserves wider intellectual and political attention. To secure careful and caring attentiveness, we require a politics of meaningfulness which takes account of the different ways in which we each make our contribution to the work of social cooperation. This demands a form of micro-politics which equips people to nurture the public good of meaningfulness, arising from the diversity of our positive values. We have good reason to find common cause in such an undertaking. Although we are now exhorted to find satisfaction and self-fulfilment in consumption, Morris's call for dignified and humane labour retains a toehold in our imaginings of what a flourishing human life ought to look like. Indeed, Morris's comment upon the purchase of goods, ''Tis the lives of men you buy',[1] indicates how we might link the moral and political dimensions of consumption and production. This is because if we acquire goods from the oppressions of others then we compromise the possibilities for our own life – if one life can be made vulnerable because of the work he or she does, then so can the life of any man or woman. Consumers can be satisfied even where producers are exploited, alienated, or otherwise harmed, but consumers are also producers with interests in not being exploited, alienated, or subjected to undignified work. This indicates that we have a shared interest in ensuring that all work is meaningful work, constituted by the goods of autonomy as non-alienation, freedom as non-domination, and social recognition as dignified work, thereby increasing the likelihood of it being the source of social bonds essential to stitching together the institutional fabric upon which we all depend.

Notes

Chapter 1   Conceptualising Meaningful Work as a Fundamental Human Need

*   This chapter has been published in *The Journal of Business Ethics* and is used here with permission from the publisher.

1   Campbell (1989) describes how, during the two world wars, German theorists sought to restore Arbeitsfreude, or the joy of work, based upon the central organising idea that work alone 'is capable of giving meaning to human existence' (ibid: 4). Arbeitsfreude was motivated by enlightenment values, but given energy by the manifest harms visited upon workers by industrialisation (ibid: 9). However, when Arbeitsfreude was united to an ideology of German Work, as a superior form of work, it became a tool in Hitler's fascist nationalism (see also Schwartz, 1998).

2   A compelling example of how interpretive differences feed into a psychopolitics of emancipation is provided by the activity of 'job crafting', which consists in 'the physical and cognitive changes individuals make in the task or relational boundaries of their work' (Wrezesniewski & Ditton, 2001). In job crafting, workers make 'unsupervised, spontaneous changes in their jobs' (Lyons, 2008: 165) through actions which are hidden from organisational view, and which therefore avoid including management in decision-making about how the job is being altered. Documented acts of job crafting have been found to be motivated by the desire to achieve the purposes of the work to best effect, and to enable workers to experience a sense of enhanced personal efficacy: 'job crafting seems to help individuals to be feel better about themselves and to enable them to perceive they have more control over what they do on the job' (Lyons, 2008: 36). An important indicator of irreducible autonomy from the most recent research on job crafting is that, rather than being marginal or the preoccupation of exceptional individuals, job crafting is both widespread and necessary to getting the work done (Berg et al, 2010).

3   Drucker (2010) points out that, whilst work organised on Fordist principles may have been experienced negatively by any individual worker, the system as a whole required elevated levels of skill, particularly social skills. Drucker argues that, by confining workers to routine tasks, Ford was motivated to 'free workers from arduous toil' (ibid: 163), thereby releasing them for active community life and for citizenship beyond the workplace.

4   Margalit (1996) identifies limits to what justice would demand with respect to meaningful work in a decent society. He argues that, to be called decent, a society is not obliged to guarantee meaningful work, but it is obliged to provide the opportunity for engaging in meaningful activities: 'A decent society is thus one that provides all its members with the opportunity to find at least one reasonably meaningful occupation' (ibid: 254). Prospects

for supplying meaningful occupation are much enhanced when the work of social cooperation is understood more broadly than paid employment, and includes the diversity of unpaid work which sustains and reproduces our common life.

5　See Council of Civil Service Unions/Cabinet Office (2004), 'Work, Stress and Health: The Whitehall II Study', London: Public and Commercial Services Union.

6　See Kaarsemaker and Poutsma (2006) for the specification of a co-ownership high performance work system which combines a philosophy of work with participatory practices such as information sharing, strong culture and values, and a clear sense of purpose.

7　One objection to this claim is that for some people meaningful work may not be a fundamental human need. And indeed, many people get by without their work being meaningful. However, it is possible that people, through disappointment and socialised expectations, may no longer come to desire the goods of meaningful work. Political theorists would call this a manifestation of 'adaptive preferences', where, faced with 'inaccessible options', it is rational to adjust one's preferences to the available choice set (Elster, 1983). In the case of the fox who desires the out of reach sweet grapes at the top of the tree, his desire is modified so that, not only does he learn to like the sour grapes at the bottom of the tree, but he loses awareness of the existence of the sweet grapes.

8　There has been some recent revival of theoretical interest in meaningful work from a Rawlsian perspective (Hsieh, 2008; Arnold, 2012), from within critical social theory (Smith, 2009; Breen, 2006), from a liberal perfectionist standpoint (Roessler, 2012), and from moral philosophy on the meaning of life (Levy, 2005).

9　Adopting a liberal perfectionist framework means giving up strict neutrality. The value of neutrality lies in the space it provides for individual autonomy and freedom of choice. Since these are also constitutive values of my concept of meaningful work, then construing meaningful work within a liberal perfectionist framework would seem to introduce a contradiction. If we specify the good life as characterised by autonomy, then do we not thereby diminish autonomy by restricting non-autonomous forms of living. However, the variety of positive values and meanings which my concept of meaningful work would allow preserves wide discretion for individuals to select the meanings that have value to them (see Roessler, 2012). Furthermore, I draw upon Sen's capability approach to specify two capabilities relevant to experiencing the value of meaningfulness which requires that, to be complete, any capability must include the freedom not to turn that capability into a functioning (Sen, 1999a). Applied to the capabilities for objective valuing and affective attachment, this means that people retain the freedom to choose not to experience meaningful work, or even to engage in meaning-making with others.

10　Wolf's specification of an objective and a subjective dimension in the value of meaningfulness indicates limits to state-sponsored meaningfulness in work. Whilst the state can acknowledge that meaningful work is a fundamental human need by supporting an organisation of work which promotes meaningfulness, it cannot guarantee that any particular individual will find their work to be meaningful. The state is obliged not to render fruitless the individual search for meaning in work; the individual is obliged to choose whether or not to exercise his capabilities for meaningfulness in work. In this way, the basic individual freedom to find some particular objectively worthy work non-meaningful is preserved.

11   The objective/subjective distinction has been identified by several writers (Ciulla, 2000; see also *Laborem Exercens*). Ciulla (2002) describes the intrinsic objective dimension of meaningful work as follows: 'meaningful work, like a meaningful life, is morally worthy work undertaken in a morally worthy organisation' (ibid: 225). I make a distinction between worthy objects and the objective dimensions of the work activity, which in my conception of meaningful work are autonomy, freedom, and dignity. A worthy object might be a material object, a person, an animal, an idea, a practice, a project, an eco-system, or some set of institutional arrangements which order the human world. However, this does not mean that we attend to the interests of these worthy objects in ways which render harm to ourselves, through whom the activity occurs (since we are also worthy objects). Instead, to be consistent with the value of meaningfulness, our actions must be structured by the objective characteristics of autonomy, freedom, and dignity. In my application of Wolf's bipartite value of meaningfulness, I am concerned to describe how objectivity and subjectivity are to be integrated. Hence, being attentive to worthy objects requires an emotional engagement which is both satisfying to us because we are able to experience the objective features of meaningful work, and represents an appropriate response to the nature of the object.

Chapter 2   Proliferating Meaningful Work: Meaning-Making and an Ethic of Care

1   The standard economic conception of work is susceptible to both negative and positive meanings of work. In public discourse and policy-making there is by no means total indifference to the quality of the work that people do. The most important international standard for the quality of work is decent work which The International Labour Organisation defines as: 'opportunities for women and men to obtain decent and productive work in conditions of freedom, equity, security and human dignity' (Report of the Director General, 1999 in International Labour Organisation (2007)). Decent work assumes that what counts as work is formal employment and fails to recognise other kinds of work or the fundamental interest that people have in work which does more than simply satisfy material needs in reasonably humane conditions. The concept of decent work does not provide sufficient resources for a critique of the way in which we organise our economic lives, whereas the more demanding concept of meaningful work yields greater emancipatory potential. See Bolle (2009) for an evaluation of the incorporation of unpaid family work into formal economic conceptions of work.

2 Elster provides a list of activities he regards as meeting the essential features for activities which promote self-realisation: 'playing tennis, playing piano, playing chess, making a table, cooking a meal, developing software for computers, constructing the Watts Towers, juggling with a chain saw, acting as a human mannequin, writing a book, discussing in a political assembly, bargaining with an employer, trying to prove a mathematical theorem, working a lathe, fighting a battle, doing embroidery, organizing a political campaign and building a boat' (Elster, 1986a: 99).

3 Sandberg (2000) suggests rationalistic approaches which ignore the inter-subjective dimensions of working set up a false separation between the worker and the work. Rather, 'worker and work form one entity through the lived experience of work. Competence is constituted by the meaning of the work takes on for the worker in his or her experience of it' (ibid: 11). Competence is arrived at through interpretative interaction with the context and with others. Sandberg illustrates how this operates through an ethnographic study of machine optimisers who develop new model car engines. He finds that machine optimisers developed different competences based upon what they understood to be the meaning of their work, so that, those who interpreted the meaning of their work to be about customer satisfaction developed different skills and knowledge bases from those who interpreted their work as keeping up with the latest technology.

4 Arneson describes market socialism as an economy characterised by: a right to a job; a right to vote within the enterprise of which one is a member; a collective right to decide how to deploy capital and profit; state policy aimed at evening out the capital over which each citizen has some degree of control; equalised tax burden (Arneson, 1987: 534).

5 Market socialism may not eliminate all non-meaningful work but this unavoidable problem can be eased if we adequately compensate those who have to undertake boring or dangerous work on our behalf (Arneson, 1987: 536).

6 Arneson quotes Marx's famous critique of the capitalist division of labour from *The German* Ideology: 'For as soon as the division of labour comes into being, each man has a particular, exclusive sphere of activity, which is forced upon him and from which he cannot escape. He is a hunter, a fisherman, a shepherd, or a critical critic, and must remain so if he does not want to lose his means of livelihood; whereas in communist society, where nobody has one exclusive sphere of activity but each can become accomplished in any branch he wishes, society regulates the general production and makes it possible for me to do one thing today and another tomorrow, to hunt in the morning, fish in the afternoon, rear cattle in the evening, criticize after dinner, just as I have a mind, without ever becoming hunter, fisherman, shepherd or critic'.

7 Arneson identifies some of the other kinds of goods that people may want from their work (apart from meaningfulness defined by non-specialisation), including: '(1) wages to be exchanged for consumer goods now or in the future; (2) pleasant companionship with work colleagues or customers; (3) the knowledge that in producing particular goods or services one is being humanly useful to others or even contributing to the fulfilment of

their vital needs; (4) interesting and challenging work that calls for discrimination, skill, and intelligence; (5) the thrill of taking financial or physical risks; (6) responsible work that requires for its successful execution the display of prized virtues; (7) solidarity with one's work mates stemming from common commitment to a cause associated either with the enterprise product or the enterprise manner of operation; etc ...' (Arneson, 1987: 528).

8 The empirical value of the public/private distinction has been reduced by new working patterns, such as homeworking and mobile communications, which cut across conventional lines of male/female work, and home/work boundaries, in the process complicating inequalities of gender and class: 'such divisions may merely have been supplanted by other means of perpetuating sex inequalities, where spatial or otherwise (Armstrong & Squires, 2002: 279; see also Armstrong, 2008).

9 Arendt's threefold distinction between labour, work, and action is influenced by Heidegger's interpretation of Aristotle's distinction between *praxis* (acting) and *poesis* (making) (Dietz, 2002: 169).

10 Arendt would deny that meaningful work is a concept which makes any sense, since meaningful action can only be enacted in the realm of action.

11 Public spaces, which reveal unique and distinct identities and enable people to act together, have been overtaken by social concerns which carry with them conformity and unfreedom (Tsao, 2002: 105). The corruption of these spontaneously emergent micro-spaces has diminished the public realm in which we appear to ourselves and to others, not as *what* we are (as functionaries or job holders in the division of labour), but as *who* we are (as distinct and unique persons) (Arendt, 1958: 181).

Chapter 3   Overcoming Alienation: Irreducible Autonomy and *Phronetic Techne* in a Practical Rationality of Caring

1 Morris (1884), for example, idealised craftwork, from which the industrialised organisation of work represents a falling away. Macintyre's attempt to revive the virtues through the device of practices also owes much to the intrinsic value of activity embodied in the craft idea. See Blauner (1964) for a Marxist approach to the loss of craftsmanship, and Inkson (1987) for an evaluation of the extent to which the craft ideal still retains a hold upon the imaginations of workers in his study of commercial potters in New Zealand. Sennett (2008) presents the most recent revival of the craft ideal, in which he also critiques the ways in which the craft ideal operates to designate forms of work as more or less valuable.

2 Team-working is often invoked as a positive example of an autonomy-promoting strategy, but such practices can be made to serve organisational purposes: Ezzy (2001: 634) identifies how team-working is used to 'appropriate workers' solidarity and support' and encourage them to 'identify their interests with the company's', and Marsh (1992), in a review of the data on Japanese manufacturers, concludes that 'systems of participatory decision-making in Japan have not led to workplace democracy' (ibid: 250), because firms appropriate workers' ideas and suggestions without giving them

authority over decision-making. Hodson (2002b) identifies how the self-disciplinary character of work teams results in the coercive extraction of higher levels of discretionary effort by increasing competition amongst co-workers, monitoring and reporting of peers, and fostering interactive behaviours designed to humiliate, criticise and ostracise: 'Team based organisations of work can thus provide the basis for an even tighter control of work life than management systems based on bureaucratic control or supervisory fiat' (Hodson, 2002b: 496; see Barker, 1999). Hodson (2002) concludes that such participatory schemes cannot be considered democratic forms of participation, they are not 'real industrial democracy wherein workers and managers share profits, ownership and high-level governance of firms' (Lincoln & Kelleberg, 1990).

Chapter 4   Confronting Domination: Freedom and Democratic Authority

1   Rothschild (2009) describes approaches to legitimate authority as 'collectivist democratic' in which 'a decision is legitimate only if it reflects the will of the involved participants, and since the participants' will can be known only through democratic dialogue, dialogue and consensus become the keys in this new form of organisation' (Rothschild, 2009: 210).

Chapter 5   Restoring Dignity: Social Recognition in Practical Identity Formation

1   Dillon (1995) distinguishes between recognition respect and evaluative respect. *Recognition self-respect* consists in 'taking appropriate account of one's own status as a person: appreciating one's fundamental moral worth and behaving accordingly' (Dillon, 1995: 293). *Evaluative self-respect* 'rests on an evaluation of oneself in terms of a normative self-conception – the view one has of the sort of person one ought to be or that it would be good to be, and of the kind of life such a person should live' (Dillon, 1997: 23).

2   Rawls does not clearly distinguish between self-respect and self-esteem, and uses the two concepts interchangeably: 'self-respect (or self-esteem)' (Rawls, 1999 [1971]: 440).

3   Relational dimensions of work are fundamental to the formation of practical identity. For example, Sluss and Ashforth (2007) identify how self-definition is affected by interpersonal relationships at work, both in terms of seeing oneself as a unique individual and in making interpersonal comparisons. Deliberative meaning-making shapes the common horizon of value by providing the political space for us to offer one another intelligible reasons for why a person, object or activity should contribute to the meaning content of our lives. In the end, organisational life is held together by both cognitive and affective dimensions of working with others: 'to work is to relate' (Flum, 2001: 262).

Chapter 6   'The Inner Workshop of Democracy': Agonistic Democratic Practices and the Realisation of Emancipatory Potentials

1   Moral arguments for economic democracy have given way to efficiency arguments which claim that participation improves economic performance. Efficiency justifications (Bowles & Gintis, 1993: 89) rely upon the superior economic efficiency of democratic firms 'in the static sense of maximising output per unit of inputs' (ibid), where workplace democracy is justified if it can be shown to make a positive contribution to organisational effectiveness in advanced technological societies (Johnson, 2006). The strains of global capitalism have created knowledge intensive, decentralised, flat organisations which are functionally flexible: 'knowledge is no longer organised through task continuity' (Johnson, 2006: 249). In such organisations, employees must collaborate across traditional functional lines, and this is impeded by hierarchies which have compliance and oppression built into them. Therefore, workplace democracy provides an efficient mechanism for facilitating autonomy, self-management, and empowerment by holding managerial hierarchies to account, and subjecting them to democratic critique (see also Kaarsemaker & Poutsma, 2006).

2   Standard arguments for workplace democracy draw upon the concept of political autonomy to justify economic and workplace democracy, using the general principle that everyone engaged in a common activity ought to have the opportunity to participate in the decision-making affecting that activity (Dewey, 1927; Dahl, 1985; Carter, 2003): 'everyone should have the opportunity to participate in making economic decisions to the degree they are affected by those decisions' (Albert & Hahnel, 2002: 20).

3   However, Pateman's spillover thesis is not securely supported by the empirical literature (Carter, 2006). For example, Greenberg et al (1996) show only a weak association between workplace participation and political participation – workers in cooperative enterprises are not more likely to be involved in voting and party activities. Greenberg et al (1996) identify a more convincing link between long-term membership of a cooperative enterprise and greater community involvement (see also Godard, 2007). Adman (2008), however, finds no relationship between political activity and the practice of civic skills at work, such as communicative and organisational capacities. The only positive spillover effect Adman is able to identify is the possibility that political tolerance may be promoted because 'exposure to differing political views is more common in working life than in voluntary organisations' (ibid: 133–4). The lack of evidence for a positive spillover effect may be because workers in democratically organised enterprises place are influenced by the wider democratic system of which they are a part. Schweizer (1995) suggests that empirical studies tend to conflate participatory (direct) with republican (representative) forms of democracy (ibid: 370): even where democratic workplaces are successful in generating a sense of political efficacy, the institutional limitations of representative democracy and a bourgeois ethos encourages people to value their private lives over an active public life, and stifles political participation (ibid: 370–4). Republican gov-

ernment monopolises public spaces, and the delegation of political power to representative government reduces the incentive to participate. Workers whose preferences and capabilities for political activity have been formed by the experience of direct democracy in their workplaces are less likely to find engaging in the limited opportunities for political participation offered by representative government, such as voting or involvement in political parties, worthwhile (ibid).

Chapter 7   Capability Justice and a Politics of Meaningfulness

1   The Scandinavian democratic dialogue tradition (Alasoini, 2006; Gustavsen, 1985; Qvale, 2002) provides an example of a society-wide attempt to create a habitual right to participate. In this context, practices of democratic dialogue are shaped by different and conflicting discourses concerning the nature of organisational life which draw upon local knowledge and provide the material for the difference and contestation upon which the creation of political moments depends: 'Within an enterprise, discourses are partly overlapping and partly disconnected. With proper channels and arenas for sharing between the different discourses, an enterprise has a capacity for generating a richer and more nuanced knowledge both of the 'realities' and their own learning processes' (Brogger, 2010: 483; see Palshaugen, 2006). Beirne (2008) suggests that a generative approach to revealing and enabling different discourses requires micro-emancipatory mechanisms and structures at the level of the task (Alvesson & Willmott, 2002) which release the autonomy potential of workers by building democratic practices out of the natural work groups, repertoires of local knowledge and established traditions developed by workers themselves (Beirne, 2008: 688).

Conclusion

1   Morris, W. (1884) *Art and Socialism*.

Bibliography

Adenzato, M. & Garbarini, F. (2006) The As If in Cognitive Science, Neuroscience and Anthropology: A Journey among Robots, Blacksmiths and Neurons. *Theory & Psychology*, 16 (6), 747–59.

Adler, P. S. (2004) Skill Trends Under Capitalism and the Socialisation of Production. In: Warhurst, Grugulis & Keep (eds) *The Skills that Matter*. Houndmills: Palgrave Macmillan.

Adman, P. (2008) Does Workplace Experience Enhance Political Participation? A Crucial Test of a Venerable Hypothesis. *Political Behaviour*, 30, 115–38.

Alasoini, T. (2006) In Search of Generative Results: A New Generation of Programmes to Develop Work Organization. *Economic and Industrial Democracy*, 27 (1), 9–37.

Albert, M. & Hahnel, R. (2002) In Defense of Participatory Economics. *Science & Society*, 66 (1), 7–21.

Alexander, J. M. (2003) Capability Egalitarianism and Moral Selfhood. *Ethical Perspectives*, 10 (1), 3–21.

Alexander, J. M. (2008) *Capabilities and Social Justice: The Political Philosophy of Amartya Sen and Martha Nussbaum*. Aldershot: Ashgate Publishing Company.

Alfes, K., Truss, C., Soane, E. C., Rees, C. & Gatenby, M. (2010) *Creating an Engaged Workforce: Findings from the Kingston Employee Engagement Consortium Project*. [Online] CIPD Report, http://www.cipd.co.uk/NR/rdonlyres/DD66E557-DB90-4F07-8198-87C3876F3371/0/Creating_engaged_workforce.pdf [Accessed 13th December 2011].

Alkire, S. (2005) *Needs and Capabilities, the Philosophy of Need*. Royal Institute of Philosophy supplement. Cambridge, New York & Melbourne: Cambridge University Press.

Allen, M. P. (2006) Hegel Between Non-Domination and Expressive Freedom: Capabilities, Perspectives, Democracy. *Philosophy & Social Criticism*, 32 (4), 493–512.

Alvesson, A. & Spicer, A. (2012) Critical Leadership Studies: The Case for Critical Performativity. *Human Relations*, 65 (3), 367–90.

Alvesson, M. & Willmott, H. (1992) On the Idea of Emancipation in Management and Organization Studies. *Academy of Management Review*, 17 (3), 432–64.

Alvesson, M. & Willmott, H. (2002) Identity Regulation as Organizational Control: Producing the Appropriate Individual. *Journal of Management Studies*, 39 (5), 619–44.

Anderson, E. S. (1995) *Value and Ethics in Economic Theory*. Cambridge, Massachusetts: Harvard University Press.

Anderson, E. S. (2010) Justifying the Capabilities Approach to Justice. In: Brighouse & Robeyns (eds) *Measuring Justice, Primary Goods and Capabilities*. Cambridge & New York: Cambridge University Press.

Anderson, J. & Honneth, A. (2005) Autonomy, Vulnerability, Recognition and Justice. In: Christman & Anderson (eds) *Autonomy and the Challenges to Liberalism*. Cambridge: Cambridge University Press.

Anthony, P. D. (1978) *The Ideology of Work*. London: Tavistock Publications.

Arendt, H. (1958) *The Human Condition*. Chicago & London: The University of Chicago Press.

Arendt, H. (1977 [1954]) What is Freedom? *Between Past and Future*. London: Penguin Books.

Aristotle (1953) *The Nicomachean Ethics*. London: Penguin Books.

Arkin, A. (2011) 'Is Engagement Working?' *People Management*, 1st November.

Armstrong, C. (2008) Collapsing Categories: Fraser on Economy, Culture and Justice. *Philosophy & Social Criticism*, 34 (4), 409–25.

Armstrong, C. & Squires, J. (2002) Beyond the Public/Private Dichotomy: Relational Space and Sexual Inequalities. *Contemporary Political Theory*, 1, 261–83.

Arneson, R. J. (1987) Meaningful Work and Market Socialism. *Ethics*, 97 (3), 517–45.

Arneson, R. J. (2000) Perfectionism and Politics. *Ethics*, 111 (1), 36–63.

Arnold, D. G. & Bowie, N. E. (2003) Sweatshops and Respect for Persons. *Business Ethics Quarterly*, 13 (2), 221–42.

Arnold, K. A., Turner, N., Barling, J., Kelloway, E. K. & McKee, M. C. (2007) Transformational Leadership and Psychological Well-Being: The Mediating Role of Meaningful Work. *Journal of Occupational Health Psychology*, 12, 193–203.

Arnold, S. (2012) The Difference Principle at Work. *Journal of Political Philosophy*, 20 (1), 94–118.

Aronson, J. & Neysmith, S. M. (2006) Obscuring the Costs of Home Care: Restructuring at Work. *Work, Employment and Society*, 20 (1), 27–45.

Ashforth, B. E. & Kreiner, G. (1999) How Can You Do It? Dirty Work and the Challenge of Constructing a Positive Identity. *The Academy of Management Review*, 24 (3), 413–34.

Ashforth, B. E. & Tomiuk, M. (2000) Emotional Labor and Authenticity: Views from Service Agents. In: Fineman (ed.) *Emotion in Organizations*. Thousand Oaks, CA: Sage.

Attewell, P. (1990) What is Skill? *Work and Occupations*, 17 (4), 422–48.

Avolio, B. J., Walumbwa, F. O. & Weber, T. J. (2009) Leadership: Current Theories, Research, and Future Directions. *Annual Review of Psychology*, 60, 421–49.

Baechtiger, A. (2010) On Perfecting the Deliberative Process: Agonistic Inquiry as a Key Deliberative Technique. *2010 Annual Meeting of the American Political Science Association, Washington DC, September 2–5, 2007*. [Online] http://papers.ssrn.com/sol3/papers.cfm?abstract_id=1642280 [Accessed 5th June 2011].

Bagchi, A. K. (2000) Freedom and Development as End of Alienation. *Economic and Political Weekly*, December 9, 4409–20.

Baier, K. (2000 [1957]) The Meaning of Life. In: Klemke (ed.) *The Meaning of Life*. New York: Oxford University Press.

Bambra, C. (2011) *Work, Worklessness and the Political Economy of Health*. Oxford: Oxford University Press.

Banks, M. (2006) Moral Economy and Cultural Work. *Sociology*, 40 (3), 455–72.

Barker, J. R. (1999) *The Discipline of Teamwork: Participation and Coercive Control.* Thousand Oaks, CA: Sage.

Barley, S. R. & Bechky, B. A. (1994) In the Backrooms of Science: The Work of Technicians in Science Labs. *Work and Occupations*, 26, 85–126.

Barley, S. R. & Kunda, G. (2001) Bringing Work Back In. *Organization Science*, 12 (1), 76–95.

Barnett, C. (2004) Deconstructing Radical Democracy: Articulation, Representation and Being-with-Others. *Political Geography*, 23 (5), 503–28.

Bartelheimer, P., Moncel, N., Verd, J. M., Vero, J. & Buttner, R. (2009) Towards Analysing Individual Working Lives in a Resource/Capabilities Perspective. European Integration Research Project CAPRIGHT. [Online] http://www.sofi-goettingen.de/fileadmin/Peter_Bartelheimer/Literatur/Net-Doc-50.pdf#page=25 [Accessed Online 20th June 2011].

Baumeister, R. F. (1991) *Meanings of Life.* New York: Guilford.

Bechky, B. (2003) Sharing Meaning across Occupational Communities: The Transformation of Understanding on a Production Floor. *Organization Science*, 14 (3), 312–30.

Beirne, M. (2008) Idealism and the Applied Relevance of Research on Employee Participation. *Work, Employment and Society*, 22 (4), 675–93.

Bench, S. W. & Lench, H. C. (2013) On the Function of Boredom. *Behavioural Sciences*, 3, 459–72.

Benjamin, J. (1990) An Outline of Intersubjectivity: The Development of Recognition. *Psychoanalytic Psychology*, 7 (Suppl), 33–46.

Benjamin, J. (2002) The Rhythm of Recognition: Comments on the Work of Louis Sanders. *Psychoanalytics Dialogues*, 12 (1), 43–53.

Berg, J. M., Wrzesniewski, A. & Dutton, J. E. (2010) Perceiving and Responding to Challenges in Job Crafting at Different Ranks: When Proactivity Requires Adaptivity. *Journal of Organizational Behavior*, 31, 158–86.

Berlin, I. (1969) Two Concepts of Liberty. In: Berlin (ed.) *Four Essays on Liberty.* London & New York: Oxford University Press.

Bernstein, P. (1976) Necessary Elements for Worker Participation in Decision-Making. *Journal of Economic Issues*, X (2), 490–522.

Blackman, L., Cromby, J., Hook, D., Papdopoulos, D. & Walkerdine, V. (2008) Creating Subjectivities. *Subjectivity*, 22, 1–27.

Blaug, R. (2007) Cognition in a Hierarchy. *Contemporary Political Theory*, 6, 24–44.

Blauner, R. (1964) *Alienation and Freedom.* Chicago and London: The University of Chicago Press.

Blumberg, P. (1968) *Industrial Democracy: The Sociology of Participation.* London: Constable.

Blustein, D. L. (2006) *The Psychology of Working: A New Perspective for Career Development, Counselling and Public Policy.* Mahwah, NJ: Erlbaum.

Blustein, D. L. (2008) The Role of Work in Psychological Health and Well-Being. *American Psychologist*, 63 (4), 228–40.

Boatright, J. R. (2004) Employee Governance and the Ownership of the Firm. *Business Ethics Quarterly*, 14 (1), 1–21.

Bohman, J. (1996) *Public Deliberation, Pluralism, Complexity and Democracy.* Boston: MIT Press.

Bohman, J. (1998) Survey Article: The Coming of Age of Deliberative Democracy. *Journal of Political Philosophy*, 6, 400–25.

Bolle, P. (2009) Labour Statistics: The Boundaries and Diversity of Work. *International Labour Review*, 148, Issue 1–2, 183–93.

Bolton, S. (2009) Getting to the Heart of the Emotional Labour Process: A Reply to Brook. *Work, Employment & Society*, 23 (3), 549–60.

Bondi, L. (2008) On the Relational Dynamics of Caring: A Psychotherapeutic Approach to Emotional and Power Dimensions of Women's Care Work. *Gender, Place and Culture*, 15 (3), 249–65.

Bonvin, J. & Farvaque, N. (2006) Promoting Capability for Work: The Role of Local Actors. In: Deneulin, Nebel & Sagovsky (eds) *Transforming Unjust Structures: The Capability Approach*. Dordrecht: Springer, 121–42.

Bonvin, J-M., & Thelen, L. (2003) Deliberative Democracy and Capabilities: The Impact and Significance of Voice. *3rd Conference on Capability Approach*, Pavia.

Borgerson, J. L. (2007) On the Harmony of Feminist Ethics and Business Ethics. *Business and Society Review*, 112 (4), 477–509.

Bosma, H., Marmot, M. G., Hemingway, H., Nicholson, A. C., Brunner, E. & Stansfeld, S. (1997) Low Job Control and Risk of Coronary Heart Disease in Whitehall II (Prospective Cohort) Study. *British Medical Journal*, 314.

Bowie, N. E. (1998) A Kantian Theory of Meaningful Work. *Journal of Business Ethics*, 17, 1083–92.

Bowles, S. (1998) Endogenous Preferences: The Cultural Consequences of Markets and Other Economic Institutions. *Journal of Economic Literature*, 36 (1), 75–111.

Bowles, S. & Gintis, H. (1993) A Political and Economic Case for the Democratic Enterprise. *Economics and Philosophy*, 9, 75–100.

Bratman, M. E. (1992) Shared Cooperative Activity. *The Philosophical Review*, 101 (2), 327–41.

Bratman, M. E. (2000) Reflection, Planning and Temporally Extended Agency. *The Philosophical Review*, 109 (1), 35–61.

Braverman, H. (1974) *Labor and Monopoly Capital: The Degradation of Work in the Twentieth Century*. New York: Monthly Review Press.

Braybrooke, D. (1987) *Meeting Needs: Studies in Moral, Political, and Legal Philosophy*. Princeton, NJ: Princeton University Press.

Braybrooke, D. (1998a) Diagnosis and Remedy in Marx's Doctrine of Alienation. In: Braybrooke (ed.) *Moral Objectives, Rules, and the Forms of Social Change*. Toronto: University of Toronto Press.

Braybrooke, D. (1998b) The Meaning of Participation and of Demands for It. In: Braybrooke (ed.) *Moral Objectives, Rules, and the Forms of Social Change*. Toronto: University of Toronto Press.

Braybrooke, D. (1998c) Work: A Cultural Ideal Ever More in Jeopardy. In: Braybrooke (ed.) *Moral Objectives, Rules, and the Forms of Social Change*. Toronto: University of Toronto Press.

Braybrooke, D. (1998d) Two Concepts of Needs in Marx's Writings. In: Braybrooke (ed.) *Moral Objectives, Rules, and the Forms of Social Change*. Toronto: University of Toronto Press.

Braybrooke, D. (2005) Where does the Moral Force of the Concept of Needs Reside and When? In: Reader (ed.) *The Philosophy of Need*, Royal Institute of Philosophy supplement. Cambridge, New York & Melbourne: Cambridge University Press.

Breen, K. (2007) Work and Emancipatory Practice: Recovering Human Beings' Productive Capacities. *Res Publica*, 13 (4), 381–414.

Breen, K. (2011) Work and Practical Reasoning: On Two Rival Visions of the Workplace. *Paper presented to the Contemporary Aristotelian Studies (CAS) Specialist Group of the Political Studies Association (PSA) 1ˢᵗ Annual Conference*, 3rd June 2011.

Brenkert, G. G. (1992) Freedom, Participation and Corporations: The Issue of Corporate (Economic) Democracy. *Business Ethics Quarterly*, 2 (3), 251–69.

Brennan, G. & Pettit, P. (2004) *The Economy of Esteem: An Essay on Civil and Political Society*. Oxford: Oxford University Press.

Brogger, B. (2010) An Innovative Approach to Employee Participation in a Norwegian Retail Chain. *Economic and Industrial Democracy*, 31 (4), 477–95.

Broom, D. H., D'Souza, R. M., Strazdins, L., Butterworth, P., Parslow, R. & Rodgers, B. (2006) The Lesser Evil: Bad Jobs or Unemployment? A Survey of Mid-Aged Australians. *Social Science & Medicine*, 63 (3), 575–86.

Brown, S. and Leigh, T. (1996) A New Look at Psychological Climate and Its Relationship to Job Involvement, Effort, and Performance. *Journal of Applied Psychology*, 81 (4), 358–68.

Bubeck, D. E. (1995) *Care, Gender and Justice*. Oxford: Oxford University Press.

Buchanan, A. E. (1985) *Ethics, Efficiency, and the Market*. Rowman & Littlefield.

Burawoy, M. (1979) *Manufacturing Consent: Changes in the Labor Process under Monopoly Capitalism*. London: University of Chicago Press.

Cacioppo, J. T. & Patrick, W. (2008) *Loneliness: Human Nature and the Need for Social Connection*. W. W. Norton & Company Inc.

Cameron, J. & Gibson-Graham, J. K. (2003) Feminising the Economy: Metaphors, Strategies and Politics. *Gender, Place & Culture*, 10 (2), 145–57.

Campbell, J. (1989) *Joy in Work, German Work: The National Debate, 1800–1945*. Princeton, New Jersey: Princeton University Press.

Camus, A. (1955) *The Myth of Sisyphus and Other Essays*. London: Penguin Books.

Card, C. (1991) *Feminist Ethics*. Lawrence: University Press of Kansas.

Carter, N. (2003) Workplace Democracy: Turning Workers into Citizens? *Paper presented at ECPR joint sessions*, Edinburgh, 28 March–2 April 2003.

Carter, N. (2006) Political Participation and the Workplace: The Spillover Thesis Revisited. *British Journal of Politics and International Relations*, 8, 410–26.

Casassas, D. (2007) Basic Income and the Republican Ideal: Rethinking Material Independence in Contemporary Societies. *Basic Income Studies*, 2 (2), 1–7.

Cathcart, A. (2009) *Directing Democracy: The Case of the John Lewis Partnership*. [Online] https://lra.le.ac.uk/handle/2381/7811 [Accessed 5th September 2011].

Chalofsky, N. (2003a) Meaningful Work. *Training and Development*, 57 (12), 52–8.

Chalofsky, N. (2003b) An Emerging Construct for Meaningful Work. *Human Resources Development International*, 6 (1), 69–83.

Chalofsky, N. (2010) *Meaningful Workplaces*. San Francisco, CA: Jossey-Bass.

Chalofsky, N. & Krishna, V. (2009) Meaningfulness, Commitment, and Engagement: The Intersection of a Deeper Level of Intrinsic Motivation, Advances in Developing. *Human Resources*, 11 (2), 189–203.

Christiano, T. (2005) An Argument for Egalitarian Justice and Against the Levelling-Down Objection. In: Campbell, O'Rourke & Shier (eds) *Law & Social Justice*. Cambridge, Mass. & London: The MIT Press.

Christman, J. (2002) *Social and Political Philosophy*. London: Routledge.

Ciulla, J. B. (2000) *The Working Life: The Promise and Betrayal of Modern Work*. New York: Random House.

Clegg, R. S., Courpasson, D. & Phillips, N. (2006) *Power and Organizations*. London & Washington, D.C.: Sage Publications.

Code, L. (1995) *Rhetorical Spaces: Essays on Gendered Locations*. New York: Routledge.

Cohen, J. (1989) The Economic Basis of Deliberative Democracy. *Social Philosophy and Policy*, 6, 25–50.

Cohen, J. & Fung, A. (2004) The Radical-Democratic Project. *Swiss Journal of Political Science*. [Online] http://www.archonfung.com/docs/articles/2004/ Cohen_Fung_Debate_SPSR2004.pdf [Accessed 9th September 2010].

Cohen, J. & Rogers, J. (1992) Secondary Associations and Democratic Governance. *Politics and Society*, 20, 393–472.

Connolly, W. E. (1991) *Identity/Difference: Democratic Negotiations of Political Paradox*. Minneapolis: Cornell University Press.

Connolly, W. E. (1995) *The Ethos of Pluralization*. Minneapolis & London: University of Minnesota Press.

Connolly, W. E. (1999) Assembling the Left. *Boundary*, 2 (26), 3.

Connolly, W. E. (2000) Speed, Concentric Cultures, and Cosmopolitan. *Political Theory*, 28 (5).

Connolly, W. E. (2004a) The Ethos of Democratization. In: Critchley & Marchart (eds) *Laclau: A Critical Reader*. London: Routledge.

Connolly, W. E. (2004b) Realizing Agonistic Respect. *Journal of the American Academy of Religion*, 72 (2), 507–11.

Connolly, W. E. (2005) *Pluralism*. Durham & London: Duke University Press.

Connolly, W. E. (2011) *A World of Becoming*. Durham & London: Duke University Press.

Cooke, M. (2004) Redeeming Redemption: The Utopian Dimension of Critical Social Theory. *Philosophy and Social Criticism*, 30 (4), 413–29.

Coole, D. (2000) Cartographic Convulsions: Public and Private Reconsidered. *Political Theory*, 28 (3), 337–54.

Copp, D. (2007) Autonomy and the Social Construction of Values. In: Ronnow-Rasumussen, Petersson, Josefsson & Egonsson (eds) *Hommage a Wlodek: Philosophical Papers Dedicated to Wlodek Rabinowicz*.

Cornelius, N. & Gagnon, S. (2002) Re-Examining Workplace Equality: The Capabilities Approach. *Human Resource Management Journal*, 10 (4), 68–87.

Council of Civil Service Unions/Cabinet Office (2004) *Work, Stress and Health: The Whitehall II Study*. London: Public and Commercial Service Union.

Courpasson, D. (2000) Managerial Strategies of Domination: Power in Soft Bureaucracies. *Organization Studies*, 21 (1), 141–61.

Courpasson, D. & Dany, F. (2003) Indifference or Obedience? Business Firms as Democratic Hybrids. *Organization Studies*, 24 (8), 1231–60.

Cox, A., Higgins, T. & Speckesser, S. (2011) Management Practices and Sustainable Organisational Performance: An Analysis of the European Company Survey 2009. *European Foundation for the Improvement of Living and Working Conditions*.

Crane, A., Matten, D. & Moon, J. (2004) Stakeholders as Citizens? Rethinking Rights, Participation and Democracy. *Journal of Business Ethics*, 53, 107–22.

Crawford, M. B. (2009) *Shop Class as Soulcraft: An Inquiry into the Value of Work*. London: Penguin Books.

Crocker, J. & Park, L. E. (2004) The Costly Pursuit of Self-Esteem. *Psychological Bulletin*, 130 (3), 392–414.

Crouch, C. (1993) *Co-operation and Competition in an Institutionalised Economy: The Case of Germany*. The Political Quarterly Publishing Co. Ltd.

Csikszentmihalyi, M. (1991) *Flow: The Psychology of Optimal Experience*. Harper Perennial.

Dagger, R. (2006) Neo-Republicanism and the Civic Economy. *Politics, Philosophy & Economics*, 5 (2), 151–73.

Dahl, R. (1985) *A Preface to Economic Democracy*. Berkley, LA: University of California Press.

Dale, K. (2005) Building a Social Materiality: Spatial and Embodied Politics. *Organizational Control*, 12 (5), 649–78.

Daly, M. (1973) *Beyond God the Father*. Boston: Beacon Press.

Daniellou, F. (2005) The French-Speaking Ergonomists' Approach to Work Activity: Cross-Influences of Field Intervention and Conceptual Models. *Theoretical Issues in Ergonomics Science*, 6 (5), 409–27.

Daniels, N. (1990) Equality of What: Welfare, Resources, or Capabilities? *Philosophy and Phenomenological Research*, 1 (Suppl.), 273–96.

Darwall, S. (1995) Two Kinds of Respect. In: Dillon (ed.) *Dignity, Character and Self-Respect*. London: Routledge.

Darwall, S. (1999) Valuing Activity. *Social Philosophy & Policy*, 16 (1), 176–96.

Davies, J. B. (2006) The Normative Significance of the Individual in Economics: Freedom, Dignity and Human Rights. In: Clary, Dolfsma & Figart (eds) *Ethics and the Market: Insights from Social Economics*. London & New York: Routledge.

Davies, K. (2001) Responsibility and Daily Life: Reflections over TimeSpace. In: May & Thrift (eds) *TimeSpace: Geographies of Temporality*. London: Routledge.

De Beauvoir, S. (1986 [1948]) *The Ethics of Ambiguity*, Frechtman (trans.). New York: Citadel Press.

De Munck, J. & Ferreras, I. (2004) Collective Rights, Deliberation and Capabilities: An Approach to Collective Bargaining in the Belgian Retail Industry. In: Salais & Villeneuve (eds) *Europe and the Politics of Capabilities*. Cambridge: Cambridge University Press.

Deakin, S. & Koukiadaki, A. (2009) The Capability Approach and Corporate Restructuring: UK Sectoral and Enterprise-Based Case Studies. *EU Sixth Research and Development Framework Programme: Integrated Project 'Resources, Rights and Capabilities in Europe'*. Centre for Business Research, University of Cambridge.

Deci, E. L. & Ryan, R. M. (2000) The What and Why of Goal Pursuits: Human Needs and the Self-Determination of Behavior. *Psychological Inquiry*, 11 (4), 227–68.

Dejours, C. (1998) *Souffrance en France. La Banalisation de l'injustice sociale*. Paris: Seuil.

Dejours, C. (2006) Subjectivity, Work and Action. *Critical Horizons*, 7 (1), 45–62.

Deranty, J-P. (2006) Repressed Materiality: Retrieving the Materialism in Axel Honneth's Theory of Recognition. *Critical Horizons*, 7 (1), 137–63.

Deranty, J-P. (2009) What is Work? Key Insights from the Psychodynamics of Work. *Thesis Eleven*, 98, 69–87.

Deranty, J-P. & Renault, E. (2007) Politicizing Honneth's Ethics of Recognition. *Thesis Eleven*, 88, 92–111.

Dewey, J. (1927) *The Public and Its Problems*. Swallow Press & Ohio University Press.

Dietz, M. G. (2002) *Turning Operations: Feminism, Arendt, and Politics*. New York & London: Routledge.

Dillon, R. S. (1995) Toward a Feminist Conception of Self-Respect. In: Dillon (ed.) *Dignity, Character & Self-Respect*. London: Routledge.

Dillon, R. S. (1997) Self-Respect: Moral, Emotional, Political. *Ethics*, 107 (2), 226–49.

Dillon, R. S. (2010) Respect. *Stanford Encyclopedia of Philosophy*.

Doherty, M. (2009) When the Working Day is Through: The End of Work as Identity? *Work, Employment & Society*, 23 (1), 84–101.

Doppelt, D. (1984) Paradigms of Human Freedom and the Problem of Justification. *Inquiry*, 27 (1–4).

Doppelt, D. (2009) The Place of Self-Respect in a Theory of Justice. *Inquiry*, 52 (2), 127–54.

Drucker, P. (2010) *Men, Ideas and Politics*. Boston, Massachusetts: Harvard Business Review Press.

Dryzek, J. S. (2000) *Deliberative Democracy and Beyond*. Oxford: Oxford University Press.

Dryzek, J. S. (2001) Legitimacy and Economy in Deliberative Democracy. *Political Theory*, 29 (5), 651–69.

Dryzek, J. S. (2009) Democratization as Deliberative Capacity Building. *Comparative Political Studies*, 42 (11), 1379–402.

Du Gay, P. (1996) *Consumption and Identity at Work*. London: Sage.

Du Gay, P. (2007) *Organizing Identity*. London: Sage.

Dundon, T. & Gollan, P. J. (2007) Reconceptualising Voice in the Non-Union Workplace. *The International Journal of Human Resource Management*, 18 (7), 1182–98.

Dundon, T., Wilkinson, A., Marchington, M. & Ackers, P. (2004) The Meanings and Purpose of Employee Voice. *The International Journal of Human Resource Management*, 15 (6), 1149–70.

Dunne, J. (1993) *Back to the Rough Ground: 'Phronesis' and 'Techne' in Modern Philosophy and in Aristotle*. Notre Dame, Indiana: University of Notre Dame.

Durkheim, E. (1933) *The Division of Labour in Society*. London: The Macmillan Press Ltd.

Dzur, A. W. (1998) Liberal Perfectionism and Democratic Participation. *Polity*, 30 (4), 667–90.

Elias, M. V. (2008) Governance from the Ground Up: Rediscovering Mary Parker Follett. *Public Administration and Management*, 15 (1), 9–45.

Elster, J. (1983) *Sour Grapes: Studies in the Subversion of Rationality*. Cambridge: Maison des Sciences de l'Homme and Cambridge University Press.

Elster, J. (1985) *Making Sense of Marx*. Cambridge: Cambridge University Press.

Elster, J. (1986a) Self-Realisation in Work & Politics: The Marxist Conception of the Good Life. *Philosophy & Social Policy*, 3 (2), 99–100.

Elster, J. (1986b) *An Introduction to Karl Marx*. Cambridge: Cambridge University Press.

England, K. & Lawson, V. (2005) Feminist Analyses of Work: Rethinking the Boundaries, Gendering, and Spatiality of Work. In: Nelson & Seager (eds) *A Companion to Feminist Geography*. Malden & Oxford: Wiley-Blackwell.

England, P. (2003) Separative and Soluble Selves: Dichotomous Thinking in Economics. In: Ferber & Nelson (eds) *Feminist Economics Today: Beyond Economic Man*. Chicago & London: Chicago University Press.

Engster, D. (2005) Rethinking Care Theory: The Practice of Caring and the Obligation to Care. *Hypatia*, 20 (3), 50–74.

Estlund, C. (2003) *Working Together: How Workplace Bonds Strengthen a Diverse Democracy*. Oxford & New York: Oxford University Press.

Ettlinger, N. (2003) Cultural Economic Geography and a Relational and Microspace Approach to Trusts, Rationalities, Networks, and Change in Collaborative Workplaces. *Journal of Economic Geography*, 3, 145–71.

Ettlinger, N. (2004) Toward a Critical Theory of Untidy Geographies: The Spatiality of Emotions in Consumption and Production. *Feminist Economics*, 10 (3), 21–54.

Eyerman, R. & Shipway, D. (1981) Habermas on Work and Culture. *Theory and Society*, 10 (4), 547–66.

Ezzy, D. (1997) Subjectivity and the Labour Process: Conceptualising Good Work. *Sociology*, 31 (3), 427–44.

Ezzy, D. (2001) A Simulacrum of Workplace Community: Individualism and Engineered Culture. *Sociology*, 35 (3), 631–50.

Fairhurst, G. T. & Grant, D. (2010) The Social Construction of Leadership: A Sailing Guide. *Management Quarterly*, 24 (2), 171–210.

Feltham, O. & Clemens, J. (2003) An Introduction to Alain Badiou's Philosophy. In: Feltham & Clemens (eds) *Infinite Thought Truth and the Return to Philosophy*. London & New York: Continuum.

Ferber, M. A. & Nelson, J. A. (eds) (2003) *Feminist Economics Today: Beyond Economic Man*. London & Chicago: Chicago University Press.

Ferree, M. M. (1990) Beyond Separate Spheres: Feminism and Family Research. *Journal of Marriage and the Family*, 52 (4), 866–84.

Fisher, B. & Tronto, J. (1990) Toward a Feminist Theory of Caring. In: Abel & Nelson (eds) *Circles of Care: Work and Identity in Women's Lives*. Albany: State University of New York Press.

Flanagan, O. (2007) *The Really Hard Problem: Meaning in a Material World*. Cambridge, Massachusetts: The MIT Press.

Fleming, P. (2012). 'Down with Big Brother!': The End of 'Corporate Culturism'? *Journal of Management Studies*, published online 13 June, doi: 10.1111/j.1467-6486.2012.01056.x.

Flum, H. (2001) Dialogues and Challenges: The Interface Between Work and Relationships in Transition. *Counselling Psychologist*, 29, 259–70.

Follett, M. P. (1998 [1918]) *The New State: Group Organization the Solution of Popular Government*. Pennsylvania: The Pennsylvania State University Press.

Follett, M. P. (1919) Community is a Process. *The Philosophical Review*, 28 (6), 576–88.

Follett, M. P. (1930 [1924]) *Creative Experience*. London: Longmans, Green & Co.

Follett, M. P. (1973 [1940]) Dynamic Administration: The Collected Papers of Mary Parker Follett. In: Fox & Urwick (eds) *Dynamic Administration*. London: Pitman Publishing.

Ford, J. D. (1999) Organizational Change as Shifting Conversations. *Journal of Organizational Change Management*, 2 (6), 480–500.

Form, W. (1980) Resolving Ideological Issues on the Division of Labor. In: Blalock (ed.) *Sociological Theory and Research*. New York: Free Press.

Fossen, T. (2008) Agonistic Critiques of Liberalism: Perfection and Emancipation. *Contemporary Political Theory*, 7, 376–94.

Fourier, C. (1983) The Utopian Vision of Charles Fourier: Selected Texts on Work, Love, and Passionate Attraction. Beecher & Bienvenu (eds). Columbia: University of Missouri Press.

Francis, H., Ramdhony, A., Reddington, M. & Staines, H. (2013) Opening Spaces for Conversational Practice: A Conduit for Effective Engagement Strategies and Productive Working Arrangements. *The International Journal of Human Resource Management*, 24 (14), 2713–40.

Frankfurt, H. (1982) The Importance of What We Care About. *Synthese*, 53, 257–72.

Frankfurt, H. (2002) Reply to Susan Wolf. In: Buss & Overton (eds) *Contours of Agency: Essays on Themes from Harry Frankfurt*. Cambridge, Massachusetts & London: The MIT Press.

Frankfurt, H. (2004) *The Reasons of Love*. Princeton: Princeton University Press.

Frankl, V. E. (1978) *The Unheard Cry for Meaning: Psychotherapy and Humanism*. New York: Simon & Schuster.

Frankl, V. E. (1984) *Man's Search for Meaning*. New York: Washington Square Press.

Frankl, V. E. (1988) *The Will to Meaning*. New York: New American Library.

Frankl, V. E. (2004) Logos, Paradox, and the Search for Meaning. In: Freeman, Mahoney & DeVito (eds) *Cognition and Psychotherapy*. Springer Publishing Company.

Fraser, N. (1985) What's Critical about Critical Theory? The Case of Habermas and Gender. *New German Critique: Special Issue on Jurgen Habermas*, 33, 97–131.

Fraser, N. (1989a) Talking about Needs: Interpretive Contests as Political Conflicts in Welfare-State Societies. *Ethics*, 99 (2), 291–313.

Fraser, N. (1989b) *Unruly Practices: Power, Discourse, and Gender in Contemporary Social Theory*. Minnesota: University of Minnesota Press.

Fraser, N. (1994) After the Family Wage: Gender Equality and the Welfare State. *Political Theory*, 22 (4), 591–618.

Fraser, N. (2005) Reframing Justice in a Globalizing World. *New Left Review*, No. 36.

Fraser, N. & Gordon, L. (1994) A Genealogy of Dependency: Tracing a Keyword of the U.S. Welfare State. *Signs: A Journal of Women in Culture and Society*, 19 (1), 1–29.

Fraser, N. & Honneth, A. (2003) *Redistribution or Recognition? A Political-Philosophical Exchange*. London & New York: Verso.

Fredrickson, B. L. (1998) What Good are Positive Emotions? *Review of General Psychology*, 2 (3), 300–19.

Freeman, S. (2007) *Rawls*. London and New York: Routledge.

Frege, C. (2005) The Discourse of Industrial Democracy: Germany and the US Revisited. *Economic and Industrial Democracy*, 26 (1), 151–75.

Freire, P. (1970) *Pedagogy of the Oppressed*. London: Penguin Books.

Friedman, A. (1977) Responsible Autonomy versus Direct Control over the Labour Process. *Capital and Class*, 1 (1), 43–57.

Fromm, E. (1945) *The Fear of Freedom*. London: K. Paul, Trench, Trubner & Co.

Fromm, E. (1947) *Man for Himself: An Inquiry into the Psychology of Ethics*. New York: Rinehart.

Fromm, E. (1955) *The Sane Society*. New York: Rinehart.

Fromm, E. (1976) *To Have or to Be?* New York: Harper & Row.

Gal, S. (2002) A Semiotics of the Public/Private Distinction. *A Journal of Feminist Cultural Theories*, 15 (1), 77–95.

Gallie, D., Felstead, A. & Green, F. (2004) Changing Patterns of Task Discretion, Work. *Employment & Society*, 18 (2), 243–66.

Gallie, D. & White, M. (1993) *Employee Commitment and the Skills Revolution*. London: PSI.

Garrety, K. (2008) Organisational Control and the Self: Critiques and Normative Expectations. *Journal of Business Ethics*, 82 (1), 93–106.

Gasper, D. (2007) What is the Capability Approach? Its Core Rationale, Partners and Dangers. *Journal of Socioeconomics*, 36 (3), 335–59.

Gaus, G. F. (1981) The Convergence of Rights and Utility: The Case of Rawls and Mill. *Ethics*, 92, 57–72.

Gebauer, J. & Lowman, D. (2008) *Closing the Engagement Gap: How Great Companies Unlock Employee Potential for Superior Results*. New York: Penguin Group.

Gewirth, A. (1998) *Self-Fulfillment*. Princeton: Princeton University Press.

Ghai, D. (2003) Decent Work: Concepts and Indicators. *International Labour Review*, 142 (2), 113–45.

Gibson-Graham, J-K. (1996) *The End of Capitalism (as We Knew It): A Feminist Critique of Political Economy*. Oxford: Blackwell.

Gibson-Graham, J-K. (2003) Enabling Ethical Economies: Cooperativism and Class. *Critical Sociology*, 29 (2), 123–61.

Gibson-Graham, J-K. (2008) Diverse Economies: Performative Practices for 'Other Worlds'. *Progress in Human Geography*, 32 (5), 613–32.

Gilligan, C. (1982) *In a Different Voice*. Cambridge: Harvard University Press.

Giovanola, B. (2005) Personhood and Human Richness: Goods and Well-Being in the Capability Approach and Beyond. *Review of Social Economy*, 63 (2), 249–67.

Glucksmann, M. (1995) Why Work? Gender and the Total Social Organization of Labour. *Gender, Work and Organization*, 2 (2), 63–75.

Godard, J. (2007) Is Good Work Good for Democracy? Work, Change at Work and Political Participation in Canada and England. *British Journal of Industrial Relations*, 45 (4), 760–90.

Goffman, E. (1959) *The Presentation of the Self in Everyday Life*. Harmondsworth: Penguin.

Gollan, P. J. & Wilkinson, A. (2007) Contemporary Developments in Information and Consultation. *The International Journal of Human Resource Management*, 18 (7), 1133–44.

Gomberg, P. (2007) *How to Make Opportunity Equal: Race and Contributive Justice*. Malden MA: Blackwell Publishing.

Goodin, R. E. & Niemeyer, S. J. (2003) When Does Deliberation Begin? Internal Reflection versus Public Discussion in Deliberative Democracy. *Political Studies*, 15 (4), 627–47.

Gorz, A. (1999) *Reclaiming Work: Beyond the Wage-Based Society*. Cambridge: Polity.

Gould, C. (1990) *Rethinking Democracy: Freedom and Social Cooperation in Politics, Economics and Society.* Cambridge: Cambridge University Press.

Gould, C. (1996) Diversity and Democracy: Representing Difference, in Democracy and Difference: Contesting the Boundaries of the Political. In: Benhabib (ed.) *Democracy and Difference: Contesting the Boundaries of the Political.* Princeton, New Jersey: Princeton University Press.

Graham, L. (1995) *On the Line at Subaru-Isuzu: The Japanese Mode and the American Worker.* Ithaca, NY: Cornell University Press.

Granter, E. (2009) *Critical Social Theory and the End of Work.* Surrey & Burlington: Ashgate Publishing.

Green, F. (2004) Why Has Work Effort Become More Intense? *Industrial Relations: A Journal of Economy and Society,* 43 (4), 709–41.

Green, F. (2006) *Demanding Work: The Paradox of Job Quality in the Affluent Economy.* Princeton & Oxford: Princeton University Press.

Greenberg, E. S., Grunberg, L. & Daniel, K. (1996) Industrial Work and Political Participation: Beyond 'Simple Spillover'. *Political Research Quarterly,* 49 (2), 305–30.

Gronn, P. (2002) Collective Influence Strategies as a Unit of Analysis. *The Leadership Quarterly,* 13, 423–51.

Gurtler, S. (2005) The Ethical Dimension of Work: A Feminist Perspective. *Hypatia,* 20 (2), 119–34.

Gustavsen, B. (1985) Workplace Reform and Democratic Dialogue. *Economic and Industrial Democracy,* 6 (4), 461–79.

Gustavsen, B. (1992) *Dialogue and Development: Theory of Communication, Action Research and the Restructuring of Work Life.* Assen & Stockholm: Van Gorcum.

Gustavsen, B. (2007) Work Organization and the 'Scandinavian Model'. *Economic and Industrial Democracy,* 28 (4), 650–71.

Habermas, J. (2002 [1971]) *Knowledge and Human Interests.* Boston, MA: Beacon Press.

Habermas, J. (1974) *Labour and Interaction, in Theory and Practice.* London: Heinemann.

Habermas, J. (1984) *The Theory of Communicative Action.* Boston: Beacon.

Habermas, J. (1987) *Theory of Communicative Action, Volume 2, Lifeworld and System: A Critique of Functionalist Reason.* Boston: Beacon.

Habermas, J. (1990) *Reconstruction and Interpretation in the Social Sciences, in Moral Consciousness and Communicative Action.* Cambridge, Mass.: MIT Press.

Habermas, J. (1993) *Remarks on Discourse Ethics in Justification and Application, in Justification and Application.* Malden & Cambridge: Polity Press.

Halford, S. & Leonard, P. (2006) Place, Space and Time: Contextualizing Workplace Subjectivities. *Organization Studies,* 27 (5), 657–76.

Hall, M. and Purcell, J. (2012) *Consultation at Work: Regulation and Practice.* Oxford: Oxford University Press.

Hall, P. & Soskice, D. (2001) *Varieties of Capitalism.* Cambridge, MA: MIT Press.

Hancock, P. & Tyler, M. (2001) Managing Subjectivity and the Dialectics of Self-Consciousness: Hegel and Organisation Theory. *Organization,* 8 (4), 565–85.

Hardimon, M. O. (1994) Role Obligations. *Journal of Philosophy,* 91, 333–63.

Hardt, M. (1999) Affective Labor. *Boundary 2,* 26 (2).

Hare, R. M. (1972) *Essays on the Moral Concepts.* California: University of California Press.

Harley, B., Hyman, J. & Thompson, P. (eds) (2005) *Participation and Democracy at Work*. Basingstoke: Palgrave Macmillan.

Harter, J. K., Schmidt, F. L. and Hayes, T. L. (2002) Business-Unit-Level Relationship between Employee Satisfaction, Employee Engagement, and Business Outcomes: A Meta-Analysis. *Journal of Applied Psychology*, 87 (2), 268–79.

Hauser, R. M. & Roan, C. L. (2007) *Work Complexity and Cognitive Functioning at Midlife: Cross-Validating the Kohn-Schooler Hypothesis in the American Cohort*. CDE Working Paper No. 2007–08, Center for Demography and Ecology, University of Wisconsin-Madison.

Held, V. (2006) *The Ethics of Care: Personal, Political and Global*. Oxford & New York: Oxford University Press.

Heller, F. (2003) Participation and Power: A Critical Assessment. *Applied Psychology: An International Review*, 52 (1), 144–63.

Hicks, J. A. & King, L. A. (2009) Meaning in Life as a Subjective Judgement and Lived Experience, Social and Personality Psychology. *Compass*, 3/4, 638–53.

Hill, T. E. (1995) Self-Respect Reconsidered. In: Dillon (ed.) *Dignity, Character and Self-Respect*. New York & London: Routledge.

Himmelweit, S. (2002) Making Visible the Hidden Economy: The Case for Gender-Impact Analysis of Economic Policy. *Feminist Economics*, 8 (1), 49–70.

Himmelweit, S. & Mohun, S. (1977) Domestic Labour and Capital. *Cambridge Journal of Economics*, 1, 15–31.

Hinchliffe, G. (2004) Work and Human Flourishing. *Educational Philosophy and Theory*, 36 (5), 535–47.

Hinchman, L. P. & Hinchman, S. K. (1984) In Heidegger's Shadow: Hannah Arendt's Phenomenological Humanism. *The Review of Politics*, 46 (2), 183–211.

Hirschman, A. O. (1970) *Exit, Voice, and Loyalty: Responses to Decline in Firms, Organizations and States*. London: Harvard University Press.

Hirst, P. (1994) *Associative Democracy: New Forms of Economic and Social Governance*. Cambridge: Polity Press.

Hochschild, A. R. (1983) *The Managed Heart: Commercialisation of Human Feeling*. Berkeley: University of California Press.

Hochschild, A. R. (1985) *The Managed Heart: The Commercialization of Human Feeling*. California: University of California Press.

Hodgson, G. M. (2006) What are Institutions? *Journal of Economic Issues*, 40 (1), 1–25.

Hodson, R. (1996) Dignity in the Workplace Under Participative Management: Alienation and Freedom Revisited. *American Sociological Review*, 61 (5), 719–38.

Hodson, R. (1998) Organizational Ethnographies: An Underutilized Resource in the Sociology of Work. *Social Forces*, 76 (4), 1173–208.

Hodson, R. (2002) Worker Participation and Teams: New Evidence from Analyzing Organizational Ethnographies. *Economic and Industrial Democracy*, 23 (4), 491–528.

Holbrook, D. (1977) Politics and the Need for Meaning. In: Fitzgerald (ed.) *Human Needs and Politics*. Oxford: Pergamon Press.

Holtgrewe, U. (2000) Recognition, Intersubjectivity and Service Work: Labour Conflicts in Call Centres. Industrielle Beziehungen, Zeitschrift fur Arbeit,

Organisation und Management. *The German Journal of Industrial Relations*, 8 (1), 37–54.

Honig, B. (1993) *Political Theory and the Displacement of Politics*. Ithaca, NY: Cornell University Press.

Honneth, A. (1995a) Work and Instrumental Action: On the Normative Basis of Critical Theory. In: Honneth (ed.) *The Fragmented World of the Social*. Albany: State University of New York Press.

Honneth, A. (1995b) *The Struggle for Recognition: The Moral Grammar of Social Conflicts*. Cambridge: Polity Press.

Honneth, A. (2004) Organized Self-Realization: Some Paradoxes of Individualization. *European Journal of Social Theory*, 7 (4), 463–78.

Honneth, A. & Farrell, J. M. M. (1998) Democracy as Reflexive Cooperation: John Dewey and the Theory of Democracy Today. *Political Theory*, 26 (6), 763–83.

Honohan, I. (2002) *Civic Republicanism*. London & New York: Routledge.

Howarth, D. R. (2008) Ethos, Agonism and Populism: William Connolly and the Case for Radical Democracy. *British Journal of Politics and International Relations*, 10, 171–93.

Hsieh, N. (2005) Rawlsian Justice and Workplace Republicanism. *Social Theory and Practice*, 31, 115–42.

Hsieh, N. (2006) Managers, Workers, and Authority. *Journal of Business Ethics*, 71, 347–57.

Hsieh, N. (2008) Survey Article: Justice in Production. *The Journal of Political Philosophy*, 16 (1), 72–100.

Hurka, T. (1993) *Perfectionism*. New York and Oxford: Oxford University Press.

Huseby, R. (2009) Sufficiency: Restated and Defended. *Journal of Political Philosophy*, 18 (2), 178–97.

Hussain, W. (2007) Sustaining Justice: Stability Under Rawlsian Social Institutions. *Annual Meeting of the American Political Science Association*, 30 August–7 September 2007.

Ikaheimo, H. (2007) Recognizing Persons. *Journal of Consciousness Studies*, 14 (5–6), 224–47.

Ikaheimo, H. & Laitinen, A. (2007) Analyzing Recognition: Identification, Acknowledgement and Recognitive Attitudes towards Persons. In: van den Brink & Owen (eds) *Recognition & Power: Axel Honneth and the Tradition of Critical Social Theory*. Cambridge: Cambridge University Press.

Ingold, T. (2000) Evolving Skills. In: Rose & Rose (eds) *Alas Poor Darwin*. London: Cape.

Inkeles, A. & Smith, D. H. (1974) *Becoming Modern*. Cambridge, Mass.: Harvard University Press.

Inkson, K. (1987) The Craft Ideal and the Integration of Work: A Study of Potters. *Human Relations*, 40 (1), 163–76.

International Labour Organisation (ILO) (2007) Social Dialogue. [Online] http://www.ilo.org/public/english/dialogue/themes/sd.htm [Accessed 30th January 2012].

Johnson, P. (2006) Whence Democracy? A Review and Critique of the Conceptual Dimensions of the Business Case for Organizational Democracy. *Organization*, 13 (2), 245–74.

Joske, W. D. (1974) Philosophy and the Meaning of Life. In: Klemke (ed.) *The Meaning of Life*. New York: Oxford University Press.

Joyce, P. (1987) The Historical Meanings of Work: An Introduction. In: Joyce (ed.) *The Historical Meanings of Work*. Cambridge: Cambridge University Press.

Kaarsemaker, E. & Poutsma, E. (2006) The Fit of Employee Ownership with Other Human Resource Management Practices: Theoretical and Empirical Suggestions Regarding the Existence of an Ownership High-Performance Work System. *Economic and Industrial Democracy*, 27 (4), 669–85.

Kahn, W. A. (1990) Psychological Conditions of Personal Engagement and Disengagement at Work. *The Academy of Management Journal*, 33 (4), 692–724.

Kant, E. (1983 [1797]) *Metaphysical Principles of Virtue*. Bobbs-Merrill Co.

Karagiannis, N. & Wagner, P. (2008) Varieties of Agonism: Conflict, the Common Good, and the Need for Synagonism. *Journal of Social Philosophy*, 39 (3), 323–39.

Kauppinen, A. (2008) Why the Shape of a Life Matters. [Online] http://www.philosophy.northwestern.edu/conferences/moralpolitical/08/papers/Kauppinen.pdf [Accessed 30th July 2011].

Keane, J. (1975) On Tools and Language: Habermas on Work and Interaction. *New German Critique*, 6, 82–100.

Keat, R. (2006) Liberalism, Neutrality, and Varieties of Capitalism. [Online] http://www.russellkeat.net/research/ethicsmarkets/keat_liberalism_neutrality_vocs.pdf [Accessed 17th January 2011].

Keat, R. (2009a) Choosing Between Capitalisms: Habermas, Ethics and Politics. *Res Publica*, 15, 355–76.

Keat, R. (2009b) Anti-Perfectionism, Market Economics and Meaningful Work. [Online] http://www.russellkeat.net/research/ethicsmarkets/keat_antiperfectionism.pdf [Accessed 17th January 2011].

Keenan, A. (2003) *Democracy in Question: Democratic Openness in a Time of Political Closure*. Stanford: Stanford University Press.

Kekes, J. (1986) The Informed Will and the Meaning of Life. *Philosophy and Phenomenological Research*, 47 (1), 75–90.

Kildal, N. (1998) The Social Basis of Self-Respect: A Normative Discussion of Politics Against Unemployment. *Thesis Eleven*, 54, 63–77.

Kioupkiolis, A. (2009) Three Paradigms of Modern Freedom. *European Journal of Political Theory*, 8 (4), 473–91.

Knights, D. & Vurdubakis, T. (1994) Foucault, Power and All That. In: Jermier, Knights & Nord (eds) *Resistance and Power in Organizations*. London: Routledge.

Knights, D. & Willmott, H. (1989) Power and Subjectivity at Work: From Degradation to Subjugation at Work. *Sociology*, 23 (4), 535–58.

Knops, A. (2012) 'Interrogating Agonism with Deliberation – Realising the Benefits'. iFILOZOFIJA I DRU_TVO XXIII (4), 2012. DOI: 10.2298/FID1204151K.

Kocyba, H. (2011) Recognition, Cooperation and the Moral Presuppositions of Capitalist Organizations of Work. *Paper presented to the 'Work After Liberalism: the significance of work for political theory' conference*, Institut fur Sozialforschung, Frankfurt, 24th–25th February 2011.

Kohn, M. L. (1976) Occupational Structure and Alienation. *The American Journal of Sociology*, 82 (1), 111–30.

Kohn, M. L., Kazinmierz, M. & Slomczynski, K. (1997) Social Structure and Personality under Conditions of Radical Social Change: A Comparative Analysis of Poland and Ukraine. *American Sociological Review*, 62, 614–38.

Kohn, M. L. & Schooler, C. (1983) *Work and Personality: An Inquiry into the Impact of Social Stratification*. Norwood: Ablex Publishing.

Kohn, M. L. & Slomczynski, K. M. (1990) *Social Structure and Self-Direction: A Comparative Analysis of the United States and Poland*. Oxford, UK: Blackwell.

Kornhauser, A. (1965) *Mental Health of the Industrial Worker: A Detroit Study*. Oxford: John Wiley.

Korsegaard, C. M. (1996) *The Sources of Normativity*. Cambridge: Cambridge University Press.

Korsegaard, C. M. (2009) *Self-Constitution: Agency, Identity and Integrity*. Oxford: Oxford University Press.

Koukiadaki, A. (2010) The Establishment and Operation of Information and Consultation Arrangements in a Capability-Based Framework. *Economic and Industrial Democracy*, 31, 365–88.

Kovacs, G. (1986) Phenomenology of Work and Self-Transcendence. *The Journal of Value Inquiry*, 20 (3), 195–207.

Kunda, G. (1992) *Engineering Culture*. Philadelphia: Temple University Press.

Kusterer, K. C. (1978) *Workplace Knowhow: The Important Working Knowledge of Unskilled Workers*. Boulder, CO: Westview.

Kutz, C. (2000) Acting Together. *Philosophy and Phenomenological Research*, 61 (1), 1–31.

Kymlicka, W. (2002) *Contemporary Political Philosophy: An Introduction*. Oxford: Oxford University Press.

Laborem Exercens (1981) Encyclical on Human Work, Pope John Paul II.

Laitinen, A. (2002) Interpersonal Recognition: A Response to Value or a Precondition of Personhood? *Inquiry*, 45, 463–78.

Laitinen, A. (2003) Social Equality, Recognition and Preconditions of Good Life. *Social Inequality Today*, Macquarie University, CRSI 2003 Conference Proceedings.

Laitinen, A. (2007) Sorting Out Aspects of Personhood: Capacities, Normativity and Recognition. *Journal of Consciousness Studies*, 14 (5–7).

Landemore, H. (2010) Deliberation, Representation, and the Epistemic Function of Parliamentary Assemblies: A Burkean Argument in Favor of Descriptive Representation. *International Conference on Democracy as Idea and Practice*, University of Oslo, Oslo, 13–15 January 2010.

Landes, J. B. (1995) The Public and the Private Sphere: A Feminist Reconsideration. In: Landes (ed.) *Feminism: The Public and the Private*. Oxford & New York: Oxford University Press (1998).

Lane, R. E. (1991) *The Market Experience*. Cambridge: Cambridge University Press.

Lane, R. E. (1992) Work as Disutility and Money as Happiness: Cultural Origins of a Basic Market Error. *The Journal of Socio-Economics*, 21 (1), 43–64.

Langley, A. & Sloan, P. (2012) Organizational Change and Dialectic Process. In: Boje, Burnes & Hassard (eds) *The Routledge Companion to Organizational Change*. Oxford & New York: Routledge.

Latour, B. & Venn, C. (2002) Morality and Technology: The Ends of the Means, Theory. *Culture & Society*, 19, 247–60.

Lawrence, G. (1977) Management Development ... Some Ideals, Images and Realities. *Journal of European Industrial Training*, 1, (2), 21–5.

Lawson, V. (2007) Geographies of Care and Responsibility. *Annuals of the Association of American Geographers*, 97 (1), 1–11.

Lazzerato, M. (1996) Immaterial Labor. In: Virno & Hardt (eds) *Radical Thought in Italy: A Potential Politics*. Minneapolis: University of Minneapolis Press.

Lazzeri, C. & Caille, A. (2006) Recognition Today: The Theoretical, Ethical and Political Stakes of the Concept. *Critical Horizons*, 7 (1).

Leach, B. (1998) Industrial Homework, Economic Restructuring and the Meaning of Work. *Labour/Le Travail*, 41, 97–115.

Lee, R. (2006) The Ordinary Economy: Tangled Up in Values and Geography. *Transactions of the Institute of British Geographers*, 31 (4), 413–32.

Lenz, C. (2005) The End or the Apotheosis of 'Labor'? Hannah Arendt's Contribution to the Question of the Good Life in Times of Global Superfluity of Human Labor Power. *Hypatia*, 20 (2), 135–54.

Levy, N. (2005) Downshifting and Meaning in Life. *Ratio*, XVIII, 2nd June, 176–89.

Lincoln, J. R. & Kalleberg, A. L. (1990) *Culture, Control and Commitment*. New York: Cambridge University Press.

Lindkvist, L. (2005) Knowledge, Communities and Knowledge Collectivities: A Typology of Knowledge Work in Groups. *Journal of Management Studies*, 26 (6), 1189–210.

Lipman, M. (1995) Caring as Thinking. *Inquiry: Critical Thinking Across the Disciplines*, 15 (1), 1–13.

Lips-Wiersma, M. & Morris, L. (2009) Discriminating Between 'Meaningful Work' and the 'Management of Meaning'. *Journal of Business Ethics*, 88, 491–511.

Littler, C. (1982) *The Development of the Labour Process in Capitalist Societies*. London: Heinemann.

Lovett, F. (2010) *General Theory of Domination and Justice*. Oxford: Oxford University Press.

Lovett, F. & Pettit, P. (2009) Neorepublicanism: A Normative and Institutional Research Program. *Annual Review of Political Science*, 12, 11–29.

Lukacs, G. (1971 [1922]) *History and Class Consciousness: Studies in Marxist Dialectics*. Cambridge, MA: The MIT Press.

Lukes, S. (2005) *Power: A Radical View* (2nd edition). London: Macmillan.

Luscher, L. S. & Lewis, M. W. (2008) Organizational Change and Managerial Sensemaking: Working Through Paradox. *Academy of Management Journal*, 51 (2), 221–40.

Lutz, M. A. (1995) Centering Social Economics on Human Dignity. *Review of Social Economy*, LIII (2), 163–80.

Lyons, P. (2008) The Crafting of Jobs and Individual Differences. *Journal of Business Psychology*, 23, 25–6.

Macey, W. & Schneider, B. (2008) The Meaning of Employee Engagement. *Industrial and Organisational Psychology*, 1, 3–30.

MacIntyre, A. (1981) *After Virtue: A Study in Moral Theory*. London: Duckworth.

MacKenzie, C. (2008) Relational Autonomy, Normative Authority and Perfectionism. *Journal of Social Philosophy*, 39 (4), 512–33.

Maddi, S. R. (1970) The Search of Meaning. *Nebraska Symposium on Motivation 1971*. University of Nebraska Press.

Maguire, S. (1999) The Discourse of Control. *Journal of Business Ethics*, 19 (1), 109–14.

Manin, B. (2005) Democratic Deliberation: Why Should We Promote Debate Rather than Discussion. *Program in Ethics and Public Affairs Seminar*, Princeton University, 13 October 2005.

Mansbridge, J. (1998) Forward: Mary Parker Follett: Feminist and Negotiator. *The New State: Group Organization the Solution of Popular Government*. Pennsylvania: The Pennsylvania State University Press.

Mansbridge, J. (2010) *The Deliberative System Disaggregated*. APSA 2010 Annual Meeting Paper, 2010.

March, J. G. (1962) The Business Firm as a Political Coalition. *The Journal of Politics*, 24 (4), 662–78.

Marchand, T. (2010) Making Knowledge: Explorations of the Indissoluble Relation between Minds, Bodies and Environment. *Journal of the Royal Anthropological Society*, Vol. 16, Supplement 1, 1–21.

Marchington, M., Wilkinson, A., Ackers, P. & Goodman, J. (1994) Understanding the Meaning of Participation: Views from the Workplace. *Human Relations*, 47 (8), 867–94.

Marcuse, H. (1964) *One-Dimensional Man*. New York & Oxford: Routledge & Kegan Paul.

Marcuse, H. (1973) On the Philosophical Foundation of the Concept of Work in Economics. *Telos*, 16 (Summer), 9–37.

Margalit, A. (1996) *The Decent Society*. Cambridge Massachusetts & London: Harvard University Press.

Margalit, A. & Honneth, A. (2001) Recognition. *Proceedings of the Aristotelian Society*, Supplementary Volumes, 111–39.

Marglin, S. A. (1974) What Do Bosses Do? The Origins and Functions of Hierarchy in Capitalist Production. *Review of Radical Political Economics*, 6 (2), 60–112.

Markell, P. (2008) The Insufficiency of Non-Domination. *Political Theory*, 36 (1), 9–36.

Marsh, R. M. (1992) The Difference Between Participation and Power in Japanese Factories. *Industrial and Labor Relations Review*, 45 (2), 250–70.

Martsolf, D. S. & Mickley, J. R. (1998) The Concept of Spirituality in Nursing Theories: Differing World-Views and Extent to Focus. *Journal of Clinical Nursing*, 27, 294–303.

Marx, K. (1978 [1844]) Economic and Philosophical Manuscripts. In: Tucker (ed.) *The Marx-Engels Reader (2nd edition)*. New York & London: W. W. Norton & Company.

Marx, K. (1848) *The Communist Manifesto*.

Marx, K. (1978 [1867]) Capital, Vol. 1: The Process of Production of Capital. In: Tucker (ed.) *The Marx-Engels Reader (2nd edition)*. New York & London: W. W. Norton & Company.

Massey, D. (1992) Politics and Space/Time. *New Left Review*, I/196.

Massey, S. J. (1983) Is Self-Respect a Moral or a Psychological Concept? *Ethics*, 93 (2), 246–61.

May, D., Gilson, R. & Harter, L. (2004) The Psychological Conditions of Meaningfulness, Safety and Availability and the Engagement of the Human Spirit at Work. *Journal of Occupational and Organizational Psychology*, 77, 11–37.

Maynor, J. (2002) Another Instrumental Republican Approach? *European Journal of Political Theory*, 1 (1), 71–89.

McAllister, D. J. & Bigley, G. A. (2002) Work Context and the Definition of Self: How Organisational Care Influences Organisation-Based Self-Esteem. *The Academy of Management Journal*, 45 (5), 894–904.

McCabe, D. (2007) Individualism at Work? Subjectivity, Teamworking and Anti-Unionism. *Organization*, 14 (2), 243–66.

McCall, J. J. (2001) Employee Voice in Corporate Governance: A Defense of Strong Participation Rights. *Business Ethics Quarterly*, 11 (1), 195–213.

McMahon, C. (1994) *Authority and Democracy: A General Theory of Government and Management*. Princeton, NJ: Princeton University Press.

McMahon, C. (1995) The Political Theory of Organizations and Business Ethics. *Philosophy and Public Affairs*, 24 (4), 292–313.

McMahon, C. (2007) Comments on Hsieh, Moriarty and Oosterhout. *Journal of Business Ethics*, 71, 371–9.

McManus, H. (2008) Enduring Agonism: Between Individuality and Plurality. *Polity*, 40 (4), 509–25.

McNay, L. (2009) Self as Enterprise: Dilemmas of Control and Resistance in Foucault's The Birth of Biopolitics. *Theory, Culture & Society*, 26 (6), 55–77.

Meda, D. (1996) New Perspectives on Work as Value. *International Labour Review*, 135 (6), 633–43.

Metz, T. (2001a) The Concept of a Meaningful Life. *American Philosophical Quarterly*, Issue 38, No. 2, 137–53.

Metz, T. (2001b) Respect for Persons and Perfectionist Politics. *Philosophy and Public Affairs*, 30 (4), 417–42.

Metz, T. (2003) Utilitarianism and the Meaning of Life. *Utilitas*, 15, 50–70.

Metz, T. (2007) New Developments in the Meaning of Life. *Philosophy Compass*, 2 (2), 196–217.

Meyers, D. T. (1995) Self-Respect and Autonomy. In: Dillon (ed.) *Dignity, Character and Self-Respect*. London: Routledge.

Meyers, D. T. (2000) Intersectional Identity and the Authentic Self?: Opposites Attract! In: Mackenzie & Stoljar (eds) *Relational Autonomy: Feminist Perspectives on Autonomy, Agency and the Social Self*. New York and Oxford: Oxford University Press.

Michaelson, C. (2008) Work and the Most Terrible Life. *Journal of Business Ethics*, 77 (3), 335–45.

Michaelson, C., Pratt, M. G., Grant, A. M. & Dunn, C. P. (2013) Meaningful Work: Connecting Business Ethics and Organization Studies. *Journal of Business Ethics* (published online, March 2013).

Mill, J. S. (1974 [1859]) *On Liberty*. London: Penguin Books.

Mill, J. S. (1994 [1871]) *Principles of Political Economy and Chapters on Socialism*. Oxford & New York: Oxford University Press.

Miller, D. (1987) *Material Culture and Mass Consumption*. Oxford: Blackwell.

Miller, D. (1999) *Principles of Social Justice*. Cambridge, Massachusetts & London: Harvard University Press.

Miller, P. & Rose, N. (1995) *Production, Identity, and Democracy: Theory and Society*, 24 (2), 427–67.

Miller, R. W. (2003) Capitalism & Marxism. In: Frey & Wellman (eds) *A Companion to Applied Ethics*. Malden, MA & Oxford: Blackwell Publishing.

Milliken, F. J., Morrison, E. W. & Hewlin, P. F. (2003) An Exploratory Study of Employee Silence: Issues that Employees Don't Communicate Upwards and Why. *Journal of Management Studies*, 40 (6), 1453–76.

Mills, C. W. (1951) *White Collar*. Oxford: Oxford University Press.

Moll, K. N. (2009) The Enduring Significance of Axel Honneth's Critical Conception of Work. *Emergent Australian Philosophers*, Issue 2, 1–16.

Moore, A. (2011) Expert Authority in a Deliberative System. *2011 General Conference of the European Consortium for Political Research, Reykjavik*, 25–27 August 2011.

Moriarty, J. (2005) On the Relevance of Political Philosophy to Business Ethics. *Business Ethics Quarterly*, 15, 455–73.

Moriarty, J. (2009) Rawls, Self-Respect, and the Opportunity for Meaningful Work. *Social Theory and Practice*, 35 (2), 441–59.

Morris, W. (1884) Art and Socialism. [Online] http://www.marxists.org/archive/morris/works/1884/as/as.htm [Accessed 16th October 2011].

Morris, W. (1993 [1890]) *News from Nowhere and Other Writings*. London: Penguin Books.

Morrison, E. (2011) Employee Voice Behavior: Integration and Directions for Future Research. *Academy of Management Annals*, 5, 373–412.

Moynagh, P. (1997) A Politics of Enlarged Mentality: Hannah Arendt, Citizenship, Responsibility, and Feminism. *Hypatia*, 12 (4), 27–53.

Muirhead, R (2004) *Just Work*. Cambridge, Massachusetts & London: Harvard University Press.

Murphy, J. B. (1993) *The Moral Economy of Labor: Aristotelian Themes in Economic Theory*. New Haven & London: Yale University Press.

Mutz, D. C. & Mondak, J. J. (2006) The Workplace as a Context for Cross-Cutting Political Discourse. *The Journal of Politics*, 68 (1), 140–55.

Nagel, T. (1971) The Absurd. *Journal of Philosophy*, 68, 716–27.

Nagel, T. (1986) *The View from Nowhere*. New York: Oxford University Press.

Naoi, M. & Schooler, C. (1985) Occupational Conditions and Psychological Functioning in Japan. *American Journal of Sociology*, 90, 729–52.

Nederman, G. J. (2008) Men at Work: Poesis, Politics and Labor in Aristotle and Some Aristotelians. *Analyse & Kritik*, 30, 17–31.

Nelson, J. A. (2003) Separative and Soluble Firms: Androcentric Bias and Business Ethics. In: Ferber & Nelson (eds) *Feminist Economics Today: Beyond Economic Man*. Chicago & London: University of Chicago Press.

Nelson, J. A. (2004) Freedom, Reason, and More: Feminist Economics and Human Development. *Journal of Human Development*, 5 (3), 309–33.

Nelson, J. A. & England, P. (2002) Feminist Philosophies of Love and Work. *Hypatia*, 17 (2), 1–18.

Neysmith, S. M. & Reitsma-Street, M. (2005) 'Provisioning': Conceptualising the Work of Women for 21st Century Social Policy. *Women's Studies International Forum*, 28, 381–91.

Noggle, R. (1999) Kantian Respect and Particular Persons. *Canadian Journal of Philosophy*, 29 (3), 449–78.

Noonan, J. (2005) Modernization, Rights, and Democratic Society: The Limits of Habermas's Democratic Theory. *Res Republica*, 11, 101–23.

Nozick, R. (1974) *Anarchy, State and Utopia*. New York: Basic Books.

Nussbaum, M. C. (1987) Nature, Function, and Capability: Aristotle on Political Distribution. *World Institute for Development Economics Research*, WP 31.

Nussbaum, M. C. (1992) Human Functioning and Social Justice: In Defense of Aristotelian Essentialism. *Political Theory*, 20 (2), 202–46.

Nussbaum, M. C. (1995) Human Capabilities, Female Human Beings. In: Nussbaum & Glover (eds) *Women, Culture and Development: A Study of Human Capabilities*. Oxford: Clarendon Press.

Nussbaum, M. C. (1999) *Sex and Social Justice*. New York: Oxford University Press.

Nussbaum, M. C. (2000) Aristotle, Politics, and Human Capabilities: A Response to Antony, Arneson, Charlesworth, and Mulgan. *Ethics*, 111 (1), 102–40.

Nussbaum, M. C. (2001) *Upheavals of Thought: The Intelligence of Emotions*. Cambridge: Cambridge University Press.

Nussbaum, M. C. (2006) *Frontiers of Justice: Disability, Nationality, Species Membership*. Cambridge, Massachusetts & London: The Belknap Press of Harvard University Press.

Nussbaum, M. C. (2011) *Creating Capabilities: The Human Development Approach*. Cambridge, Massachusetts & London: The Belknap Press of Harvard University Press.

Nussbaum, M. & Glover, J. (1995) (eds) *Women, Culture and Development: A Study of Human Capabilities*. Oxford: Clarendon Press.

Nussbaum, M. C. & Sen, A. (eds) (1993) *The Quality of Life*. Oxford: Clarendon Press.

O'Neill, J. (1997) Hegel against Fukuyama: Associations, Markets and Recognition. *Politics*, 17 (3), 191–6.

Offe, C. (1977) *Industry and Inequality: The Achievement Principle in Work and Social Status*. New York: St. Martin's Press.

Offe, C. (1985) *Disorganized Capitalism*. Cambridge, MA: The MIT Press.

Orr, J. E. (1997) *Talking About Machines: An Ethnography of a Modern Job*. Ithaca, New York: ILR Press.

Overvold, G. E. (1987) The Imperative of Organizational Harmony: A Critique of Contemporary Human Relations Theory. *Journal of Business Ethics*, 6 (7), 559–65.

Palshaugen, O. (2006) Constructive Practice and Critical Theory: The Contributions of Action Research to Organisational Change and the Discourse on Organisations. *International Journal of Action Research*, 2 (3), 283–318.

Park, L. E. & Crocker, J. (2005) Interpersonal Consequences of Seeking Self-Esteem. *Personality and Social Psychology Bulletin*, 31 (11), 1587–98.

Patchen, M. (1970) *Participation, Achievement, and Involvement on the Job*. Englecliffs, NJ: Prentice Hall.

Pateman, C. (1970) *Participation & Democratic Theory*. Cambridge: Cambridge University Press.

Pateman, C. (2004) Democratizing Citizenship: Some Advantages of a Basic Income. *Politics & Society*, 32 (1), 89–105.

Pateman, C. (2007) Why Republicanism? *Basic Income Studies*, 2 (2), 1–6.

Patterson, O. (1982) *Slavery and Social Death: A Comparative Study*. Harvard: Harvard University Press.

Pearce, C. L. & Conger, J. A. (2003) All Those Years Ago: The Historical Underpinnings of Shared Leadership. In: Pearce & Conger (eds) *Shared Leadership: Reframing the Hows and Whys of Leadership* (pp. 1–18). Thousand Oaks, CA: Sage.

Pearce, C. L. & Sims, H. P. Jr. (2002) Vertical versus Shared Leadership as Predictors of the Effectiveness of Change Management Teams: An Examination of Aversive, Directive, Transactional, Transformational, and Empowering Leader Behaviours. *Group Dynamics: Theory, Research, and Practice*, 6, 172–97.

Perrons, D. (2000) Care, Paid Work, and Leisure: Rounding the Triangle. *Feminist Economics*, 6 (1), 105–14.

Petersen, A. & Willig, R. (2004) Work and Recognition: Reviewing New Forms of Pathological Developments. *Acta Sociologica*, 47 (4), 338–50.

Pettit, P. (1997) *Republicanism: A Theory of Freedom and Government*. Oxford: Oxford University Press.

Pettit, P. (2001) *A Theory of Freedom: From the Psychology to the Politics of Agency*. Cambridge: Polity Press.

Pettit, P. (2002) *Rules, Reasons, and Norms: Selected Essays*. Oxford: Oxford University Press.

Pettit, P. (2007) Free Persons and Free Choices. *History of Political Thought*, XXVIII (4), 709–18.

Pettit, P. & Schweikard, D. (2006) Joint Actions and Group Agents. *Philosophy of the Social Sciences*, 36 (18), 18–39.

Pocock, B. (2006) Jobs, Care and Justice: A Fair Work Regime for Australia. [Online] *Clare Burton Memorial Lecture 2006*, http://www.unisa.edu.au/staffdev/women/cblectures/speech2006.pdf [Accessed 5th September 2011].

Pot, F. D. & Koningsveld, E. (2009) Quality of Working Life and Organizational Performance – Two Sides of the Same Coin? *Scandinavian Journal of Work and Environmental Health*. [Online] http://www.rower-eu.eu:8080/rower/conferences/1stWorkshop/pot.pdf [Accessed 29th July 2011].

Power, M. (2004) Social Provisioning as a Starting Point for Feminist Economics. *Feminist Economics*, 10 (3), 3–19.

Prendergast, R. (2005) The Concept of Freedom and its Relation to Economic Development – A Critical Appreciation of the Work of Amartya Sen. *Cambridge Journal of Economics*, 29, 1145–70.

Proudfoot, W. (1978) Rawls on Self-Respect and Social Union. *Journal of Chinese Philosophy*, 5, 255–69.

Pruijit, H. (2000) Repainting, Modifying, Smashing Taylorism. *Journal of Organisational Change Management*, 13 (5), 439–51.

Pruijit, H. (2003) Teams between Neo-Taylorism and Anti-Taylorism. *Economic and Industrial Democracy*, 24 (1), 77–101.

Purcell, J. (2012) The Limits and Possibilities of Employee Engagement. *Warwick Papers in Industrial Relations*, Number 96.

Purcell, J., Kinnie, N., Swart, J., Rayton, B. & Hutchinson, S. (2009) *People Management and Performance*. London: Routledge.

Putterman, L. (1988) The Firm as Association versus the Firm, Economics and Association. *Economics and Philosophy*, 4, 243–66.

Pyman, A., Cooper, B., Teicher, J. & Holland, P. (2006) A Comparison of the Effectiveness of Employee Voice Arrangements in Australia. *Industrial Relations Journal*, 37 (5), 543–59.

Pyszczynski, T. & Cox, C. (2004a) Can We Really Do Without Self-Esteem? Comment on Crocker and Park. *Psychological Bulletin*, 130 (3), 425–9.

Pyszczynski, T. et al (2004b) Why do People Need Self-Esteem? A Theoretical and Empirical Review. *Psychological Bulletin*, 130 (3), 435–68.

Qvale, T. U. (2002) A Case of Slow Learning? Recent Trends in Social Partnerships in Norway with Special Emphasis on Workplace Democracy. *Concepts and Transformations*, 7 (1), 31–55.

Ramsey, H., Scholarios, D. & Harley, B. (2000) Employees and High-Performance Work Systems: Testing Inside the Black Box. *British Journal of Industrial Relations*, 38 (4), 501–31.

Radin, M. J. (1996) *Contested Commodities*. Harvard: Harvard University Press.

Rau, A. (2011) Psychopolitics and the Need for a Politics of the Sorrow of Work. *Paper presented to the 'Work After Liberalism: The Significance of Work for Political Theory' Conference*. Institut fur Sozialforschung, Frankfurt, 24th–25th February 2011.

Rawls, J. (1999 [1971]) *Theory of Justice*. Oxford: Oxford University Press.

Rawls, J. (2001) *Justice as Fairness: A Restatement*. Cambridge, Massachusetts & London: The Belknap Press of Harvard University Press.

Rawls, J. (2005) *Political Liberalism*. New York: Columbia University Press.

Raz, J. (1986) *The Morality of Freedom*. Oxford: Clarendon Press.

Raz, J. (1989) Liberating Duties. *Law and Philosophy*, 8 (1), 3–21.

Raz, J. (1996) *Ethics in the Public Domain*. Oxford: Clarendon Press.

Raz, J. (2001) *Value, Respect and Attachment*. Cambridge: Cambridge University Press.

Raz, J. (2002) *Engaging Reason*. Oxford: Oxford University Press.

Raz, J. (2003) *The Practice of Value*. Oxford: Oxford University Press.

Reader, S. (2005) Aristotle on Necessities and Needs. In: Reader (ed.) *The Philosophy of Need: Royal Institute of Philosophy Supplement*. Cambridge, New York & Melbourne: Cambridge University Press.

Reader, S. (2006) Does a Basic Needs Approach Need Capabilities? *The Journal of Political Philosophy*, 4 (3), 337–50.

Reader, S. (2007) The Other Side of Agency. *Philosophy*, 82, 579–604.

Reader, S. & Brock, G. (2004) Needs, Moral Demands and Moral Theory. *Utilitas*, 16 (3), 251–66.

Restakis, J. (2010) *Humanizing the Economy: Cooperatives in the Age of Capital*. Canada: New Society Publishers.

Rich, B. L., LePine, J. A. and Crawford, E. R. (2010) Job Engagement: Antecedents and Effects on Job Performance. *The Academy of Management Journal*, 53, 617–35.

Rigg, J. (2013) Worthwhile Concept or Old Wine? A Review of Employee Engagement and Related Concepts. *American Journal of Business and Management*, 2 (1), 31–6.

Robeyns, I. (2001) An Income of One's Own: A Radical Vision of Welfare Policies in Europe and Beyond. *Gender and Development*, 9 (1), 82–9.

Robeyns, I. (2003) The Capability Approach – An Interdisciplinary Introduction. University of Amsterdam. [Online] http://www.capabilityapproach.com/pubs/323CAtraining20031209.pdf [Accessed 18th September 2009].

Roessler, B. (2007) Work, Recognition, Emancipation. In: van den Brink & Owen (eds) *Recognition and Power*. Cambridge & New York: Cambridge University Press.

Roessler, B. (2012) Meaningful Work: Arguments from Autonomy. *Journal of Political Philosophy*, 20 (1), 71–93.

Rogers, M. L. (2008) Republican Confusion and Liberal Clarification. *Philosophy & Social Criticism*, 34 (7), 799–824.

Roland, C. E. & Fox, R. M. (2003) Self-Respect: A Neglected Concept. *Philosophical Psychology*, 16 (2), 247–88.

Rose, H. (1994) *Love, Power, Knowledge*. Cambridge: Polity Press.

Rosser, G. (1997) Crafts, Guilds and the Negotiation of Work in the Medieval Town. *Past and Present*, 154, 3–31.

Rosso, B. D., Dekas, K. H. & Wrzesniewski, A. (2010) On the Meaning of Work: A Theoretical Integration and Review. *Research in Organizational Behavior*, 30, 91–127.

Rothschild, J. (2009) Workers' Cooperatives and Social Enterprise: A Forgotten Route to Social Equity and Democracy. *American Behavioral Scientist*, 52, 1023–41.

Ruddick, S. (1998) Care as Labor and Relationship. In: Halfon & Haber (eds) *Norms and Values: Essays on the Work of Virginia Held*. Lanham, MD: Rowman & Littlefield.

Ryan, R. M. & Brown, K. W. (2003) Why We Don't Need Self-Esteem: On Fundamental Needs, Contingent Love and Mindfulness. *Psychological Inquiry*, 14 (1), 71–6.

Sachs, D. (1981) How to Distinguish Self-Respect from Self-Esteem. *Philosophy and Public Affairs*, 10 (4), 346–60.

Saks, A. (2006) Antecedents and Consequences of Engagement. *Journal of Managerial Psychology*, 21 (7), 600–19.

Salais, R. (2003) Work and Welfare: Towards a Capability Approach. In: Zeitlin & Trubeck (eds) *Governing Work and Welfare in a New Economy*. Oxford: Oxford University Press.

Salais, R. & Villeneuve, R. (eds) (2004) *Europe and the Politics of Capabilities*. Cambridge: Cambridge University Press.

Salzinger, L. (1991) A Maid by Any Other Name: The Transformation of 'Dirty Work' by Central American Immigrants. In: Burawoy et al (eds) *Ethnography Unbound: Power and Resistance in the Modern Metropolis*. Berkeley, CA: University of California Press.

Sandberg, J. (2000) Understanding Human Competence at Work: An Interpretative Approach. *Academy of Management Journal*, 43 (1), 9–25.

Sandberg, J. & Pinnington, A. (2009) Professional Competence as Ways of Being: An Existential Ontological Perspective. *Journal of Management Studies*, 46 (7), 1138–70.

Sayer, A. (2000) Moral Economy and Political Economy. *Studies in Political Economy*, 61, Spring, 2000, 79–104.

Sayer, A. (2007) Dignity at Work: Broadening the Agenda. *Organization*, 14 (4), 565–81.

Sayer, A. (2011) *Why Things Matter to People: Social Science, Values and Ethical Life*. Cambridge: Cambridge University Press.

Sayers, S. (2003) Creative Activity and Alienation in Hegel and Marx. *Historical Materialism*, 11 (1), 113–28.

Sayers, S. (2005) Why Work? Marx and Human Nature. *Science and Society*, 69 (4), 606–16.

Schaap, A. (2009) *Law and Agonistic Politics*. Aldershot: Ashgate.

Schaufeli, W. B. (2013). What is Engagement? In: Truss, Alfes, Delbridge, Shantz & Soane (eds) *Employee Engagement in Theory and Practice*. London: Routledge.

Scheffler, S. (2006) Projects, Relationships and Reasons. In: Wallace, Pettit, Scheffler & Smith (eds) *Reason and Value: Themes from the Moral Philosophy of Joseph Raz*. Oxford: Oxford University Press.

Schooler, C. (2007) Culture and Social Structure: The Relevance of Social Structure to Cultural Psychology. In: Kitayama & Cohen (eds) *Handbook of Cultural Psychology*. New York & London: The Guildford Press.

Schumacher, E. F. (1979) *Good Work*. London: Jonathan Cape.

Shuck, M. B., Rocco, T. S. & Albornoz, C. A. (2010) Exploring Employee Engagement from the Employee Perspective: Implications for HRD. *Journal of European Industrial Training*, 35 (1), 300–25.

Shuck, M. B. and Wollard, K. K. (2010) Employee Engagement and HRD: A Seminal Review of the Foundations. *Human Resource Development Review*, 9 (1), 89–110.

Schwartz, A. (1982) Meaningful Work. *Ethics*, 92 (4), 634–46.

Schwartz, M. (1998) Peter Drucker and the Denial of Business Ethics. *Journal of Business Ethics*, 17, 1685–92.

Schwarzenbach, S. A. (1996) On Civic Friendship. *Ethics*, 107 (1), 97–128.

Schweickart, D. (1980) *Capitalism or Worker Control? An Ethical and Economic Appraisal*. New York: Praeger.

Schweizer, S. L. (1995) Participation, Workplace Democracy, and the Problem of Representative Government. *Polity*, 27 (3), 359–77.

Sciaraffa, S. (2011) Identification, Meaning, and the Normativity of Social Roles. *European Journal of Philosophy*, 19 (1), 107–28.

Scott, J. C. (1990) *Domination and the Arts of Resistance: Hidden Transcripts*. Yale University Press.

Seglow, J. (2009) Rights, Contribution, Achievement, and the World. *European Journal of Political Theory*, 8 (1), 61–75.

Sen, A. K. (1977) Rational Fools: A Critique of the Behavioural Foundations of Economic Theory. *Philosophy and Public Affairs*, 6, 317–44.

Sen, A. K. (1979) Utilitarianism and Welfarism. *Journal of Philosophy*, 76, 463–89.

Sen, A. K. (1985a) Well-Being, Agency and Freedom. *Journal of Philosophy*, 32 (4), 169–221.

Sen, A. K. (1985b) The Standard of Living. In: Hawthorn (ed.) *Tanner Lectures, 1985*. Cambridge: Cambridge University Press.

Sen, A. K. (1987) *On Ethics and Economics*. Oxford: Blackwell.

Sen, A. K. (1992) *Inequality Reexamined*. New York & Oxford: Russell Sage Foundation.

Sen, A. K. (1993a) Capability and Well-being. In: Nussbaum & Sen (eds) *The Quality of Life*. Oxford: Clarendon Press.

Sen, A. K. (1993b) Markets and Freedoms: Achievements and Limitations of the Market Mechanism in Promoting Individual Freedoms. *Oxford Economic Papers*, 45, 519–41.

Sen, A. K. (1997) From Income Inequality to Economic Inequality. *Southern Economic Journal*, 64 (2), 383–401.

Sen, A. K. (1999a) *Development as Freedom*. New York: Oxford University Press.

Sen, A. K. (1999b) Democracy as a Universal Value. *Journal of Democracy*, 10 (3), 3–17.

Sen, A. K. (2000) Work and Rights. *International Labour Review*, 139 (2), 119–28.

Sen, A. K. (2002) *Rationality and Freedom*. Cambridge, Massachusetts: Belknap Press.

Sen, A. K. (2004) Elements of a Theory of Human Rights. *Philosophy and Public Affairs*, 32, 315–56.

Sen, A. K. (2005) Human Rights and Capabilities. *Journal of Human Development*, 6 (2), 151–66.

Sen, A. K. (2009) *The Idea of Justice*. London: Penguin.

Sennett, R. (1998) *The Corrosion of Character: The Personal Consequences of Work in the New Capitalism*. New York & London: W. W. Norton & Company.

Sennett, R. (2003) *Respect: The Formation of Character in an Age of Inequality*. London: Penguin Books.

Sennett, R. (2008) *The Craftsman*. New Haven & London: Yale University Press.

Sennett, R. & Cobb, J. (1972) *The Hidden Injuries of Class*. New York & London: W. W. Norton & Company.

Sevenhuijsen, S. (1998) *Citizenship and the Ethics of Care: Feminist Considerations on Justice, Morality and Politics*. London: Routledge.

Sevenhuijsen, S. (2000) Caring in the Third Way: The Relation between Obligation, Responsibility and Care in Third Way Discourse. *Critical Social Policy*, 20 (5), 5–37.

Sher, G. (1997) *Beyond Neutrality: Perfectionism and Politics*. Cambridge: Cambridge University Press.

Shershow, S. C. (2005) *The Work and the Gift*. London & Chicago: The Chicago University Press.

Shuck, B., Reio, T. G. & Rocco, T. S. (2011) Employee Engagement: An Examination of Antecedent & Outcome Variables. *Human Resource Development International*, 14 (4), 427–45.

Sitton, J. F. (1998) Disembodied Capitalism: Habermas's Conception of the Economy. *Sociological Forum*, 13 (1), 61–83.

Skinner, Q. (1998) *Liberty before Liberalism*. Cambridge: Cambridge University Press.

Sluss, D. & Ashforth, B. (2007) Relational Identity and Identification: Defining Ourselves Through Work Relationships. *Academy of Management Review*, 32 (1), 9–32.

Smart, J. J. C. & Williams, B. (1983) *Utilitarianism: For & Against*. Cambridge: Cambridge University Press.

Smith, A. (1999 [1776]) *The Wealth of Nations*. London: Penguin Books.

Smith, A. (2006 [1790]) *The Theory of Moral Sentiments*. Mineola, NY: Dover Publications.

Smith, A. M. (1994) Hegemony Trouble: The Political Theories of Judith Butler, Ernesto Laclau and Chantel Mouffe. In: Weeks (ed.) *The Lesser Evil and the Greater Good: The Theory and Politics of Social Diversity*. London: Rivers Oram Press.

Smith, N. (2009) Work and the Struggle for Recognition. *European Journal of Political Theory*, 8 (1), 46–60.

Smith, N. & Laitenen, A. (2009) Taylor on Solidarity. *Thesis Eleven*, 99, 48–70.

Sohn-Rethel, A. (1978) *Intellectual and Manual Labor*. Atlantic Highlands, NJ: Humanities Press.

Sparks, J. R. & Schenk, J. A. (2001). Explaining the Effects of Transformational Leadership: An Investigation of the Effects of Higher-Order Motives in Multilevel Marketing Organizations. *Journal of Organizational Behavior*, 22, 849–69.

Spelman, E. V. (2003) *Repair: The Impulse to Restore in a Fragile World*. MA: Beacon Press.

Spence, L. J., Schmidpeter, R. & Habisch, A. (2003) Assessing Social Capital: Small and Medium Sized Enterprises in Germany and the UK. *Journal of Business Ethics*, 47 (1), 17–29.

Spencer, D. A. (2009a) Work in Utopia: Pro-Work Sentiments in the Writings of Four Critics of Classical Economics. *The European Journal of the History of Economic Thought*, 16 (1), 97–122.

Spencer, D. A. (2009b) The 'Work as Bad' Thesis in Economics: Origins, Evolution, and Challenges. *Labor History*, 50 (1), 39–57.

Stacey, C. L. (2005) Finding Dignity in Dirty Work: The Constraints and Rewards of Low-Wage Home Care Labour. *Sociology of Health and Illness*, 27 (6), 831–54.

Starkey, C. (2006) Meaning and Affect. *The Pluralist*, 1 (2), 88–103.

Steger, M. F. & Dik, B. J. (2010) Work as Meaning: Individual and Organizational Benefits of Engaging in Meaningful Work. *Oxford Handbook of Positive Psychology and Work*.

Strauss, G. (2006) Worker Participation – Some Under-Considered Issues. *Industrial Relations*, 45 (4), 778–803.

Swanson, J. (2008) Economic Common Sense and the Depoliticization of the Economic. *Political Research Quarterly*, 61 (1), 56–67.

Swenson, D. F. (1949) The Dignity of Human Life. In: Klemke (ed.) *The Meaning of Life*. New York: Oxford University Press.

Taylor, C. (1985) The Person. In: Carrithers, Collins & Lukes (eds) *The Category of the Person*. Cambridge: Cambridge University Press.

Taylor, C. (1989) *The Sources of the Self*. Cambridge, MA: Harvard University Press.

Taylor, C. (1992) *Ethics of Authenticity*. Cambridge, MA: Harvard University Press.

Taylor, C. (1995) *Irreducibly Social Goods, Philosophy Arguments*. Cambridge, MA: Harvard University Press.

Taylor, F. W. (2003 [1911]) *The Principles of Scientific Management*. Dover Publications Inc.

Taylor, R. (1967) The Meaning of Life. In: Klemke (ed.) *The Meaning of Life*. New York: Oxford University Press.

Terkel, S. (1975) *Working*. London: Wildwood House.

Teschl, M. & Comim, F. (2005) Adaptive Preferences and Capabilities: Some Preliminary Conceptual Explorations. *Review of Social Economy*, 63 (2), 229–47.

Thackray, R. I. (1981) The Stress of Boredom and Monotony: A Consideration of the Evidence. *Psychosomatic Medicine*, 43 (2), 165–76.

Thompson, J. & Bunderson, J. (2001) Work-Nonwork Conflict and the Phenomenology of Time: Beyond the Balance Metaphor. *Work and Occupations*, 28 (1), 17–39.

Thompson, P. (2003) Disconnected Capitalism: Or Why Employers Can't Keep Their Side of the Bargain, Work. *Employment & Society*, 17 (2), 359–78.

Thompson, P. & Smith, C. (2000) Follow the Redbrick Road: Reflections on Pathways In and Out of the Labour Process Debate. *International Studies of Management and Organization*, 30 (4), 40–67.

Thompson, S. (2006) *A Political Theory of Recognition: A Critical Introduction.* Malden, MA & Cambridge: Polity Press.

Thompson, M. J. (2013) Reconstructing Republican Freedom: A Critique of the Neo-Republican Concept of Domination. *Journal of Philosophy & Social Criticism*, 39 (3), 277–98.

Thomson, G. (1987) *Needs.* London & New York: Routledge & Kegan Paul.

Thomson, G. (2003) *On the Meaning of Life.* South Melbourne: Wadsworth.

Thomson, G. (2005) *Fundamental Needs.* In: Reader (ed.) *The Philosophy of Need.* Royal Institute of Philosophy supplement. Cambridge, New York & Melbourne: Cambridge University Press.

Tilgher, A. (1931) *Work and What it Has Meant to Men Through the Ages.* London: George G. Harrap & Company Ltd.

Tirrell, L. (1993) Definition and Power: Toward Authority without Privilege. *Hypatia*, 8 (4), 1–34.

Toren, C. (1993) Making History: The Significance of Childhood Cognition for a Comparative Anthropology of Mind. *Man*, 28 (3), 461–78.

Tourish, D. (2013) *The Dark Side of Transformational Leadership: A Critical Perspective.* London and New York: Routledge.

Townsend, K., Wilkinson, A. & Burgess, J. (2014) Routes to Partial Success: Collaborative Employment Relations and Employee Engagement. *The International Journal of Human Resource Management*, 25 (6), 915–30.

Tronto, J. (1993) *Moral Boundaries: Towards a Political Ethic of Care.* New York: Routledge Press.

Tronto, J. (1999) *Care Ethics: Moving Forward. Hypatia*, 14 (1), 112–19.

Tronto, J. (2010) Creating Caring Institutions: Politics, Plurality, and Purpose. *Ethics and Social Welfare*, 4 (2), 158–71.

Truss, C. & Madden, A. (2013) Time Reclaimed: The Temporality of Meaningful Work. *The British Sociological Association: Work, Employment and Society Conference.* University of Warwick, unpublished paper.

Tsao, R. (2002) Arendt against Athens: Rereading the Human Condition. *Political Theory*, 30 (1).

Tully, J. (2002) The Unfreedom of the Moderns in Comparison to Their Ideals of Constitutional Democracy. *The Modern Law Review*, 65, 204–28.

Ulrich, D. (1997) *Human Resource Champions.* Boston, MA: Harvard Business School Press.

Van Parijs, P. (1991) Why Surfers Should be Fed: The Liberal Case for an Unconditioned Basic Income. *Philosophy and Public Affairs*, 20 (2), 101–31.

Van Parijs, P. (1997) *Real Freedom for All: What (if Anything) Can Justify Capitalism?* Oxford & New York: Oxford University Press.

Van Staveren, I. (2001) *The Values of Economics: An Aristotelian Perspective.* London & New York: Routledge.

Van Staveren, I. (2007) Beyond Utilitarianism and Deontology: Ethics in Economics. *Review of Political Economy*, 19 (1), 21–35.

Verdofer, Weber, Unterrainer & Seyr (2012) The Relationship Between Organizational Democracy and Socio-moral Climate: Exploring Effects of the Ethical Context in Organizations. *Economic and Industrial Democracy*, 0 (0), 1–27.

Vezina, M., Derriennic, F. & Monfort, C. (2004) The Impact of Job Strain on Social Isolation: A Longitudinal Analysis of French Workers. *Social Science & Medicine*, 59, 29–38.

Villa, D. R. (1999) *Politics, Philosophy, Terror: Essays on the Thought of Hannah Arendt*. Princeton, New Jersey: Princeton University Press.

Wall, S. (2001) Freedom, Interference and Domination. *Political Studies*, 49, 216–30.

Wallace, K. (1993) Reconstructing Judgement: Emotion and Moral Judgement. *Hypatia*, 8 (3), 61–83.

Walsh, A. (1994) Meaningful Work as a Distributive Good. *Southern Journal of Philosophy*, 32, 233–50.

Walzer, M. (1983) *Spheres of Justice: A Defence of Pluralism & Equality*. Oxford & Cambridge: Blackwell.

Walzer, M. (1994*) Thick and Thin*. Paris: University of Notre Dame Press.

Warr, P. (2007) *Work, Happiness, and Unhappiness*. Mahwah, NJ & London: Lawrence Erlbaum Associates, Publishers.

Warren, M. E. (1992) Democratic Theory and Self-Transformation. *American Political Science Review*, 86 (1), 8–23.

Warren, M. E. (1993) Can Participatory Democracy Produce Better Selves? Psychological Dimensions of Habermas's Discursive Model of Democracy. *Political Psychology*, 14 (2), 209–34.

Warren, M. E. (1996a) Deliberative Democracy and Authority. *American Political Science Review*, 90 (1), 46–60.

Warren, M. E. (1996b) What Should We Expect from More Democracy: Radically Democratic Responses to Politics. *Political Theory*, 24 (2), 241–70.

Warren, M. E. (1999) What is Political? *Journal of Theoretical Politics*, 11 (2), 207–31.

Warren, M. E. (2001) *Democracy and Association*. Princeton: Princeton University Press.

Warren, M. E. (2002) What Can Democratic Participation Mean Today? *Political Theory*, 30 (5), 677–701.

Watson, T. J. (2008) Managing Identity: Identity Work, Personal Predicaments and Structural Circumstances. *Organization*, 15 (1), 121–43.

Weber, M. (1930) *The Protestant Ethic and the Spirit of Capitalism*. London & New York: Routledge.

Weber, M. (1974) *Max Weber: The Interpretation of Social Reality*. London: Joseph.

Weber, M. (1978) *Economy and Society: An Outline of Interpretive Sociology*. Berkeley, CA: University of California Press.

Weber, W. G., Unterrainer, C. & Höge, T. (2008) Socio-Moral Atmosphere and Prosocial and Democratic Value Orientations in Enterprises with Different Levels of Structurally Anchored Participation. *German Journal of Research in Human Resource Management*, 22, 171–94.

Wee, L. & Brooks, A. (2010) Negotiating Gender Subjectivity in the Enterprise Culture: Metaphor and Entrepreneurial Discourses. *Gender, Work and*

Organization. [Online] http://onlinelibrary.wiley.com/doi/10.1111/j.1468-0432. 2010.00543.x/pdf [Accessed 20th October 2011].

Weeks, J. (1998) The Sexual Citizen, Theory. *Culture & Society*, 15 (3–4), 35–52.

Weeks, K. (1998) *Constituting Feminist Subjects.* Ithaca, NY: Cornell University Press.

Weeks, K. (2007) Life Within and Against Work: Affective Labor, Feminist Critique, and Post-Fordist Politics. *Ephemera*, 7 (1), 233–49.

Wegge, J., Jeppesen, H. J., Weber, W. G., Pearce, C. L., Pundt, A., Jonsson, T., Wolf, S., Wassenaar, C. L., Unterrainer, C. & Piecha, A. (2010) Promoting Work Motivation in Organisations: Should Employee Involvement in Organizational Leadership become a New Tool in the Organizational Psychologist's Kit? *Journal of Personnel Psychology*, 9 (4), 154–71.

Weick, K. E. (1995) *Sensemaking in Organizations.* California & London: Sage Publications.

Weil, S. (2006 [1955])) *Oppression and Liberty.* London: Ark.

Weil, S. (1977 [1946]) Factory Work. In: Panichas (ed.) *The Simone Weil Reader.* New York: David McKay Company.

Weil, S. (1986) Prerequisite to Dignity of Labour. In: Miles (ed.) *Simone Weil: An Anthology.* London: Virgo.

Welbourne, T. (2011) Engaged in What? So What? A Role-Based Perspective for the Future of Employee Engagement. In: Wilkinson & Townsend (eds) *The Future of Employment Relations: New Paradigms, New Developments.* Basingstoke: Palgrave Macmillan.

Wenger, E. (2000) Communities of Practice and Social Learning Systems. *Organization*, 7 (2), 225–46.

Western, S. (2008) *Leadership: A Critical Text.* London: Sage.

White, S. K. (2000) *Sustaining Affirmation: The Strengths of Weak Ontology in Political Theory.* Princeton & Oxford: Princeton University Press.

White, S. (2008) The Republican Case for Basic Income: A Plea for Difficulty. *Basic Income Studies*, 2 (2), 1–7.

Whyte, W. F. & Whyte, K. E. (1991) *Making Mondragon: The Growth and Dynamics of the Worker Cooperative Complex.* Ithaca, NY: Cornell University Press.

Wiedermann, H. (1980) Codetermination by Workers in German Enterprises. *The American Journal of Comparative Law*, 28 (1), 79–82.

Wiggins, D. (1988) Truth, Invention, and the Meaning of Life. In: Sayre-McCord (ed.) *Essays on Moral Realism.* Ithaca: Cornell University Press.

Wiggins, D. (1998) *Needs, Values, Truth: Essays in the Philosophy of Value.* Oxford: Oxford University Press.

Wilde, L. (2007) The Concept of Solidarity: Emerging from the Theoretical Shadows? *British Journal of Politics and International Relations*, 9, 171–81.

Wilkinson, A., Dundon, T. & Grugulis, I. (2007) Information but Not Consultation: Exploring Employee Involvement in SME's. *The International Journal of Human Resource Management*, 18 (7), 1279–97.

Wilkinson, A., Dundon, T., Marchington, M. & Ackers, P. (2004) Changing Patterns of Employee Voice: Case Studies from the UK and Republic of Ireland. *The Journal of Industrial Relations*, 46 (3), 298–322.

Wilkinson, R. & Pickett, K. (2009) *The Spirit Level: Why More Equal Societies Almost Always Do Better.* London: Allen Lane.

Williams, B. (1981) Persons, Character and Morality. In: Williams (ed.) *Moral Luck*. Cambridge: Cambridge University Press.

Williams, C. C. & Nadin, S. (2010) Rethinking the Commercialisation of Everyday Life: A Whole Economy Perspective. *Foresight*, 12 (6), 55–68.

Williams, G. (2006) 'Infrastructures of Responsibility': The Moral Tasks of Institutions. *Journal of Applied Philosophy*, 23 (2), 207–21.

Williams, G. (2008) Responsibility as a Virtue. *Ethical Theory and Moral Practice*, 11 (4), 455–70.

Williamson, T. (2004) The Relationship Between Workplace Democracy and Economic Democracy: Three Views. *Annual Meeting of the American Political Science Association*, 2–5 September 2004, Chicago.

Willig, R. (2009) Self-Realization Options: Contemporary Marching Order in the Pursuit of Recognition. *Acta Sociologica*, 52 (4), 350–64.

Willmott, H. (1993) Strength is Ignorance; Slavery is Freedom: Managing Culture in Modern Organizations. *Journal of Management Studies*, 30 (4), 515–52.

Willmott, H. (1994) Bringing Agency (Back) into Organizational Analysis: Responding to the Crisis of (Post)Modernity. In: Hassard & Parker (eds) *Towards a New Theory of Organizations*. London & New York: Routledge.

Wingenbach, E.C. (2011) *Institutionalizing Agonistic Democracy: Post-Foundationalism and Political Liberalism*. Surrey, England & USA: Ashgate.

Wisner, A. (1995) Understanding Problem-Building: Ergonomic Work Analysis. *Ergonomics*, 38 (3), 595–605.

Wolin, S. S. (1996) Fugitive Democracy, in Democracy and Difference: Contesting the Boundaries of the Political. In: Benhabib (ed.) *Democracy & Difference: Contesting the Boundaries of the Political*. Princeton, New Jersey: Princeton University Press.

Wolf, S. (1982) Moral Saints. *The Journal of Philosophy*, 79 (8), 419–39.

Wolf, S. (1997a) Happiness and Meaning: Two Aspects of the Good Life. *Social Philosophy & Policy*, 14, 207–25.

Wolf, S. (1997b) Meaningful Lives in a Meaningless World. *Quaestiones Infinitae*, 19. Utrecht: Utrecht University.

Wolf, S. (2002) The True, the Good, and the Lovable: Frankfurt's Avoidance of Objectivity. In: Buss & Overton (eds) *Contours of Agency: Essays on Themes from Harry Frankfurt*. Cambridge, Massachusetts & London: The MIT Press.

Wolf, S. (2007) The Meanings of Lives. [Online] New York University, http://www1.law.nyu.edu/clppt/program2003/readings/wolf.pdf [Accessed 25th July 2009].

Wolf, S. (2010) *Meaning in Life and Why It Matters*. Princeton, New Jersey: Princeton University Press.

Wong, W. (2008) Meaningfulness and Identities. *Ethical Theory and Moral Practice*, 11 (2), 123–48.

Wood, A. (1981) *Karl Marx*. London: Routledge and Kegan Paul.

Wood, S. J. (1982) *The Degradation of Work?* London: Hutchinson.

Wrzesniewki, A. (2002) 'It's Not Just a Job': Shifting Meanings of Work in the Wake of 9/11. *Journal of Management Inquiry*, 11 (3), 230–4.

Wrzesniewski, A. & Dutton, J. (2001) Crafting a Job: Revisioning Employees as Active Crafters of Their Work. *Academy of Management Review*, 26 (2), 179–201.

Wrzesniewski, A., Dutton, J. & Debebe, G. (2003) Interpersonal Sensemaking and the Meaning of Work. *Research in Organisational Behaviour*, 25, 93–135.

Wrzesniewski, A., McCauley, C. & Rozin, P. (1997) Jobs, Careers, and Callings: People's Relations to Their Work. *Journal of Research in Personality*, 31 (1), 21–33.

Young, I. M. (1979) Self-Determination as a Principle of Justice. *The Philosophical Forum*, XI (1), 30–46.

Young, I. M. (1990) *Justice and the Politics of Difference*. Princeton: Princeton University Press.

Young, I. M. (2006) Taking the Basic Structure Seriously. *Perspectives on Politics*, 4 (1), 91–7.

Zerilli, L. (2005) 'We Feel Our Freedom': Imagination and Judgement in the Thought of Hannah Arendt. *Political Theory*, 33 (2), 158–88.

Zimmermann, B. (2006) Pragmatism and the Capability Approach: Challenges in Social Theory and Empirical Research. *European Journal of Social Theory*, 9 (4).

Zink, J. R. (2007) Reconsidering Rawls's Special Conception of Self-Respect. *Paper presented at the Annual General Meeting for The Midwest Political Science Association, 2007*. Chicago, IL.

Zurn, C. F. (2005) Recognition, Redistribution, and Democracy: Dilemmas of Honneth's Critical Social Theory. *European Journal of Philosophy*, 13 (1), 89–126.

Index

Printed and bound by CPI Group (UK) Ltd, Croydon, CR0 4YY